SPIRITUAL HEALING

There has recently been much interest in the relationship between science and religion, and how they combine to give us a 'binocular' perspective on things. One important phenomenon which has been neglected in recent work is the concept of spiritual healing. This edited collection explores a variety of approaches to spiritual healing from different religious points of view, identifying both what it is and how it works. The authors also explore the biological and psychological processes, open to scientific enquiry, through which healing may be mediated. As such, this book indicates the central proposition that religious and scientific perspectives answer different questions about healing, and there is not necessarily any conflict between them.

FRASER WATTS is a reader in theology and science at the Faculty of Divinity, University of Cambridge. He is the editor of *Creation, Law and Probability* (2008), *Jesus and Psychology* (2007) and *The Dialogue between Science and Religion* (2006), and the author of *Theology and Psychology* (2002). He is also an ordained minister in the Church of England, and Vicar-Chaplain of St Edward's Church in Cambridge.

SPIRITUAL HEALING

Scientific and Religious Perspectives

EDITED BY

FRASER WATTS

University of Cambridge

CAMBRIDGE
UNIVERSITY PRESS

CAMBRIDGE UNIVERSITY PRESS
Cambridge, New York, Melbourne, Madrid, Cape Town, Singapore,
São Paulo, Delhi, Dubai, Tokyo, Mexico City

Cambridge University Press
The Edinburgh Building, Cambridge CB2 8RU, UK

Published in the United States of America by Cambridge University Press, New York

www.cambridge.org
Information on this title: www.cambridge.org/9780521197939

First published 2011

Printed in the United Kingdom at the University Press, Cambridge

A catalogue record for this publication is available from the British Library

Library of Congress Cataloging-in-Publication Data
Spiritual healing : scientific and religious perspectives / edited by Fraser Watts.
p.   cm.
ISBN 978-0-521-19793-9 (Hardback)
1. Spiritual healing.   2. Healing–Religious aspects–Christianity.   3. Medicine–Religious aspects–
Christianity.   4. Healing–Religious aspects.   5. Medicine–Religious aspects.   6. Religion and
science.   I. Watts, Fraser N.   II. Title.
BT732.5.S667 2011
203′.1–dc22
2010028680

ISBN 978-0-521-19793-9 Hardback

Contents

Figures

Contributors

MICHAEL J. BOIVIN is Associate Professor in the International Neurologic and Psychiatric Epidemiology Program (INPEP) at Michigan State University College of Osteopathic Medicine (MSU-COM). He is also an adjunct research investigator in the Neuropsychology Section at the University of Michigan. He is presently the principal investigator on a study of spiritual well-being, emotional well-being, neuropsychological function, and quality of life for newly diagnosed breast cancer patients (Templeton Advanced Research Program, Metanexus Institute). He served as a Fulbright senior research scholar to DR Congo (1990–1) and Uganda (2003–4), and is presently an NIH-funded investigator on several Ugandan-based studies in pediatric severe malaria and HIV. He has a PhD from Western Michigan University in the experimental analysis of behaviour, and a Masters in Public Health (MPH) degree from the University of Michigan. In addition to his breast cancer research at MSU, his international research has focused on health factors, especially severe malaria and HIV, that influence the neuropsychological development of children in Africa.

CHARLES BOURNE studied Engineering and then Theology at the University of Cambridge, graduating in 2003. During his time in Cambridge he investigated spiritual healing under the supervision of Fraser Watts and this prompted him to seek practical experience of a healing modality. He subsequently trained in Traditional Chinese Acupuncture at the College of Integrated Chinese Medicine, Reading, and now has a private acupuncture practice in West London. Alongside this, he maintains a longstanding involvement in sport, working as a rowing coach at St Paul's School, London.

PHILIP CLAYTON is a philosopher and theologian who works across the broad range of issues that arise at the various intersections between science, religion, and theology. Over the last several decades he has published and lectured on many of the major branches of this debate, including the history of modern philosophy, philosophy of science, comparative religions, and constructive theology. His scientific interests include evolutionary biology, emergent complexity, and the neural correlates of consciousness. Clayton received the PhD jointly from the Philosophy and Religious Studies departments at Yale University and is currently Ingraham Professor at Claremont School of Theology and Professor of Religion and Philosophy at Claremont Graduate University. He is the author or editor of 17 books and over 100 articles, mostly recently *The Oxford Handbook of Religion and Science* (2008), *Adventures in the Spirit* (2008), and *In Quest of Freedom: the Emergence of Spirit in the Natural World* (2009).

SIMON DEIN is a Senior Lecturer in Anthropology and Medicine, University College London. He is an Honorary Consultant Psychiatrist, Princess Alexandra Hospital, Harlow. He completed his PhD thesis in 1999 on Religious Healing among Lubavitcher Hasidim in London at University College. His main interests are millennialism, religion and health, and psychological aspects of religious experience. He has written sixty papers and three books, including *Religion and Healing among the Lubavitch Community of Stamford Hill: A Case Study in Hasidism* (2004). He is one of the editors of the *Journal of Mental Health, Religion and Culture*. He is the Director of a Master's Degree in Culture and Health at University College London.

HANNAH GILBERT has a degree in Anthropology from the University of Durham, and has recently completed a PhD at the University of York that explored the social and performative aspects of British spirit mediumship. She also runs a researcher network for research into extraordinary experiences, entitled 'Exploring the Extraordinary'. She is a member of AERU – www.york.ac.uk/depts/soci/research/aeru.htm.

PAUL GILBERT is Professor of Clinical Psychology at Derbyshire Mental Health Trust and the University of Derby. He is a fellow of the British Psychological Society, with research interests in shame, self-criticism and compassion-focused therapy. In 2007 he set up the Compassionate Mind Foundation (www.compassionatemind.co.uk) with a mission statement of 'promoting well-being through the scientific understanding and application of compassion'.

BRUCE KINSEY studied Theology and Ecclesiastical History at King's College in the University of London, and is Senior Tutor, and Head of

Philosophy and the Study of Religion at the Perse School in Cambridge. He is also a practising psychoanalytic psychotherapist, a qualified supervisor with the Society for Analytical Psychotherapy, a former Chairman of the psychoanalytical psychotherapy section of the UK Council for Psychotherapy, and Advisor in Pastoral Care and Counselling for the Diocese of Ely. His research is on the interface of religion and psychoanalysis and he is currently working on the psychodynamics of spiritual healing. He is a member of the Psychology and Religion Research Group in the University of Cambridge.

DAVID LEECH is currently a postdoctoral research fellow (Philosophy) at the University of Paris X-Nanterre, Paris. After receiving his PhD (Philosophy of Religion) from the University of Cambridge he worked as a postdoctoral researcher first in the Psychology of Religion Research Group, University of Cambridge and then on a joint project between the Ian Ramsey Centre and the Department of Evolutionary Anthropology, University of Oxford. He has published on various topics spanning the areas of philosophy of religion, science and religion, and intellectual history.

JUSTIN MEGGITT is University Senior Lecturer in the Study of Religion and the Origins of Christianity at the Institute of Continuing Education, and Affiliated Lecturer in New Testament Studies at the Faculty of Divinity, University of Cambridge. He is also a Fellow and Director of Studies in Theology and Religious Studies at Hughes Hall, a member of the Reykjavik Academy and a Fellow of the Jesus Project. He has published widely on the origins of Christianity, including *Paul, Poverty and Survival* (1998) and *The Madness of King Jesus* (forthcoming) and has a particular interest in the intersection between ancient popular culture in the early Roman Empire and the emergence of the earliest Christian churches. Meggitt also has a longstanding interest in the study of seventeenth-century religious radicalism and inter-religious encounter, evident in his recent monograph *Quakers and Muslims in the Seventeenth Century: Apocalypse and Anomaly* (forthcoming).

MARILYN SCHLITZ is a clinical research scientist, medical anthropologist, thought leader, and change consultant. Her work over the past three decades explores the interface of consciousness, science, and healing. She received her PhD in Anthropology from the University of Texas, Austin. She is the President and CEO for the Institute of Noetic Sciences, Senior Scientist at the Research Institute, California Pacific

Medical Centre, and co-founder of the Integral Health Network. She has published numerous articles on consciousness studies in scholarly and popular journals and has given talks at the United Nations, the Smithsonian Institution, and the Explorers Club. She has taught at Trinity University, Stanford University, and Harvard Medical Centre. Marilyn possesses a rare ability to translate complex ideas into a common-sense language that excites the imaginations of audiences worldwide. Her books include *Consciousness and Healing: Integral Approaches to Mind Body Medicine* (2005) and *Living Deeply: The Art and Science of Transformation in Everyday Life* (2008).

FRASER WATTS has a background in clinical and experimental psychology. He has been a Senior Scientist at the UK Medical Research Council's Applied Psychology Unit, and has also served as President of the British Psychological Society. In 1994 he became Starbridge Lecturer in Theology and Natural Science in the University of Cambridge, and is now Reader in Theology and Science. His research focuses on the dialogue between theology and psychology, and on the psychological study of religion. He is Director of the Psychology and Religion Research Group, and a Fellow of Queens' College Cambridge. He is also an ordained minister in the Church of England and Vicar-Chaplain of St Edward's Church in Cambridge. His most recent books are *Theology and Psychology* (2002) and *Forgiveness in Context* (2004; both edited with Liz Gulliford), *Jesus and Psychology* (2007), and *Creation: Law and Probability* (2008).

BURTON WEBB is Professor of Biology and Chair of the Division of Natural Sciences and Mathematics at Indiana Wesleyan University. He holds degrees from Olivet Nazarene University, Ball State University, and the Indiana University School of Medicine. Trained as a molecular immunologist, Dr Webb's research interests range from cancer immunology to the implicit theology of the universe around us. The recipient of numerous teaching awards, Dr Webb is most proud of his students, who are working in research laboratories and medical facilities around the globe. Dr Webb is married with two children and resides in central Indiana, USA.

Preface

Spiritual healing is a topic that has been strangely neglected in the academic literature. Most books on spiritual healing are written by enthusiasts, and make no attempt to advance our understanding of it in a dispassionate way. Spiritual healing is being increasingly widely practised, in both religious and non-religious contexts, and there is an urgent need to understand it better.

The present book is a contribution from the joint perspectives of science and religion. The dialogue between science and religion has become a rich field of interdisciplinary enquiry in recent years. However, rather surprisingly, spiritual healing is a topic that has so far been completely neglected in that literature. That is all the more surprising as the related topic of divine action has attracted particular attention. I hope that the chapters of this book advance our understanding of spiritual healing from the perspectives of both science and religious studies. The basic assumption is that, if spiritual healing is to be understood, it is important not to neglect the perspectives of either science or religion. It is implicit that neither science nor religion can provide a complete account of spiritual healing on their own. Some of the most interesting issues about spiritual healing arise at the point where these two perspectives intersect.

This book had its origins in a three-day symposium, jointly chaired by Sarah Coakley and me, which took place under the aegis of the John Templeton Foundation's Humble Approach Initiative. Thirteen medical and social scientists, philosophers, and theologians met at Queens' College, Cambridge in January 2004 to consider a broad range of issues raised about the concept of 'spiritual healing' and its relation to conventional medicine. The discussion was sufficiently fruitful to produce two books: this one, which focuses mainly on spiritual healing as divine action; and a companion volume edited by Sarah Coakley, *Spiritual Healing: Science, Meaning and Discernment* (Grand Rapids,

Eerdmans, forthcoming), which focuses on healing as hermeneutics and secondary causation.

Both editors are grateful to everyone who met at Queens' College for beginning to frame the issues. Many of the original participants have contributed to one or other volume, but we are also pleased to have been able to attract other authors who were willing to wrestle, from the perspective of a variety of different disciplines, with the key issues that spiritual healing raises. We are also grateful to the John Templeton Foundation for its generosity in facilitating the exploration of the big questions raised by a topic like spiritual healing, and helping to making the fruits of that discussion available to a wider public.

I am grateful to the many people who have helped me to clarify my thoughts about spiritual healing, and to three in particular. Conversations with Sarah Coakley surrounding the Cambridge colloquium were enormously helpful in sharpening the approach to spiritual healing that I wished to take. Philip Clayton helped me to clarify things further during his very fruitful sabbatical stay in Cambridge, from which I benefited greatly. I also owe a debt of gratitude to my friend and local colleague, Bruce Kinsey, for many helpful conversations about spiritual healing over an extended period. Of course, none of them should be held responsible for the approach to spiritual healing that I have taken here.

Fraser Watts
University of Cambridge

CHAPTER I

Conceptual issues in spiritual healing

Fraser Watts

Spiritual healing raises challenging issues. Religious traditions such as Christianity make strong claims about healing. The gospels are full of healing stories, and it is claimed that the followers of Jesus continued such healings. In the twentieth century and into the twenty-first there has been a marked revival of interest in healing within various faith traditions, and in non-religious settings too. Is it credible that spiritual healing takes place? If so, how are such healings to be understood and explained in our scientific culture?

First, though, there are really difficult problems of definition about spiritual healing. What do we mean by 'spiritual' healing? In considering this, it may be helpful to make a distinction between different things that 'spiritual' can be applied to in this context. There can be:

1 Healing in which spiritual practices play a role
2 Healing in which spiritual aspects of the human person are presumed to be involved
3 Healing that is explained in terms of what are presumed to be spiritual processes

I will consider each of these in turn. In doing so, it is important to remember that spiritual healing now occurs in both religious and non-religious settings. On the one hand, there is an explicitly Christian spiritual healing movement, most evident in charismatic churches, but also found in pilgrimages to Lourdes and other such sites. On the other hand, there is an explicitly secular spiritual healing movement, with links to 'New Age' culture. Some of what needs to be said about spiritual healing applies equally to healing in religious and non-religious settings; some of it is specific to spiritual healing that occurs in one setting or the other.

THE ROLE OF SPIRITUAL PRACTICES IN HEALING

Spiritual healing can be seen as healing in which spiritual practices play a role. The concept of spiritual practices is fairly straightforward. There is now quite an extensive and rigorous academic literature on the definition of spirituality, and on the distinction between spirituality and religion (Zinnbauer and Pargament 2005, pp. 21–42). Though there are various possible approaches to the definition of spirituality, it generally includes participation in spiritual practices, such as meditation or prayer, though it often shifts the emphasis away from the structure of beliefs in which those spiritual practices might be embedded. Spiritual practices are found within all of the major world faith traditions, but are also now found outside any established faith tradition.

It is easy to see how spiritual practices could enhance healing processes, and some of the evidence for that is reviewed in this book (see Larson *et al.* 1998; Koenig *et al.* 2001). On this view, healings might be deemed to be spiritual simply because of the spiritual practices involved. That would neither invoke any kind of spiritual ontology of the human person, nor require any kind of spiritual explanation. Healing that is facilitated by spiritual practices could be explained entirely in terms of the impact of spiritual practices on psychosomatic processes. It seems highly likely that this provides an adequate account of at least some of what is regarded as 'spiritual' healing. It is also likely that psychosomatic processes play at least some role in all cases of spiritual healing.

It is worth noting that spiritual practices can be used not on their own but in conjunction with medical or surgical interventions. There are indications that the effectiveness of ordinary treatments can be enhanced by the explicit use of spiritual practices; medical and surgical treatments tend to work better when a 'whole-person' approach is taken. There are also indications that attending to spiritual aspects of the healing process can enhance the overall effectiveness of medical and surgical treatment, just as there is increasing recognition of the importance in psychotherapy of addressing religious issues constructively. So there is a strong pragmatic case for attending to the spiritual dimension of healing. The suggestion that spiritual practices play a useful auxiliary role in healing makes no strong or difficult assumptions.

Spiritual practices are now to be found both in religious and non-religious contexts. (By a 'religious' context, I mean the context provided by the structures, practices and assumptions of one of the world's recognized faith traditions.) It will be apparent that spiritual healing, in the sense of healing that is facilitated by spiritual practice, may or may not be explicitly 'religious' in the sense of occurring in such a setting. Some healing takes place in religious settings and is embedded within religious assumptions, but much does not. Equally, healing that takes place in a recognizably religious setting may or may not involve spiritual practice. Surgery can be undertaken in a hospital with an explicitly religious ethos. The religious context of healing and the role of spiritual practice in healing are conceptually independent. In practice, however, there is a close association between religious and spiritual healing, in that most religious healing also uses spiritual practices.

A similar distinction could be made between religious and spiritual experience, though those concepts are not always distinguished. Religious experiences, I suggest, are experiences that are interpreted in a religious way. Spiritual or mystical experiences, in contrast, are experiences with a distinct quality, such as a strong sense of unity. In terms of this distinction, experiences can be either religious, or spiritual/mystical, or both. It seems likely that experiences that are both religious and spiritual have the most far-reaching consequences for the people concerned.

There was no doubt a time when it was unnecessary to make these distinctions, as the religious frame of reference was used so comprehensively in Western culture that no one would have considered the possibility of spiritual healing that was not interpreted religiously. However, with the breakdown of the comprehensive application of a religious frame of reference in the latter part of the nineteenth century, it has become increasingly common for spiritual healing to occur outside the context of religious practice, and to be interpreted without a religious frame of reference.

Some spiritual practices that can contribute to healing, such as meditation, are general spiritual practices. They are most commonly practised outside any explicit healing context, but can nevertheless contribute to healing. Other spiritual practices, such as the laying on of hands, are used with the specific intention of bringing healing about. The latter raise complex questions to which I will return in the concluding chapter of this book.

I suggest that spiritual practices such as prayer, meditation and laying on of hands, can contribute to spiritual healing in a way that parallels how psychotherapy can contribute to psychological healing. There may also be a particular role for the religious minister or healer in spiritual healing that is parallel to, but different from, that of the psychotherapist in psychological healing. Paul Tillich makes such a point when he distinguishes the role of the psychologist in removing neurotic anxiety from the role of

the minister in 'mediating the essential' (Dourley 1997, pp. 211–22).
However, there is nothing specifically religious or theological here.
A secular spiritual healer can also 'mediate the essential', and secular
spiritual healing can also be enhanced by spiritual practices.

HEALING THAT INVOLVES THE SPIRITUAL ASPECTS
OF THE PERSON

My second way of understanding the concept of spiritual healing is
healing that involves the 'spiritual' aspects of the person being healed.
But what are they? This is a question that has not been much addressed
recently, but there are some useful pointers to draw on.

One comes from the Jungian psychologist James Hillman, who in his
paper 'Peaks and vales' (1979) makes a strong case for the distinction
between spirit and soul, and uses it to make a parallel distinction between
spiritual direction and psychotherapy. For Hillman, spirit is the aspect
of a person that tends to 'rise above' the problems of life, whereas soul
tends to 'go deep'. Spirit desires and brings liberation, whereas soul is
attentive to pathology. Spirit is single-minded, whereas soul values
complexity.

This distinction of Hillman's between soul and spirit can yield a
distinction between two kinds of healing: psychological and spiritual.
Psychological healing operates best where there are problems that have a
psychosomatic component, and would normally proceed through psychotherapy. The kind of healing that would be associated with what Hillman
calls spirit might be related to what psychotherapists call a 'flight into
health', a concept that is discussed by Bruce Kinsey in Chapter 6.

Though 'flight into health' is a disparaging phrase, the fact that it is a
recognized concept suggests that there is a real phenomenon here, albeit
one that is not yet well understood. I suggest that flight into health
(or rising above illness) may not always be pathological. There may well
be relatively healthy or unhealthy forms of this process. The main concern
about flight into health is that such healing tends to be transitory.
However, there may be ways of making it more enduring. There may
be ways in which the benefits of spiritual healing can be extended by
spiritual practice. Also, the relationship with a human healer can be
replaced by a healing relationship with God that is more permanent
and independent of circumstances. There may be other ways in which
the processes that lead to spiritual healing can be internalized in a way that
makes them enduring.

It needs to be emphasized that the distinction between soul and spirit can be made within a holistic view of the human person, and of how spiritual healing takes place. I see spiritual healing as being holistic, in that it involves body, mind and spirit. I do not assume that mind or spirit are *separate* from body; the concept of spiritual healing need not imply a return to substance dualism (or to a three-substance view).

Let us assume an emergentist view of mind in which mental powers are seen as emerging from the physical body (Clayton 2006). In a similar way, spirit can be seen as emerging from body and mind. Philosophical theology has learned the lessons of post-war philosophy of mind, and recognizes that mind should not be seen as a substance that is separate from body. First, it is best seen in adjectival terms, as mental properties or powers, rather than as referring to a thing called 'mind'. Second, though there is a conceptual distinction between mind and brain (or body), they cannot actually be separated or divided; as Coleridge often insisted, distinctions do not imply divisions. Third, though mental properties and powers are real enough, they arise from body and brain, and do not have a separate origin.

There can be healing that is psychological (i.e. healing that can be explained psychologically), and such healing can be formulated in a way that is consistent with all the above assumptions about mind. It does not imply healing by a mind that is separate from the body. On the contrary, the concept of psychosomatic medicine is remarkably holistic, and built on the idea that psychological processes are closely intertwined with physical ones. Psychosomatic healing does not rest on a flight into radical mind–body dualism.

The concept of spiritual healing should be approached in a similar way. I have argued elsewhere that the lessons of recent philosophy of mind should be applied to how we think about soul qualities (Watts 2001). Soul and spirit are not separate from body and mind, any more than mind is separate from body. Mind and spirit are distinguishable aspects of the human person, but not separate entities. So talk of 'spiritual' healing does not assume that 'spirit' is something separate and distinct from the rest of a person. It is spiritual in the sense of being healing in which the spiritual aspects of the person are significant, rather than being healing that is exclusively spiritual. Indeed, it makes no sense to suggest that healing could be purely spiritual.

The issues that arise here seem fairly similar whether spiritual healing is undertaken in religious or non-religious contexts. There is a longer tradition of debate in Christianity than in contemporary secular culture about whether to make a twofold distinction between body and soul or spirit, or a threefold distinction between body, soul and spirit, but the issues are essentially the same. I have suggested that the threefold distinction is helpful, but it should not be thought of as concerning three separate substances.

SPIRITUAL EXPLANATIONS OF HEALING

The above concept of spiritual healing can in principle be understood entirely in anthropological (human) terms, even though spiritual healing may make use of human processes that are not yet well understood. However there is a further sense of spiritual healing as healing that involves transcendent resources and which requires an explanation in spiritual terms.

This radical concept of spiritual healing involves a power or energy that can be called 'spiritual' and which is central and indispensable to healing. Almost all those engaged in spiritual healing assume they can become channels of a healing energy that transcends themselves. Such healing energy is generally assumed, in some sense, to be 'spiritual'. It is an interesting point of similarity in the assumptions made by both Christian and secular healers that the healer is a channel of a healing power that transcends them, and that they are not themselves the source of this healing power (see Chapter 5). The healing power may be understood in different ways in Christian and secular forms of spiritual healing, but they agree on its dependence on transcendent resources.

Those with a religious frame of reference will want to name the source of healing energy as 'God'. Others, in secular settings, will want to conceptualize it in other ways, perhaps just as 'healing energy'. However, it is important not to confuse the question of whether or not transcendent resources for healing are conceptualized in theological terms with the quite separate question of whether or not healing depends on the grace of God. Even though secular spiritual healing may proceed outside an explicit framework of religious belief, it should not be assumed to proceed independently of God. A Christian theologian would surely recognize that all human efforts at healing take place within God's created order and are in accordance with His purposes. That is as true of secular spiritual healing as it is of medical science. Secular healing may be outside faith or theology, but it is surely not outside God.

This is a point made very clearly by Paul Meehl in one of the most rigorous books published so far on psychology and theology (1958).

Meehl rejects the distinction between spiritual healing and all other modes of healing. The fundamental distinction, he argues, is between direct cures (such as the miracles described in Jesus' ministry) and indirect cures through medicine, psychotherapy and the like. 'The important thing to remember is that God is always the primary cause in restoring health' (Meehl 1958, p. 307).

Bringing God into the discussion radically transforms the sense in which spiritual healing can be deemed to be 'spiritual'. Philosophically, the sense in which God is spiritual is very different from that in which humans are spiritual. We can take an emergentist view of human spirituality in which the spiritual aspect of humans is grounded in the physical and mental aspects, distinguishable from them, but not independent or separable. However, it is not appropriate to take a similar emergentist view of the sense in which God is spirit (Clayton 2006). Theologically, the world emerges from God, not God from the world. So the involvement of God in spiritual healing can make it radically spiritual, in a way that is quite different from the involvement of human spirituality in healing.

Theologically, spiritual healing seems to be a particular example of divine action in the natural world, and divine action is a topic that has recently been much discussed by those concerned with the interface between science and religion (Saunders 2002). Most participants in this discussion have wanted to avoid either eliminating the concept of divine action altogether or, on the other hand, seeing it as a supernatural intervention in the natural world that overturns the laws of nature. To eliminate special divine action is to jettison a concept that has been central to the Judeo-Christian tradition. However, there are both theological and scientific reasons for refraining from seeing it as a divine intervention that contravenes the laws of nature.

From a scientific standpoint, 'intervention' by God looks improbable, and there appears to be no scientific evidence for it. From a theological point of view it is unattractive because it involves the assumption that God overturns laws of nature that emanate from Him, and which it would be more consistent with his faithfulness and constancy to uphold. It also risks marginalizing God's action in the world to a few occasions when exceptional things occur, and neglecting the sense that the ordinary world depends constantly on God's general providence.

Healing raises particular issues beyond those raised by other cases of divine action, issues that have not been adequately considered. Unlike many cases of divine action, spiritual healing is often explicitly sought.

Those seeking healing, whether seeking it for themselves or others, often use spiritual practices such as laying on of hands to bring healing about. So there is a distinctive combination of human initiative and presumed divine action involved in spiritual healing.

TRANSCENDENCE AND SCIENCE

Let us suppose that spiritual healing actually occurs, in the radical sense of healing that is dependent on transcendent resources, whether or not they are conceptualized theologically. How does spiritual healing in that sense relate to a scientific worldview?

It is a mistake to ask whether spiritual healing should be understood scientifically *or* theologically. They represent complementary perspectives on spiritual healing, an approach which I have argued elsewhere is essential to a proper conception of the relationship between theology and science (Watts 1998). There are certainly aspects of spiritual healing that need to be conceptualized theologically rather than scientifically. However, there are other aspects that need to be conceptualized scientifically rather than theologically. Spiritual healing can be understood more adequately when it is approached both theologically and scientifically, rather than by either discipline alone.

I want to avoid making a sharp distinction between healing phenomena that are amenable to naturalistic explanation, and other 'spiritual' or supernatural healing phenomena that are not so amenable. That distinction arises from a rigid view of what the laws of nature permit and, historically, it is only since the scientific revolution that a rigid view of the laws of nature has been widely considered. I suggest that there are no good reasons for regarding the laws of nature as invariant laws to which no exceptions are possible. Only if we believe that we know the full range of phenomena permitted by the laws of nature can we presume to identify certain phenomena as 'natural', and other phenomena as lying outside them and therefore 'supernatural'. The Medical Bureau at Lourdes seems wrong-headed from this point of view, in that it only regards healing as 'spiritual' if it is totally inexplicable in natural terms.

It is better to see healing in terms of a subtle interpenetration of the natural and the spiritual, rather than in terms of a sharp disjunction between them. I see healing as representing an enhancement of what normally happens under the laws of nature rather than an overturning of those laws. Science is gradually becoming increasingly emancipated in its ontology and the range of processes it is prepared to accept. As it does so, there will be less and less reason for regarding exceptional phenomena as outside the laws of nature.

SCIENTIFIC PARADIGMS AND SPIRITUAL HEALING

There seems no reason why spiritual healing, in a radical sense, should not be studied by natural science and to some degree understood by it. Some see spiritual healing as, by definition, lying outside natural science. However, I would argue that whether or not this is so depends on how broadly natural science is conceived. Natural science at present may be unable to comprehend spiritual healing in a radical sense, but there is no reason why natural science should remain limited in that way. I would want to press the case for an emancipated natural science that will be able to study and understand whatever forms of spiritual healing occur.

The pressure for an emancipation of science comes at least as much from within science as from outside it. The task of science is to investigate and understand whatever is present or occurs in the world. If science encounters genuine phenomena (and I assume spiritual healing to be one of these), its task is to investigate and understand. If it finds its present theoretical frameworks inadequate for doing that, the theoretical frameworks must be expanded.

In any particular period, science works with particular paradigms. It is a feature of scientific methodology that it tries to explain phenomena as simply as possible. Science often adopts a working hypothesis of the form that all real phenomena can be explained within a certain framework. Such frameworks are only particular scientific paradigms, they are not science itself. When a paradigm proves inadequate for understanding a genuine phenomenon, science has no alternative but to replace it with a broader paradigm that is more consistent with known phenomena. Though I assume that spiritual healing can, to some extent, be understood scientifically, I concede that the science needed to understand spiritual healing is not yet fully available at the beginning of the twenty-first century. We are only at the foothills of the human sciences and are not yet in any position to lay down the law about what is/is not credible scientifically. There is still much too much that we don't understand.

There is nothing reductionist about my claim that spiritual healing can be understood scientifically. It is not a claim of the form, 'spiritual healing is nothing but xyz'. I am not claiming that spiritual healing can be adequately understood in terms of the theoretical frameworks currently adopted by science. For example, I am not claiming that spiritual healing is really just a psychological phenomenon. I want both to admit the reality and power of spiritual healing, but also to assert that science is potentially capable of taking steps towards understanding it. A complementary theological account will always remain essential in any comprehensive understanding of the phenomenon.

My approach here is influenced by my general view of the development of science, and the place of paradigm shifts within it. Following Kuhn and his concept of paradigm shifts (Kuhn 1962; Gutting 1980), I see no reason to accept that modern medical science is definitive, and that the current paradigmatic assumptions will reign for all time. Indeed, it seems clear that there are signs of strain within the current paradigm that may lead to it being revised in significant ways. The inconvenient fact that some 'alternative' approaches to healing, such as acupuncture, seem to be effective, at least in certain contexts (Vickers 1996, pp. 303–11), is a major problem for the current paradigm, as it often cannot make any sense of the assumptions on which they are based.

Paradigm shifts are always an uncomfortable matter. Kuhn originally suggested that paradigms were incommensurable, and that non-rational factors determined the shift from one paradigm to another. However, I think the consensus would now be that both rational and non-rational factors are involved. On the rational side, there is a judgement to be made about whether there is a sufficient accumulation of inconvenient facts that defy incorporation within current assumptions to justify a paradigm shift. On the non-rational side, there is the hostility to new thinking that comes from those who fear that their approach will have to undergo radical readjustment, and the opportunism of those who hope to make their names spearheading a new paradigm.

Among those who are committed to a dialogue between religious and scientific approaches concerning spiritual healing there are at least two significant points of debate. One concerns how broad or narrow a version of science to adopt; the other concerns the methodology of relating science and religion, and whether science is allowed to dictate what can legitimately be said from a religious viewpoint, to the extent that it becomes what Polkinghorne calls 'assimilation' rather than 'consonance' (1996).

It may be helpful here to make an analogy with debates about evolution, where one can distinguish three broad positions. There are narrow Darwinians who assume that everything in evolution can be attributed to natural selection. There are broad Darwinians such as Stephen Jay Gould and Simon Conway Morris who operate within Darwinian assumptions but who think that other factors apart from natural selection are important. Thirdly, there are anti-Darwinians, who reject natural selection, and indeed evolution altogether. This leads to two rather different debates, one between those who are for and against evolution, and another more subtle debate between broad and narrow Darwinian theories of evolution.

The interesting debate about science and spiritual healing is not about whether or not to try to understand healing in scientific terms at all, but about whether to employ a narrow or an emancipated science in this context. I believe the more interesting debate about medical science and spiritual healing is not between those who espouse physicalism and those who reject it, but between those who want a narrow or a broad version of physicalism. Even among those who want to remain within a relatively conservative version of the modern medical paradigm, there are ways in which some aspects of spiritual healing can be understood.

COMPLEMENTARY ACCOUNTS

It is in the nature of reality that it often requires multiple, overlapping accounts. That point has often been made within scientific discourse, for example in terms of quantum complementarity. We may need to describe a quantum entity as both wave and particle; neither description will do on its own. There is also a complementarity of the sciences of mind and brain that is less exact, and so may be more like the complementarity of natural and spiritual.

I propose that to understand healing we need not just different, complementary scientific explanations (as in quantum mechanics or the mind/brain sciences), but theological and scientific accounts. The key question is not whether spiritual healing is to be understood scientifically *or* theologically, but what the relationship should be between theological and scientific accounts.

Theological and scientific approaches to healing are complementary in that they answer different questions. It has often been remarked that theology and science address, respectively, 'why' and 'how' questions. In cosmology, for example, theology can be seen as answering 'why' questions, in that it places the creation of the universe within the purposes of God. Science, in contrast, is answering 'how' questions, such as how the big bang occurred in a quantum vacuum. The why/how distinction provides a useful initial clarification of the contributions of theology and science to understanding spiritual healing.

As with cosmology, theology characteristically places healing within the purposes of God, purposes that are both revelatory and pastoral. The gospel healing narratives are the primary source material for a Christian theology of healing. Three of the seven 'signs of glory' stories around which the first half of St John's Gospel is constructed are healing stories; the story of the healing of the blind man in John 9 is most explicit in its claim that Jesus healed to reveal God's glory. Other healing stories seem to be as much a response to pastoral need as a deliberate act of revelation, but it would be a mistake to pit pastoral and revelatory purposes against one another.

There are also many other important issues about what the healings represent (e.g. that they are signs of the wholeness that God's kingdom brings), what human qualities they depend on (faith, urgent desire), and what principles they illustrate (e.g. that healing is more important than keeping the Sabbath). It is not my purpose here to develop a theology of healing in detail, but simply to indicate the nature of the questions with which such a theology is concerned.

The scientific approach to healing deals with very different questions, which can conveniently be subdivided into outcome and process questions. The most basic scientific question is whether spiritual healing actually takes place, and that calls for the careful keeping of records, for information about the nature of the problems that are presumed to be healed, and for a comparison with what remission might have taken place without spiritual healing.

More interestingly, there are also process questions about how healing takes place. For example, if pain is alleviated by spiritual healing questions arise about exactly how the pain reduction occurred. It is possible in principle to compare how pain is alleviated through spiritual healing with the effects of medication on pain. If pain relief occurs at all, it must be possible to address such questions scientifically, and it is hard to see why that should be resisted, unless it is thought that theology and science are so radically irreconcilable that a theological approach to spiritual healing renders a complementary scientific account completely inappropriate.

It rarely, if ever, happens that scientific data rule out a theological approach; keeping science and theology in dialogue influences the details of how the theological approach is worked out. Dialogue between theology and science generally leads to a process of mutual revision, rather than the acceptance or rejection of theological positions. We will normally need to offer both theological and scientific accounts of spiritual healing.

There is a related example in the work on grace by the Jesuit psycho-analyst William Meissner (1987) who proposes a theology of grace, indebted to Karl Rahner, in terms of relationship with a transcendent God, who is the source of grace. However, alongside that, he proposes a psychological account of how grace works itself out at the human level. There is no contradiction between those two accounts, but they answer different questions. The theological account is more about *what* grace is; the psychological account is more about *how* it works. In the same way, a theological account of healing might focus mainly on God as the source of healing, and a psychological account on how healing works.

It has been an assumption of Christians involved in spiritual healing, at least since the revival of spiritual healing that took place in the twenti-eth century, that special divine action is more likely to be involved in spiritual healing than in medical or psychological healing. Both arise within the general providence of God, but spiritual healing involves a deliberate seeking of divine action, and special divine action seems more likely to occur when God is acknowledged, sought and invoked. It is in the nature of God to work with people, rather than independently of them, and the most significant cases of special divine action arise when humans are explicitly open to God and are co-operating with him (Watts 2002, ch. 8). The spiritual practices in which people engage when seeking healing may set up a resonance or attune-ment with God, rather as I have suggested prayer does (Watts 2001), following Polkinghorne's earlier suggested analogy with a nuclear resonance (1989).

In this sense, the theological account is especially important to spiritual healing, even though a general theological explanation can be offered of all healing. With medical healing, the naturalistic account of how healing takes place is primary, in the sense that it is this that guides the actions of doctors and surgeons, even though it is possible to offer a more general theological view of how medical healing is embedded in God's creation and purposes. In contrast, with spiritual healing the theological account is the primary one in the sense that it is the one that explicitly guides the actions of those involved. It is also possible to offer a naturalistic version, for example of how the alleviation of pain is mediated when spiritual healing takes place. With spiritual healing the theological explanation is primary, whereas for medical healing it is the naturalistic one. Comple-mentary versions are possible in both cases, but the priority attached to them is reversed.

THE ACADEMIC LITERATURE ON SPIRITUAL HEALING

Despite the importance of spiritual healing, there is only a small and scattered academic literature about it. The vast majority of books published are by advocates and practitioners, and are written either to persuade or to be of practical benefit. Some are discussed by Bourne and Watts in Chapter 5. A pioneering dispassionate treatment of spiritual healing was the thorough examination of religious and psychological healing undertaken by Leslie Weatherhead in the post-war period, *Psychology, Religion and Healing* (1951).

Among historical books, Amanda Porterfield's *Healing in the History of Christianity* (2005) surveys the contribution of Christians to healing of various kinds, not just spiritual healing. There is an excellent set of historical case studies in a volume on *The Church and Healing* published for the Ecclesiastical History Society (Sheils 1982), and Harrell (1975) has contributed a study of the revival of charismatic healing in post-war America.

Taking a social-scientific approach, John Pilch has looked at New Testament healing from an anthropological point of view (2000). Thomas Csordas has provided the richest anthropological studies of contemporary healing, including *The Sacred Self: A Cultural Phenomenology of Charismatic Healing* (1997) and *Body/Meaning/Healing* (2002). Gary Easthope has undertaken a sociological examination with the merit of considering a broad range of settings and approaches (1986). Simon Dein has contributed a valuable study of the role of healing in the Lubavitch Community in North London (2004). Two edited books that contain valuable social-scientific material on religious healing are *The Performance of Healing* (Lademan and Roseman 1996) and *Religion and Healing in America* (Barnes and Sered 2005).

The theological strand on healing is represented by Evelyn Frost (1940), who looked at what the pre-Nicene Church Fathers have to say about healing. Morton Kelsey has undertaken a broader historical survey of theologies of healing in *Psychology, Medicine and Christian Healing* (1988), exploring the story of the decline and revival of spiritual healing. Ronald Kydd has identified conceptual and theological models for healing in *Healing Through the Centuries* (2001) and Stephen Pattison has considered the modern revival of religious healing in *Alive and Kicking* (1989, ch. 3).

Daniel Benor has reviewed the scientific literature relevant to spiritual healing very fully (1993). For a briefer and more up-to-date overview see

Benor (2005). David Larson and colleagues edited a consensus report on spirituality and health (1998), and Harold Koenig and colleagues have edited a *Handbook of Religion and Health* (2001). Coakley and Shelemay (2007) have recently edited *Pain and its Transformations*, a fascinating interdisciplinary book on pain that has implications for spiritual healing.

OVERVIEW OF THE BOOK

The next few chapters of this book look at religious and theological aspects of healing. Justin Meggitt, in Chapter 2, considers the healings described in the gospels. Like many recent scholars he is persuaded that those healings are historical facts, though there are open questions about how they were achieved. In Chapter 3, Philip Clayton contributes a Christian historical theology of healing. There have been considerable changes over the centuries in both the practice and conceptualization of spiritual healing, and that is important background for any contemporary attempt to make sense of the subject.

The next two chapters broaden the story beyond Christianity. Chapter 4, by Simon Dein, plays two important roles in the book. First it provides a detailed examination of contemporary spiritual healing in another faith tradition, a conservative Jewish community. It also takes a social-scientific perspective, and shows how the social sciences can elucidate the role of spiritual healing in a religious community. Chapter 5 by Charles Bourne and Fraser Watts analyses spiritual healing in the non-religious as well as the Christian world. Its method is to examine representative books about healing by Christian and secular writers, and to see how far they share common assumptions, despite their different contexts and language.

Then follow a group of chapters that focus on some of the psychological and biological processes by which healing might be mediated. In Chapter 6, Bruce Kinsey brings a psycho-analytical perspective to bear, and uses it to elucidate the psychological significance of illness and healing, and the dynamics of the healing relationship. The next two chapters switch the focus to biology. Chapter 7, by Paul and Hannah Gilbert, focuses on the development of interpersonal relationships, and how the empathy and compassion that are a marked feature of spiritual healing might be mediated biologically. Michael J. Boivin and Burton Webb, in Chapter 8, focus on breast cancer, review recent research on psychoneuroimmunology, and investigate immune response and how it can affect the progress of the disease. In Chapter 9 Marilyn Schlitz looks at the empirical evidence that bears on the hypothesis that various parapsychological processes might play a role in spiritual healing. She includes a review of controversial empirical research on the efficacy of prayer for healing. David Leech's chapter considers, from a more philosophical point of view, the relationship between parapsychological and theological approaches to spiritual healing.

In a final chapter, I draw together how spiritual healing might be mediated at a biological and psychological level, and place the current interest in spiritual healing in a broad social and historical context.

CHAPTER 2

The historical Jesus and healing: Jesus' miracles in psychosocial context

Justin Meggitt

The healing miracles of the historical Jesus may seem, at first sight, an unpromising, if not fanciful subject for critical study. Those unfamiliar with current scholarship might wonder how supernatural phenomena, such as *miracles*, can be the subject of serious *historical* scrutiny in the twenty-first century. In fact, regardless of what one thinks about the possibility of miracles (and, of course, this very much depends upon what one means by a miracle) most of those specializing in the study of the origins of Christianity believe that there are good grounds for holding that the historical Jesus was thought by his contemporaries, including both supporters and critics, to be an effective healer and exorcist. It is in this sense that the healings and exorcisms can be considered to constitute *historical* data and can be open to examination. Although subsequent generations of Christians would become almost fixated by Jesus' reputation as a miracle worker (Mathews 1999, pp. 54–91) and produced ever more elaborate and fantastical traditions, there are good reasons to look closely at the earliest records of this activity. Indeed, it is my contention that they can stand rather more scrutiny than they have so far received: if we look closely at the psychosocial dynamics that seem to characterize the healing activity of the *historical* Jesus as recounted in formative traditions about him, largely embedded in the synoptic gospels, we can go some way towards understanding how and why he acquired this reputation as an effective healer.

But first it is necessary to clarify the grounds that lead many biblical critics to believe that the historical Jesus was, in his own day, thought to be an effective and miraculous healer. There are a number of reasons for this conviction. Jesus' healings and exorcisms are attested in all the major sources that we possess for Jesus' life, both Christian and non-Christian, both supportive and hostile. The evidence is comprehensively surveyed elsewhere (e.g. Blackburn 1994; Twelftree 1999) and not much would be gained by repeating it all here (although it is important to note, in the

light of Eve's recent work (2005), that the multiple attestation of traditions does not give us quite the degree of historical certainty that is often
assumed). However, it is helpful to give a few indicative examples of
material that is judged vital in arriving at such a position. Two specific
traditions that are often ascribed to the 'Q' source (a hypothetical source
that is normally thought to predate the canonical gospels and to reflect the
earliest traditions about the historical Jesus) are usually taken as particularly strong evidence that the *historical* Jesus thought himself to be a healer
and exorcist whose activities were visible to all, and to corroborate the
broader pictures evident in the gospels and other material. The first of
these is the tradition that John the Baptist sent some of his disciples to ask
Jesus whether he was 'the one who is to come', a question that produced
the following, affirmative answer:

And he answered them, 'Go and tell John what you have seen and heard: the
blind receive their sight, the lame walk, the lepers are cleansed, the deaf hear,
the dead are raised, the poor have good news brought to them. And blessed is
anyone who takes no offence at me.' (Luke 7:22–3; Matthew 11:4–5)

As it stands, in both Matthew and Luke, the question by the Baptist and the
subsequent response are particularly awkward as John is described as having
already recognized Jesus' true status in both gospels: in Matthew, at his
baptism (3:14) and in Luke, even earlier, from within his mother's womb
(1:41). Such incongruity is usually taken by biblical scholars as evidence that
the gospel writers have preserved a primitive tradition – and so it is all the
more likely to be authentic. Jesus' answer to John the Baptist is also a
problematic one as healing miracles were not associated with any significant messianic expectations within Judaism in this period and so it comes as
something of a surprise, not withstanding one sliver of evidence from the
Dead Sea Scrolls (4Q521). So, as it stands, this incident is unlikely to have
been created by the early Church and is most likely to have had its origins in
a specific incident. If that is the case, then the belief that Jesus carried out
healings belongs in the earliest stratum of our knowledge about this figure.

The second key tradition takes the form of a saying in which Jesus
explicitly linked the arrival of the Kingdom of God, the chief preoccupation of his preaching (e.g. Matthew 3:2, Mark 1:15), with his exorcisms:

But if it is by the finger of God that I cast out the demons, then the kingdom of
God has come to you. (Luke 11:20; Matthew 12:28)

Although brief, this saying too has a good claim to authenticity although
in this case, primarily on the grounds that it is a 'Q' logion and seems to

cohere with what we know of characteristics of Jesus' ministry from elsewhere. Davies and Allison call the authenticity of this second saying 'one of the assured results of modern criticism' (1991, p. 339).

To those unfamiliar with the conventions of current historical critical scholarship, the significance placed on these two traditions might seem odd. However, when we combine such early sayings with traditions about his healings and exorcisms that appear to be very early and multiply attested but evidently did not originate with either Jesus or the early Church, such as the tradition that Jesus expelled demons by the power of Beelzebul, the prince of demons (found in Matthew 12:24, Mark 3:22, Luke 11:15), the notion that he was thought to be a healer and exorcist seems all but established.

The fact that non-Christian sources, both Jewish and pagan, also depict Jesus as a figure famed for his ability to heal and exorcise, makes such a picture almost irrefutable and undermines any argument that sees them, *in toto*, as the invention of subsequent Christians. We find, for example, his healings and exorcisms the subject of the earliest anti-Christian polemics of which we have a record, those of Trypho and Celsus (found in Justin Martyr and Origen respectively), who seem to have access to traditions about Jesus independent of the gospels. Both critics attacked the character of Jesus' miracles and his motivations in performing them, but neither claimed that they had not taken place. Criticisms of a similar kind, in which Jesus' miracles were clearly being equated with the miracles of magicians, seem to lie behind the accusations that provoked the earliest work of Christian apologetic literature, that of Quadratus of Athens (in Eusebius, *The History of the Church*, 4.3). The healings and exorcisms also appear to be alluded to in Josephus' *Testimonium Flavianum* (found in *Jewish Antiquities*, 18.63–4), or rather in the likely kernel of authentic material that lies at the heart of this much edited passage by the famous Jewish historian (Carleton Paget 2001, pp. 539–624). Indeed, it is fair to say that if Jesus was famous for anything amongst his contemporaries, it was for his healing miracles and exorcisms: the unidentified exorcists who are recorded as using Jesus' name in Mark 9:38 and Luke 9:49, and the tradition in Acts 19:13 that the seven sons of Sceva attempted something similar, point to the antiquity of this estimation (see Meggitt 2006, pp. 89–114).

So it is reasonable to say that the historical Jesus was perceived by his contemporaries to have been a healer. Indeed, as Meier, observes in his work *A Marginal Jew: Rethinking the Historical Jesus*, 'Put dramatically, but with not too much exaggeration: if the miracle tradition from Jesus' public ministry were to be rejected *in toto* as unhistorical, so should every other Gospel tradition about him' (Meier 1991, p. 630). This explains why virtually all scholars of the historical Jesus, whatever their ideological persuasion, accept that the historical Jesus was indeed believed to be a miraculous healer in his own lifetime: Geza Vermes (1973), E. P. Sanders (1985, 1993), John Dominic Crossan (1991), Gerd Theissen (with A. Merz 1998), E. S. Fiorenza (1995a, 1995b), Luke T. Johnson (1997), David Flusser (1998), Robert Funk and the Jesus Seminar (1998), Paula Fredriksen (2000), J. D. G. Dunn (2003), John P. Meier (1991–2009) and Graham Stanton (2002). It has not always been so (Avalos 1999, p. 6) and most reconstructions of the historical Jesus still fail to deal adequately with the healing miracles (Davies 1995, p. 15), but in recent decades this consensus has emerged and looks stable.

However, before scrutinizing the psychosocial dynamics of the events that lie at the heart of this estimation of the historical Jesus, we need to make some important, preliminary remarks.

First, the fact that Jesus was thought to have been a healer and exorcist in his own lifetime does not, in itself, set him apart from his contemporaries. Others were also believed to have such abilities. For example, from literary sources of the time we hear of Eleazar, a Jewish exorcist who carried out an exorcism in front of Vespasian (Josephus, *Jewish Antiquities*, 8.45–8), and an unnamed Syrian exorcist and Chaldean healer who were reputed to have done similar things (Lucian, *Lover of Lies*, 16, 11). It is clear that a number of those who inhabited the first-century world, both Jew and gentile, were believed to be able to carry out such things. Indeed, there were many people who 'in return for a few coins ... will expel demons from men, and dispel diseases' by miraculous means (Celsus in Origen, *Contra Celsum*, 68). And in addition to living people, shrines and statues that were believed to effect miraculous cures were found everywhere. A cursory examination of the literary and archaeological records of the cult of Asklepios indicates as much (see, for example, Edelstein *et al.* 1998; Hart 2000) – indeed, according to Josephus, even Jews could, on occasion, avail themselves of such sites (Josephus, *The Jewish War*, 2.21.6 and *Jewish Antiquities*, 18.2.3). Claims could be made about the healing powers of some of the most unlikely of subjects – for example, Athenagoras, in his *A Plea for the Christians* (26), informs us that a statue of Peregrinus, an apostate Christian ridiculed by Lucian of Samosata as a religious charlatan, was regarded as having curative powers. The gospels themselves are insistent that Jesus did not have a monopoly on such miraculous activity. They record Jesus himself saying as much. 'If I cast out demons by Beelzebul, by whom do your sons cast them out?' (Matthew 12:27, Luke 11:19 and Mark 13:22; Matthew 24:24).

Second, in saying this I would not like to appear to be arguing that everyone in the ancient world believed in supernatural healings and exorcisms, or that those who did believe in them, believed in them in the same way. There was considerable diversity in the nature and extent of belief in the supernatural in antiquity (Remus 1983, pp. 7–47), and there was also significant scepticism too. The New Testament itself contains evidence of just such variegated belief. The gospel of John, for example, although containing a number of healings, does not contain any exorcisms at all. Although a number of explanations for this anomaly have been suggested (e.g. Twelftree 2007, pp. 183–205; Piper 2000, pp. 253–78), the most likely explanation is that the author (or those who first brought together the traditions upon which the author was dependent) evidently did not share the same notions about demons as did the other three gospel writers and, indeed, the historical Jesus himself.

Third, it is important to note that it is impossible to say anything for certain historically about any *specific* healing or exorcism. That is not the same as saying that they were not thought to have occurred in ways that resemble the accounts found in the gospels, but we really do not have sufficient grounds to say that any particular miracle tradition is based on a particular historical incident. Others are not so circumspect in this respect. For example Twelftree lists twenty-two miracles that he believes 'can be judged with high confidence to reflect an event or events most likely in the life of the historical Jesus' (1999, p. 328) – of which nineteen are healing miracles (see also Sterling 1993, pp. 67–93). It is possible that the recent work of Bauckham (2006) might yet lead us to place rather more weight on the claim that the gospel writers based their narratives on direct eyewitness testimony (Luke 1:2) and so open the door to exploring the unique psychosocial dynamics of individual healings in future years. But for now such undertakings, seen for example in the influential work of Donald Capps (2000, pp. 165–217; 2008), can look historically naive and almost pre-critical. Our analysis will have to remain at the level of generality if it is to have historical credibility and we will work with Norman Perrin's assertion that 'we cannot, today, reconstruct a single authentic healing or exorcism narrative from the tradition we have' (1976, p. 137). This is a minimalist position, but one that can at least allow us to proceed somewhat further with the question.

DID JESUS EVER CURE ANYBODY?

If Jesus was thought to be a healer and exorcist by his contemporaries, it seems reasonable to go further and ask the question asked by John Pilch (2000, p. 142) 'Did Jesus ever cure anybody?' New Testament scholars, almost without exception (though see Remus 1997, pp. 104–18), would consider this question unacceptable. Meier, for example, believes questions about whether miracles actually happened are only legitimate in philosophy or theology and should not concern someone interested in the *historical* Jesus: 'they are illegitimate or at least unanswerable in a historical investigation that stubbornly restricts itself to empirical evidence and rational deductions or inferences from such evidence' (Meier 1991–2009, vol. 2, p. 511). Instead, most would say that questions should be kept modest and we should limit ourselves to trying to understand what Jesus or his contemporaries meant in Christological terms when they claimed he was a miracle worker, and leave it at that. But, as Meier himself notes, avoiding this question looks disingenuous to everyone but New Testament scholars themselves (1994, p. 511).

So it is refreshing that a minority of scholars have, in relatively recent years, been unwilling to leave the question unasked. However, most who have asked it have answered it in the negative. Pilch, for example, answered the question that he posed so candidly with a definitive 'No' (Pilch 2000, p. 142). However, in saying this, Pilch does not deny that Jesus *healed* people. In fact, his book could be said to be, in part, dedicated to explaining how this happened. This apparent contradiction is explicable because for Pilch *curing* and *healing* are not synonyms. *Curing* is 'the strategy of destroying or checking a pathogen, removing a malfunctioning or non-functioning organ, restoring a person to health or well-being' (Pilch 2000, p. 153), whereas *healing* he defines as 'the restoration of meaning to life. It is the strategy of restoring social and personal meaning for life problems that accompany human health misfortunes.' (Pilch 2000, p. 155). The former, Pilch maintains, rarely occurs, even with the benefits of modern medicine, while the latter always occurs, in the sense that 'All people . . . eventually come to some resolution' (2000, p. 141) – and, for Pilch, Jesus seems to have been particularly effective at facilitating this process.

In claiming that Jesus *healed* but did not *cure* (for example 2000, p. 142), Pilch is saying something which, with varying degrees of sophistication, has been said by other New Testament scholars although without the conceptual rigour he brings to the discussion (for example Crossan

1994, p. 82; 1998, pp. 293–304). He should be commended for his honesty on this matter and his clarity, as well as his valuable appropriation of perspectives that originate in the field of medical anthropology. Although I am unconvinced by the homogenization of cultures that his particular approach to the 'Mediterranean' world entails (for much the same reasons I am unconvinced by the work of Bruce Malina on which he is dependent; see Meggitt 1998, pp. 215–19), and remain perplexed by his assertion that human beings *always* achieve 'healing' (not something I recognize in my own experience), the basic distinction between *healing* and *curing* is obviously an important one.

Nonetheless, there are two ways in which Pilch's answer to the question that he asks about Jesus seems inadequate. Pilch claims to use the New Testament texts in a manner analogous to that of an anthropologist's 'field report' (2000, p. 76) and calls on readers to take seriously what anthropologists term *emic* (that is *insider*) accounts of reality as part of the interpretative process. Yet in what follows Pilch seems unwilling to engage with the *emic* claims that are made about Jesus. Jesus was not thought by his contemporaries solely to provide resolutions to the social and personal problems of meaning created by *illness* (the social experience of a sickness). He was also thought to cure *disease* (the physical experience of a sickness). Pilch is quite wrong to ignore this. He appears to do so because of his belief that someone can only think in terms of disease if they think in terms of contemporary biomedical models, which obviously first-century people did not. Hence his rather odd assertion that 'in the Bible there is no interest at all in disease' (Pilch 2000, p. 76). This is an indefensible position and one that would not be supported by leading medical anthropologists in the field. Kleinman and Sung, for example, make it clear in their survey of historical and traditional healthcare systems that these are concerned not just with affecting the meaning of an illness but also with attempts to limit disease (1979, p. 22; see also Webb 2006, p. 195, Eve 2002, p. 354). As we saw at the outset, Jesus' healings were regarded by his contemporaries as unexpectedly efficacious with tangible consequences: the blind, it is claimed, received their sight, the lame walked, people with leprosy were cleansed, and the deaf heard. These results look to the modern reader, as they would to one of Jesus' contemporaries, suspiciously like *cures*.

How can such unusual claims be explained? Given the above, it will not do to dismiss them as legendary accretions to our traditions about Jesus. They seem to go too far back and be too widespread in our records for that (hence the unusual consensus amongst scholars that we noted).

Of course, for some, the explanation lies mostly in unwitting self-deception on the part of many of those 'cured'. They may have been swept up in the exhilaration of events, and temporarily ceased to be conscious of their symptoms. Or their belief in the reputation of the healer might have convinced them that their symptoms had been alleviated when, by any objective assessment, they had not (a well-attested phenomenon – see Kleinman and Sung 1979, p. 13). However, self-deception seems unlikely in most cases. Although it might be possible where a person is suffering from certain chronic, degenerative, biomechanical disorders, it is hard to see how a paralytic can forget their symptoms or a blind person see, however swept up they are in events or impressed by a charismatic individual. To label Jesus' cures self-deception seems a crude way of understanding the nature of such experiences and the long-term results that Jesus was claimed to have had. So, for example, Quadratus, according to Eusebius a disciple of the apostles, wrote an apology to Hadrian in 124 or 125 allegedly claiming that

Our Saviour's works, moreover, were always present: for they were real, consisting of those who had been healed of their diseases, those who had been raised from the dead; who were not only seen whilst they were being healed and raised up, but were afterwards constantly present. Nor did they remain only during the sojourn of the Saviour on earth, but also a considerable time after His departure; and, indeed, some of them have survived even down to our own times. (Quadratus in Eusebius, *The History of the Church*, 4.3)

So if such 'cures' were not the result of self-deception, can we suggest any alternative explanations?

PSYCHOSOMATIC EXPLANATIONS

For many New Testament scholars it is not unthinkable that the historical Jesus did indeed *cure* people of diseases as well as heal them of illnesses. Some are, of course, happy to account for this by affirming their belief that Jesus did indeed carry out miraculous cures by supernatural means (Twelftree 1999, p. 345). There is a great deal that could be said about this kind of reasoning, but I do think that a couple of points need to be made.

1 Scholars should not assume, as Twelftree seems to, that establishing the historicity of the miracle traditions necessarily implies that Jesus carried out what would usefully be called a miracle by a modern reader. For those in antiquity, a miracle can be best defined, as Remus suggests, as an event that is 'perceived to be extraordinary and beyond human

capability; ... inexplicable except by attributing it to or associating it in some way with superhuman agency' (Remus 1992, p. 859). But while such a definition might be consonant with perspectives in the early Roman empire, clearly the judgement of a twenty-first-century person on what exactly constituted an event that is inexplicable would be markedly different.

2 I find it somewhat disingenuous that I have yet to find a biblical scholar who believes that the miracles of Jesus are only explicable in supernatural terms and who also believes that the miracles that allegedly occurred in the shrine of Asklepios should also be ascribed to such a cause, or that the emperor Vespasian's healings in Alexandria can be explained in such a way (Tacitus, *The Histories*, 4.81; Suetonius, *Vespasian*, 7.2; and Cassius Dio, *Roman Histories*, 65.8; Eve 2008). If someone really wishes to claim supernatural causality in explaining the miracles of Jesus – a claim that would look rather unusual in any other field of historical enquiry – then they should at least be as generous as the historical Jesus appears to have been, and allow for others being able to effect genuine miracles by such means in the first century (Matthew 12:27, Luke 11.19; see also Mark 9:38–9, Luke 9:49–50). In saying this I am not saying anything new – Paul Achtemeier said as much in his 1975 article on the tradition about the healing of the boy with epilepsy (2008, pp. 138–9).

However, most scholars of the New Testament believe that the historical Jesus did indeed *cure* people of diseases as well as heal them of illnesses but assume that the events were not 'miraculous' in the sense that they do not require modern interpreters to believe that what happened in the past is beyond modern, rational explanation, however astonishing and inexplicable they might have been to Jesus' contemporaries. For them Jesus' healings did not 'violate the laws of Nature' and therefore constitute a miracle according to Hume's familiar criterion. At the core of traditions about the historical Jesus it is claimed are events in which the sick were cured of disorders that were psychosomatic, or to use an increasingly common term, psychophysiologic, in their origins. That is, the symptoms that were successfully alleviated by the historical Jesus, such as blindness, paralysis, or possession, did not have a physical or organic origin but were the bodily manifestation of intense psychological disturbances.

The notion that the healing miracles and exorcisms of the historical Jesus were of disorders that had psychosomatic aetiologies is often central to arguments made by a broad range of scholars in support of their belief that the historical Jesus was viewed as a healer during his lifetime and for the reliability, at least in general terms, of such traditions. The likely authenticity of these traditions is often contrasted with the likely inauthenticity of the other major category of miraculous activity ascribed to Jesus, the so-called 'nature miracles' such as walking on water (Matthew 14:24–33, Mark 6:47–52, John 6:16–21) which are regularly dismissed as patently unhistorical. As David Aune, for example, remarks 'Since most of the healings and exorcisms found in the tradition can be construed as psychosomatic cures, their occurrence is not an *a priori* historical impossibility' (1980, p. 1525). Morton Smith said much the same in his controversial work *Jesus the Magician* (1978, p. 8) and similar sentiments are expressed by Robert Funk in a book detailing the findings of the influential Jesus Seminar: 'During his lifetime Jesus was considered a healer. From today's perspective, Jesus' cures are related to psychosomatic maladies' (Funk and the Jesus Seminar 1998, pp. 530–1). Funk and his notoriously sceptical colleagues even go on to identify six specific healings in the earliest traditions about Jesus that they believe are evidence of this: the healing of Peter's mother-in-law (Matthew 8:14–15, Mark 1:29–31, Luke 5:38–9); the man with 'leprosy' (Matthew 8:1–4, Mark 1:40–5, Luke 5:12–16, Papyrus Egerton 2:1–4); the paralysed man (Matthew 9:1–8, Mark 2:1–12, Luke 5:17–26); the woman with a haemorrhage (Matthew 9:20–2, Mark 5:24b–34, Luke 8:42b–48); a blind man (Mark 8:22–6) and blind Bartimaeus (Matthew 20:29–34, Mark 10:46–52, Luke 18:35–43). The exorcisms are often singled out as the cures most readily explicable by recourse to psychosomatic explanation (see, for example Sanders 1993, p. 159).

Having raised the possibility that psychosomatic explanations can be given for the healing traditions associated with the historical Jesus, most scholars have been unwilling to pursue this idea much further, assuming that the case is self-evident and no more can be gained by following this line of inquiry. An example of this tendency can be seen in Graham Stanton's cautious remark:

Few doubt that Jesus possessed unusual gifts as a healer, though of course varied explanations are offered. Some suggest that many of the illnesses and disabilities has psychosomatic roots. While this may well have been the case, we have no ways of investigating the matter further. (Stanton 2001, p. 67; see also Twelftree 1999, p. 256)

However, rather more sophisticated psychosomatic explanations have begun to emerge, in which scholars have tried to describe and characterize the factors and mechanisms that might have led to the alleviation of the physical symptoms that the historical Jesus encountered. For example, in recent years there has been a growing tendency to interpret possession as a psychosocial disorder caused by the internalization of oppression, and more specifically the political oppression that the inhabitants of Palestine endured under the Romans (e.g. Crossan 1991, pp. 313–32; Myers 1990, pp. 192–4; Hollenbach 1981, pp. 567–88). A person's anguish at colonial subjugation might become repressed and turned in on itself in a self-destructive manner, as Franz Fanon depicted in his seminal work *The Wretched of the Earth*, a study of mental illness during the Algerian revolutionary war against France (Fanon 1965). Such a person might manifest abnormal behaviour because it offered a socially acceptable form of protest and rebellion in preference to other, more 'sane' and dangerous options. After all, it is noted, the Gerasene demoniac inflicted violence on *himself* (Mark 5:5) and the demons in this story, according to the accounts in Mark and Luke, call themselves 'Legion' (Mark 5:1–20, Luke 8:26–39).

Others have seen the ailments as a consequence of broader economic and social context. Gerd Theissen, for example, notes that the miracles stories

present themselves as forms of expression of lower classes, in the simplicity of their theology, the simplicity of their narrative, but above all their subject matter. Belief in miracles is concentrated here on specific situations of distress, on possession, disease, hunger, lack of success and danger, in other words on situations which do not strike as hard in all social groups. (1983, p. 249)

He then goes on to claim that socio-economic factors may have helped create the plethora of possessed individuals that Jesus faced:

while possession as such could not be class-specifically conditioned, its mass appearance could be. In a society which expresses its problems in mythical language groups under pressure may interpret their situation as threats from demons. (Theissen 1983, p. 250)

For Theissen there is a distinct connection between social class and possession. As a result he can argue that exorcisms challenged more than just demons. Healings and exorcisms are class specific and have class-specific implications (Theissen 1983, p. 251).

Although the insights of Crossan, Theissen and others are suggestive, and should not be dismissed lightly, it is only with the work of Stevan Davies in 1995 that we encounter a sustained and sophisticated examination of the psychosocial characteristics of the healing traditions associated with the historical Jesus by a New Testament scholar. Davies, for example, maintains that those who suffered from specific physical ailments and were cured by the historical Jesus were in fact experiencing 'somatization' or 'conversion' disorders (1995, pp. 70–1). A 'somatization' disorder is a psychiatric disorder that manifests itself in recurrent and multiple physical symptoms. A 'conversion' disorder refers more specifically to the impairment of voluntary motor or sensory functions which appears to suggest neurological or other organic causes but is believed to be associated with psychological stressors (Moene and Roelofs 2008, pp. 625–45). Conversion disorders are often classified as a type of somatoform disorder, as in the influential *Diagnostic and Statistical Manual of Mental Disorders IV* (American Psychiatric Association 1994), but they are also classified as a dissociative disorder, as is the case in the *International Classification of Diseases-10* (World Health Organization 1992–4). Apart from differences in symptoms, there is actually little that distinguishes conversion disorders and somatization disorders (Brown 2004, pp. 793–812). For Davies, the causes that he posits for the physical ailments Jesus allegedly healed provide a cogent reason for his apparent success.

Davies' treatment of the exorcism traditions is also extremely helpful. He dismisses socio-political or economic explanations of possession, maintaining that it could not have had a socio-political or economic cause because the experiences of colonialism and economic oppression were not actually as intense in first-century Galilee and Judea as the likes of Crossan and Theissen maintain (he refers to Sanders 1992 and 1993 to demonstrate this). 'Whatever was happening to cause demon-possession in Galilee it was not discontent with the Roman troops in Judea, nor was it a form of response to indebtedness and taxation' (Davies 1995, p. 81). Rather he provides two different explanations of its occurrence. He draws upon cross-cultural studies to suggest that 'demon-possession is usually a means by which an individual in a socially subordinate role can respond to and cope with circumstances that cannot be effectively dealt with otherwise – most of the time, those circumstances arise from intrafamily conflicts' (1995, p. 81). In addition, he also suggests, following a brief analysis of the literature relating to the origins of multiple personality disorder (MPD), that sufferers 'may have been under the influence of alter-personae that originated in the past, during childhood, as a defence mechanism resulting from abuse' (1995, p. 89).

Donald Capps is another scholar who has posited more detailed psychophysiological explanations for Jesus' efficacy as a healer and exorcist, although unlike Davies he is a psychologist of religion rather than a New Testament scholar. His *Jesus: A Psychological Biography* (2000) and his more recent work *Jesus the Village Psychiatrist* (2008) contain much of value which could be helpful in reconceptualizing our understanding of the healing traditions and contain a far more sophisticated understanding of the relationship between 'disease' and 'illness' than that assumed by scholars working more strictly within the field of New Testament studies. Indeed, he quite rightly takes to task New Testament scholars, such as John Dominic Crossan, who have assumed too rigid a dichotomy between 'disease' and 'illness' as a consequence of their erroneous reading of the influential work of Arthur Kleinman (Capps 2000, p. 168). However, for all their strengths, Capps' psychophysiological explanations of the healings and exorcisms of Jesus are of limited utility, primarily because they are predicated upon his belief in the veracity of classical psychoanalytical theory. So, for example, he can maintain that 'the common element in the cases of persons who were either exorcised or healed was anxiety, a reaction to an externally or internally induced sense of danger, manifesting itself in meaningful symptoms' (2000, p. 170). Unless one already has a prior commitment to such psychoanalytical assumptions, some of Capps' exegesis appears unacceptably speculative. For instance, he says of Jesus' healing of a the paralytic man:

In my view what Jesus has done here is to confront the anxiety of the paralytic man, commanding him not to be undone by perceived dangers (external or internal), but to have confidence that these dangers, whatever they may be, do not warrant an immobilized existence. The command to the man in Mark 2:1–12 to 'go to your home' suggests that the perceived danger is located there, either because he feels threatened at home (e.g. having been treated abusively by his father), or because he is concerned about what he may do to someone at home (e.g. strike his father, take sexual license with a sister). (Capps 2000, p. 195)

Despite its creativity, Capps' work has some other failings that make it problematic. His speculations about Jewish physiology and concurrent psychological disorders evinces an ahistorical and homogenized understanding of Jewish ethnic and cultural identity through time, retrojecting into the first century CE ideas found in ideologically charged medical discourse that developed at the turn of the twentieth century (2000, pp. 196–207).

Despite the increasing sophistication of the analysis by the likes of Crossan, Theissen, Davies, Capps, and others (notably Howard 2001), unfortunately psychophysiological explanations of the healings and exorcisms of the historical Jesus produced to date are of limited value.

They may explain *some* of Jesus' success as a healer but they have significant weaknesses.

Firstly, we do not know with any certainty what kind of disorders were suffered by those whom Jesus healed. As has long been noted, the gospels are notoriously short on detailed clinical description and medical terminology (despite the often repeated claim that Luke's gospel is clearly the work of a physician with the name mentioned in Colossians 4:14; see Cadbury 1926 contra Hobart 1882). When someone is described in these texts as suffering from possession, fever, dysentery, paralysis, blindness, having a flow of blood, a withered hand, leprosy or being 'moonstruck', we can only guess at what is being described (Amundsen and Ferngren 1995, p. 2944). The descriptions of the predicaments of those healed adhere to clear oral and redactional conventions in their depiction of symptoms. Diagnosis is a far from easy undertaking, even with the benefit of modern technology – blood tests and MRIs, X-rays, CAT scans, and endoscopes – and even when one has a body rather than just a text to hand. Even today, of those deaths that are autopsied in the United States (approximately 6 per cent) about 40 per cent reveal that the cause of death has been misdiagnosed – a figure that has stayed roughly the same over the last one hundred years (see Graber *et al.* 2002). Given that it is so difficult for us to have any real idea of the nature of the symptoms that those seeking healing presented to the historical Jesus, it seems unreasonable to claim that we can know anything much about the specific aetiologies of these complaints (and, of course, a specific symptom, such as blindness, can have a myriad of possible causes, physical, organic as well as psychological). It seems all the more unreasonable to posit a *psychological* cause for a particular ailment when the gospels give us so little insight into the interior life of those that Jesus encountered (so it is hard to know whether they were psychologically conflicted or traumatized in any way). Even if we could trust the records that we have as accurate records of historical events, we rarely find anything that can even vaguely approximate to a case history. The closest we seem to get is the occasional reference to the duration of an illness, such as Mark 5:25, 9:21, Luke 13:16, and the rare mention of how those seeking healing have failed to achieve it by other means (Mark 5:26, 9:18).

Even where there is an interesting correlation between the kind of symptoms presented by those healed in the gospels and those associated with somatization and conversion disorders listed in works such as the influential *Diagnostic and Statistical Manual of Mental Disorders* (*DSM-IV*, American Psychiatric Association 1994), such as a loss of voice, deafness, blindness, paralysis, or muscle weakness and excessive menstrual bleeding, this is not in itself conclusive evidence of the presence of psychosomatic disorder. For example, how can the exegete know whether the paralysed man (Matthew 9:1–8, Mark 2:1–12, Luke 5:17–26) suffered from the pseudoneurologic symptoms indicative of a somatization disorder (Davies 1995, p. 71) or was paralysed because of other far more common congenital or acquired disorders (whether, for example, organic, infective, degenerative, malignant or traumatic in origin).

Secondly, from what limited information we can deduce about the disorders that Jesus encountered it seems unlikely that their aetiologies were predominantly psychosomatic. The earliest records that we possess of Jesus' healing ministry do not indicate that he gained his reputation by *only healing a small percentage of those that came to him.* Yet, it is clear that if the success of Jesus was limited to those individuals presenting with symptoms that have a psychosomatic basis *alone* surely such a pattern should be discernible in the records. However, only in the tradition about Jesus' healings in Nazareth do we get the indication that Jesus could only heal a few of those that came to him (Matthew 13:58, Mark 6.5). The sources also emphasize that a number of the ailments that Jesus cured had been suffered since birth (Mark 9:21; John 9:1) so they cannot have had a psychophysiological aetiology. In the light of this it seems rather unwise of scholars, such as Sanders, to maintain 'Once one grants that Jesus healed, the prominence of cures of the lame, the dumb and the blind is not surprising. Those diseases respond to faith-healing' (Sanders 1985, p. 163).

It should be said, at this point, that it most certainly is not the case that demons are the major cause of sickness in the New Testament, something which has encouraged some to believe in the likelihood of psychosomatic explanations for Jesus' healings, the logic being that if the explanation for a disorder is itself, from our perspective, something fantastical, then it is all the more likely to indicate an affliction that is not physical in its origins. Amundsen and Ferngren are right to observe that in most of the healings performed by Jesus, not only is there no mention of demonic involvement, but the symptoms are usually clearly distinguished from demonic possession and naturalistic explanations of a person's predicament seem to predominate (Amundsen and Ferngren 1995, p. 2950). The only exception to this appears to be the case of the boy suffering from epilepsy (Matthew 17:14–20, Mark 9:14–29, Luke 9:37–43) – a condition that remained popularly ascribed to demonic causation – as we can see in the Hippocratic text *On the Sacred Disease* (Longrigg 2000).

THE MEANING RESPONSE

If psychosomatic interpretations are not able to explain how the historical Jesus effected cures, is there anything more that can be said? In one sense the psychosomatic explanations, although they fall down in assuming that only those phsyiological disorders with a psychological aetiology can have been cured by the historical Jesus, at least alert us to the potential relationship between psychological states and physiological disease. And when we examine this more closely it seems quite plausible that the historical Jesus could have been thought to have caused dramatic changes in the course of a wide range of diseases, with diverse aetiologies, whether of a predominately psychological origin or not. Particularly, I maintain, if we recognize his place in generating a particularly powerful form of what the medical anthropologist Daniel Moerman (2002) refers to as the 'meaning response' in many of those who sought healing from him.

This is perhaps a rather odd statement to make, which can easily be misunderstood and which will require some clarification. Before I do this, I should immediately make it clear that in saying this, I am not making a special case for the historical Jesus. Indeed our case is dependent, in part, on empirical studies of the efficacy of a range of different forms of non-medical therapeutic interventions of different kinds in different cultures (Moerman 2002) and so could be applicable in making sense of claims about the efficacy of other healing traditions in antiquity (such as those associated with the shrine of Asklepios).

Moerman's work is essentially the consequence of trying to explicate what is often referred to as the placebo effect in modern medicine. To date I have found only one New Testament scholar who has made a direct link between this phenomenon and the healings in the New Testament, Harold Remus (1997), although those studying other epochs have been rather less reticent about making such connections when trying to explain the efficacy of non-empirically based therapeutic traditions (see, for example, McMahon 1975). Unfortunately Remus' analysis is somewhat impressionistic and although there is much of value in what it says, it is based in part on the kind of anecdotal data from popularizing and somewhat sensational modern texts that bedevils the discussion of this subject, and does not appear to have had much effect on assumptions within the field.

The 'placebo effect' is well known in Western societies, as indeed is its negative corollary, the nocebo effect (Cohen 1985; Hahn and Kleinman 1983). Placebos, inert medications or 'sham' procedures that can only be effective by the power of suggestion, were, until relatively recently, regularly prescribed by doctors. Indeed, in 1953 it was estimated by the Royal Society of Medicine that approximately 40 per cent of prescriptions given by general practitioners were placebos (Brody 2000, p. 25). However, their use has become rather less common in recent decades or, rather, less overt (see Tilburt *et al.* 2008). This decline is partly the result of developments in medical ethics (for example, at the heart of a placebo lies a deception on the part of the person prescribing it; see Bulger 1990; Brody 1995), research methodologies (placebo-induced therapeutic changes are those changes that are screened out by researchers trying to test the efficacy of new treatments rather than studied in their own right; Kaptchuk 1998) and the fact that placebos have been tainted by association with various complementary therapies (any complementary therapy with rather shaky empirical foundations is often dismissed as having achieved its success by the placebo effect). But, despite this neglect we need to remember that the placebo effect is indeed tangible: it is something that is clearly discernible above and beyond that which would be visible as a result of the self-limiting nature of many illnesses or so called 'regression to the mean' (chronic diseases, left to themselves, often wax and wane) and yet cannot be explained as a direct consequence of a specific medication or treatment. Indeed, despite its decline in recent years, it is still used widely by many modern medical practitioners. As Spiegel comments in an edition of the British Medical Journal, 'We cannot afford to dispense with any treatment that works, even if we are not certain how it does' (2004, p. 928).

The degree of efficacy of the placebo effect can be quite dramatic and the range of ailments for which clinical data exist from double bind randomized controlled trials to demonstrate this is extremely broad. There are plenty of studies that illustrate this, and Moerman (1983, 2002) provides a good survey (as do Shapiro and Shapiro 1997; Benson and Epstein 1975, pp. 1225–7; Benedetti 2008). Placebo-induced symptom relief has been reported in an impressively wide range of illnesses, including allergies, angina pectoris, asthma, cancer, cerebral infarction, depression, diabetes, enuresis, neurosis, ocular pathology, Parkinsonism, prostatic hyperplasia, schizophrenia, skin diseases, ulcers and warts and so on (see, for example, Harrington 1997; White *et al.* 1985; Benedetti *et al.* 2004). Indeed, as it stands it appears that placebo responses can be seen in virtually all conditions (although the clinical data has tended to be focused, for historical reasons, upon symptoms related to pain). The point to note here is that placebos have been shown to affect not just a patient's subjective *perception* of a symptom (such as pain) but also bodily processes that are objectively observable and measurable.

It is worth emphasizing to those unfamiliar with the literature that such effects are not anecdotal but as much clinical results (however awkward) as those for the drugs or procedures which are being trialled. And we should remember this when we read, for example, that a placebo alone has nearly the efficacy of a well-known and effective medication for gastric ulcers, or that a 'sham' surgery for a form of coronary heart disease has proven more efficacious than a common procedure (Moerman 2002, pp. 9–10, 55–61), as have 'sham' versions of arthroscopies, a common treatment for osteoarthritis of the knee (Moseley *et al.* 1996). The standard claim that the placebo effect is a fixed constant amounting to about 30 per cent of any given treatment effect, based upon the classic study by Beecher (1955), something that was widely taught for much of the second half of the twentieth century, has quite rightly been shown to be untenable and based upon rather sloppy research (see Kienle and Kiene 2001), but nonetheless the significance of the placebo effect has become established (with some occasional dissent, see Hrobjartsson and Gøtzsche 2001). Although its impact is variable across conditions and contexts, and some have been rather too indiscriminate in their claims (see, for example, Humphrey 2002), it is now regarded by most clinicians as demonstrably and universally present in any therapeutic intervention where the person is treated (see Adler and Hammett 1973). The only necessary factor is that the intervention is one of which the sufferer (or those about them) is conscious (Colloca *et al.* 2004 proved that knowledge on the part of the patient of the administration of a placebo in a clinical setting). It is not, as commonly assumed, only effective whether the underlying aetiology is a psychological one, an 'imagined' illness, 'the fact is that hypochondriacs, depressives, individuals with somatic pain and virtually all other types of patients can respond to placebo' (Ernst 2001, p. 22). It does not appear that a particular personality type could be labelled a placebo responder (Kamper *et al.* 2008), whether a person responds or not seems 'to be primarily determined by the situation or setting' – its effect is not limited to only one small group within a population (Brody 2000, p. 36). Nor is its effect only on the subjective perceptions of symptoms (such as pain). Objective measurements of various bodily processes have established its capacity to change other aspects of the course of a disease. Nor does its effect appear to be transient (see, for example, Miller and Rosenstein 2006).

Perhaps a useful way of demonstrating the potential efficacy of the placebo effect is to look at what could be described as the other side of the same phenomenon – the nocebo effect (Hahn and Kleinman 1983). In its most extreme case, known as 'voodoo death' or 'hex death', belief in the power of a curse can lead to the death of an individual – a phenomenon found in a range of cultures present in Europe, Latin America, Africa, the Pacific, the Caribbean and Australasia – and famously presented in Walter Cannon's 1942 article. Within a short period of being declared 'socially dead' (something that usually happens to people after biological death, through the rituals associated with a funeral) the individual dies, not as a consequence of any physical act by those that have cursed him but as a consequence of the powerful combined efficacy of the beliefs, values, fears, anxieties and expectations of the community within which he or she lived (despite Cannon's arguments, the physiological mechanisms remain unknown; though see Lester 1972; Engel 1978; Sternberg 2002; and the criticisms of Reid and Williams 1984). Lévi-Strauss described such a case:

Shortly thereafter sacred rites are held to dispatch him to the realm of shadows. First brutally torn from all his family and social ties and excluded from all functions and activities through which he experienced self-awareness, then banished by the same forces from the world of the living, the victim yields to the combined terror, the sudden total withdrawal of the multiple reference systems provided by the support of the group, and finally the group's decisive reversal in proclaiming him – once a living man, with rights and obligations – dead and an object of fear, ritual and taboo. (in Helman 2001, p. 14)

But while the consequences of the placebo effect are well known and clinically demonstrable, the expression 'placebo effect' is unfortunate and used carelessly for a broad range of phenomena and there are calls to abandon it in both medical anthropology and amongst clinicians and medical researchers (see Miller and Kaptchuk 2008). The expression focuses undue attention on the substance (or procedure) prescribed as the placebo (the one thing that does not cause the placebo effect is the placebo itself, which is, by definition, inert) rather than the complex interaction of biology and meaning in human life that produces these effects – a complex interaction that also plays a significant part in *any* therapeutic intervention. As Helman notes,

In medical anthropology, the concept of 'placebo effect' is not confined only to medications: to chemically inactive substances used in double-blind studies. It includes any 'pill, potion or procedure' (Wolf 1959) where belief plays an important part. This is because all forms of healing – whether medical or non-medical, orthodox or complementary, modern or traditional – make use of this phenomenon to some extent. (Helman 2001, p. 6)

The placebo clearly tells us something remarkable and puzzling about the capacity for human beings to activate, through the power of knowledge, symbols and their associated meanings, a rich and complex repertoire of healing processes by which they may be able to 'heal' themselves.

Exactly how this effect comes about and what factors facilitate it has been the subject of study by a number of medical anthropologists and healthcare professionals over the last thirty years (for surveys see, for example, Helman 2001 and Miller and Kaptchuck 2008). There has been a range of reasons for this growth in scholarship (which rather paradoxically has coincided with a decline in its use), but at least part of the motivation for this interest is the increasing desire to translate knowledge about this phenomenon into improved outcomes for patients.

However, it is with Moerman's work that the role of the person healed and the significance of meaning in causing these beneficial physiological changes has finally been given centre stage (Moerman 2002, p. 14), and the effect examined independently of the conceptual confusion that is caused by the emphasis on the placebo itself. Moerman's work provides us with the most thorough analysis of the phenomenon to date and I will make use of his terminology and perspective in what follows.

For Moerman the 'meaning response' can be created by a number of factors and can be induced by a range of actions and behaviours within specific micro and macro contexts (micro context here refers to the specific setting of a healing and macro context to its location within a broader culture). Context is, of course, vital, though not completely determinative (and certainly the 'clinical encounter', the micro context, should not be given undue prominence as I believe Miller and Kaptchuck have done in their recent work).

Let us briefly look at some of those elements that are known to combine to constitute the 'meaning response' and affect its efficacy before returning to the conundrum of Jesus' cures.

(1) *Knowledge.* What people know (or think they know) about a disease or medicine or therapeutic intervention of some kind can enhance both the autonomous healing of their bodies (the organic response of immunological and related systems) and also behavioural responses (the things they do to enhance their own healing or to assist someone else). It is important to note that this knowledge is not knowledge of empirical reality, it does not need, by modern biomedical standards to be 'true', it is just necessary for the individual or group to believe that it is. It needs to be true within the shared cultural script, the macro context that validates such understandings (Helman 2001, p. 11; although such scripts are dynamic and always open to chance and individual interpretations of them may well be affected by the consequences of the therapeutic encounter itself, see Meggitt 2006). So, for example, volunteers in a trial in which

some were given placebos which were inscribed with the name of a famous analgesic perceived their sham medication to be only slightly less effective in combating headaches than those given the real medication only without the customary the branding (and significantly more so than those given the placebo without the branding; Moerman 2002, p. 19). The widespread 'knowledge' of the efficacy of the specific brand and general belief in the efficacy of healing chemicals (something Helman notes is an essential component of Western forms of the 'placebo effect' (2001, p. 11) and a key characteristic of the Western script) were evidently central factors in explaining the results.

(2) *The therapist.* The meaning response is not just moderated by the patient and their knowledge; the *therapist* is also crucial as an agent. Confidence (or the appearance of confidence) of the therapist in the efficacy of the intervention has a demonstrable influence on long-term outcomes. Of course, the importance of the way that the therapist presents her- or himself in healing has been known for a long time – at least since Hippocrates and Galen (Nutton 2002, pp. 237–8). As Galen reportedly remarked 'He cures most successfully in whom the people have the most confidence' (quoted in Harrington 1997, p. 13). W. R. Houston's famous address to the American College of Physicians in 1938 spelt this out clearly when he called for 'the doctor himself, as therapeutic agent, [to] be refined and polished to make himself a more potent agent' (in Moerman 2002, p. 36; see also Novack 1987 and Brody 1997). A description of a doctor from George Bernard Shaw's 1911 play *The Doctor's Dilemma* illustrates, albeit humorously, this well-known aspect of medicine through the ages. 'Cheering, reassuring, healing by the mere incompatibility of disease or anxiety with his welcome presence. Even broken bones, it is said, have been known to unite at the sound of his voice' (Shaw 1911, p. 20). Indeed, the healing power of the words of a therapist is something acknowledged in classical literature, and in particular in Plato (Entralgo 1970).

(3) *The form of the therapeutic intervention.* Although the content of an intervention, the biomedical efficacy of the prescription or procedure, is obviously important, the *form* of the intervention and its culturally specific symbolic associations are also vital. It is well known and experimentally verified, for example, that the colour of a medication makes a difference to its effectiveness and the outcome of an intervention (so, for instance, blue placebo sedatives were three times as effective as the same substance coloured pink; Moerman 2002, p. 48). Stimulant medications tend to be marketed in red, orange or yellow tablets in Europe and North America, while depressants or tranquilizers tend to be marketed in blue, green or

purple (Moerman 2002, p. 49). This might sound somewhat inconsequential but it illustrates the vital effect of culture in the interpretation of the form of an intervention and its subsequent efficacy. What is true of colours is also true of the other rituals and techniques associated with healing (placebos administered by injections are, for example, particularly efficacious; Colloca and Benedetti 2001). It may be odd to think in this way, but pills and needles are, in one sense, ritual symbols, and 'most forms of healing, in different communities, employ a whole cluster of these symbols, they may not be only specific objects, equipment, documents, decorations, but also certain standardized types of body language, movement, posture, dance, clothing, speech and sound' (Helman 2001, p. 6).

In saying this it is important to note that this does not require the patient to share the same understanding of the intervention as that of the therapist, or the same understanding of the key symbols he or she might use – they can have a powerful meaning but by virtue of being reinscribed in the patient's own cultural script. For example, whilst a practitioner of traditional Chinese medicine may use symbols that reference and evoke tradition to effect a cure, the Western consumer may consume these symbols not as 'traditional' but as exotic but the weight placed on the significance of the exotic within their own script may result in the symbols having an equally significant effect. Many of the most enthusiastic advocates of the efficacy of acupuncture in the West have little grasp of the system of Chinese medicine underlying it and indeed in one famous study it was shown that when acupuncture was administered in a manner that deliberately did not cohere with the underlying assumptions of that particular therapy it was equally efficacious (Ernst 2001, p. 25).

(4) *Expectancy on the part of the patient* can also be an important role in the meaning response. Anticipations of one's own automatic reactions to various situations and behaviours are important in understanding outcomes, as Kirsch and Weixel have demonstrated (1988), as are the expectancies of those around you. However, in saying this there are many examples of evidence of the efficacy of meaning response that do not seem to involve any clear notions of expectancy on the part of the recipient – people respond to what things mean whether they 'expect' them or not (Evans 1985).

The work of Moerman is almost totally unknown to New Testament scholars (Pilch 2000, p. 35 does make a brief reference to Moerman 1983) and none have related it in any direct way to what we know about the healings and exorcisms of Jesus. Certainly no one, to date, has made a connection between 'meaning response' and the apparent efficacy of the historical Jesus' activities – and few, other than Remus, have even raised the question in relation to the narrower and less useful notion of placebo. But from what we have just seen, there seem to be good reasons for thinking that this may prove a fruitful area of investigation. A number of historically defensible characteristics of the healing stories associated with Jesus of Nazareth can be correlated with factors that might well have combined to create effective 'meaning responses' on the part of those healed.

(1) For example, *knowledge* of Jesus and the kind of healing he offered seems important to the healing and exorcism stories. His healings were equated by many of his contemporaries, from early in the tradition, with the famous and efficacious miracle traditions of Israel, notably those of the eschatological figure Elijah (Matthew 16:14, Mark 8:28, Luke 9:19; Mark 6:15, Luke 9:8; see Malachi 4:5 and Matthew 17: 11–13; Mark 9:11–12). In addition the healings and exorcisms were probably understood by many of his contemporaries in the context of apocalyptic beliefs of some kind, as evidence of the arrival of the Kingdom of God and, perhaps, associated notions concerning the abolition of death and disease (2 Baruch 21:22–3, 4 Ezra 8:53–4; cf. Revelation 21:4) – an expectation that on occasion seems to have been associated with messianic ideas (see, for example, 4Q521 in the Dead Sea Scrolls). Such associations created a specific and efficacious 'knowledge' about Jesus in the eyes of those who sought healing. Although in saying this we should also be aware that that the acclamation 'Son of David', which is often associated with his healings, may not reveal messianic expectations on the part of those seeking healing but may well be a reference to Solomon, the 'Son of David' believed widely to have power over the demons and celebrated in both popular literature, such as the *Testament of Solomon*, and countless amulets from the period (Berger 1973, 1974; Duling 1975) – but if this is the case, this too would form a particularly efficacious form of 'knowledge' about Jesus and his therapeutic activity.

It is also the case that if we rid ourselves of the assumption that people whose religious identities are not given or implied are Jesus' co-religionists, if we take seriously the alleged locations of the healings and the alleged origins of the crowds that came for healing (see, for example, Matthew 4:23–5; Mark 3:7–8; Luke 6:17–18), then non-Jews who sought out cures, for themselves or others, such as the Syrophoenician woman or the centurion, were not necessarily exceptions amongst those who encountered Jesus. Although we must be careful not to exaggerate the degree of diversity within Galilee, the key region within which the historical Jesus operated (Meyers 1997), it was not isolated and road networks allowed for far more cultural interchange than is often assumed (Strange 1997) and such encounter is particularly common in the realm of health. For such people the 'knowledge' of Jesus would not be produced and enhanced by interpreting what they knew of his activity through the symbols of prophethood or messiahship but would consist primarily of his reputation refracted through, from their perspective, his particular Jewish exoticism – as seems to be the case of those gentiles who made use of the Syrian exorcist from Palestine recorded by Lucian or Eleazar the exorcist at Vespasian's court – or even John Chrysostom's congregation who sought out purveyors of Jewish amulets whenever they fell sick, much to his anger (*Homilies against the Jews,* 8.5, 6).

(2) Jesus' likely efficacy as a *therapeutic agent* is also evident in the confidence which his contemporaries believed that he displayed (Mark 1:27 and Luke 4:36) and which he most probably shared. It seems likely, from the Q traditions with which we began this piece, that Jesus held up his healings as evidence of his status as the one expected (in language almost identical to 4Q521), and his exorcisms as evidence of the arrival of the Kingdom of God, and that he thought of himself as bringing about God's intervention in history. No doubt his confidence stemmed from such a distinctive conviction, whatever its specific implications. Whether this conviction was present at the outset, or developed over time, in a virtuous circle, fed by the growing confidence expressed by the crowds, it is of course impossible to know – and it is possible that the perspective of those seeking healing did not necessarily correlate with his own self-perception (perhaps accounting for the reluctance motif associated with some miracles; see, for examples, Mark 5:43; Matthew 12:15, 16). We should keep in mind the sobering remarks made by Cadbury many years ago, which are as relevant now:

Probably much that is commonly said about the general purpose of Jesus' life and the specific place in that purpose of detailed incidents is modern superimposition upon a nearly patternless life and upon nearly patternless records of it. (Cadbury 1937, p. 141)

However, while we cannot know for certain how and when Jesus began to think of himself as an effective healer, it is clear that the perception of others seems to have grown exponentially. Even if the New Testament accounts exaggerate the speed at which his reputation grew to heighten his significance, the fact that he established such an enduring and widespread reputation as a healer in what amounted to a brief period of activity by whatever reckoning, is telling – and would have impacted significantly on the efficacy of his therapeutic interventions.

(3) The *form* of Jesus' healing is also important from the records that we possess. There is some evidence that Jesus used techniques associated with folk practices at the time (such as the use of spittle in Mark 7:33, 8:23 and John 9:6), and used terminology and actions familiar from the work of other healers and exorcists – such as commanding demons to be silent or to come out of a victim (Mark 1:25, 5:8, 9:25), asking the name of a demon (Mark 5:9), refusing to allow a demon to return to a victim (Mark 9:25), and on one occasion transferring demons into an object – in this case a herd of pigs (Mark 5:12–14). This was established more than forty years ago by Samuel Eitrem (1966), with reference to the Greek Magical Papyri and other sources (notably Lucian and Philostratus). However, when compared to the complex behaviour of other healers and exorcists of his day (such as Eleazar the exorcist in Josephus, *Jewish Antiquities*, 8:45–8) it is surprising how little evidence of such practices is present in the traditions about Jesus. Twelftree goes too far in saying that 'in his exorcisms Jesus is reported to have availed himself of standard formulas or incantations used by the exorcists of ancient magic' (2007, p. 46) – the language employed in the accounts is far too brief and lacks the usual characteristics of such material. The use of Aramaic in healing narratives (Mark 5:41, 7:34) may well be explained by either Mark or his source believing that it was sufficiently exotic to merit being an 'incantation' but as Achtemeier rightly says, they could hardly have been uttered by the historical Jesus, an Aramaic speaker, with that intention – 'Yet if (as seems highly likely) Jesus spoke Aramaic then they were not "foreign incantations"' (Achtemeier 2008, p. 42). I really cannot find evidence of any obvious incantations present in the traditions about Jesus. One only needs to compare what is in the New Testament with, for example, the incantation recommended by Cato the Elder for mending a dislocated hip:

A dislocation can be remedied with this chant. Take a green reed, about four or five feet long, split it down the middle, and have two men hold it against their hips. Begin to chant: motas vaeta daries dardares astataries dissunapiter. Continue until the two halves of the reed come together. Wave an iron knife over the reed. When the halves have joined and are touching one another, take the reed in your hand and cut it on the right and on the left. Fasten it to the dislocation or fracture, which will the heal. Continue to chant every day: huat ista pista sista dannabo danaustra. Or: haut haut haut istasis tarsis ardannabou dannaustra. (Cato the Elder, *On Agriculture*, 160)

As a result it seems that the historical Jesus appears to have been set apart from many of his contemporaries. For some, interpreting his activity within a Jewish perspective, he may have appeared as someone who healed by means that would have struck his Jewish contemporaries as more akin to the practices of the prophets of the Hebrew Bible, a particularly efficacious group. For others, his technique would have at the very least transmitted a sense of authority.

(4) *Expectations* seem to also have been key in the earliest traditions. The 'faith' of both those healed and those around them who anticipated healing is a well-known motif in many of the healing and exorcism narratives associated with Jesus. Although the individual gospel writers clearly had different ideas about how this was to be understood, it seems present in a sufficient number of narratives to lead us to assume that it was a recurring characteristic of many of the original healings and exorcisms. Indeed, we hear, for example, of the rather awkward (and probably authentic) tradition that Jesus could not heal very many in his home town of Nazareth (Mark 6:5, Matthew 13:58) because of a lack of faith. Faith in Jesus' power to heal or the expectation that he will heal is not only present in numerous summary passages in the gospels (such as Mark 1:32–4, 3:10–11) but is a vital element to such early traditions as the story of the centurion's servant (Matthew 8:5–13, Luke 7:1–10 and John 4:45–54), the healing of a man with leprosy (Matthew 8:1–4, Mark 1:40–5, Luke 5:12–16, Papyrus Egerton 2:1–4), the paralysed man (Matthew 9:1–8, Mark 2:1–12, Luke 5:17–26), Jairus' daughter (Matthew 9:18–26, Mark 5:21–43, Luke 8:40–56), the woman with a haemorrhage (Matthew 9:20–2, Mark 5:24b–34, Luke 8:42b–48), the man with a withered hand (Matthew 12:9–14, Mark 3:1–6, Luke 6:6–11), the Syrophoenician woman's daughter (Matthew 15:21–8, Mark 7:24–30), the 'moonstruck' boy (Matthew 17:14–20, Mark 9:14–29, Luke 9:37–43) and blind Bartimaeus (Matthew 20:29–34, Mark 10:46–52, Luke 18:35–43). Indeed, as Kleinman and Sung noted, the belief of a person seeking healing on behalf of someone who does not directly encounter the healer can also have beneficial effects on the sufferer (1979, p. 9), something that might also help elucidate the small number of healings in the early Christian traditions where the beneficiary is some distance away from Jesus – the centurion's servant (Matthew 8:5–13, Luke 7:1–10, see also John 4:46–54), and the Syrophoenician woman's daughter (Mark 7:24–30, Matthew 15:21–8).

CONCLUSION

So, in brief, it seems likely that the historical Jesus was believed to have cured people but, from what we can tell, it seems unlikely that such cures were restricted to psychosomatic maladies. Moerman's concept of 'meaning response' may help us to go some way to explain his unusual and striking efficacy across a range of ailments with different aetiologies. It cannot explain everything. The historical data is so sparse, and far from being analogous to the 'field reports' that Pilch claims, we are faced with highly formulaic renderings of traditions (see, for example, Achtemeier 2008, p. 118) that cannot bear individual, close scrutiny for our historical purposes. However, Moerman's approach does give a possible explanation that is rather better than any other non-supernatural explanation of the historical events that have been proffered before and at least offers us the chance to put our understanding of this aspect of the historical Jesus' ministry on a rather surer footing. At the very least I hope it will make New Testament scholars think twice before rather glibly deciding that the efficacy of Jesus' miracles can be explained by the psychosomatic nature of the ailments that were presented to him – an argument that I noted at the outset actually plays a significant but little-examined role in the historical judgements of key scholars of the historical Jesus.

Intriguingly though, using the perspective of Moerman to make sense of the conundrum of Jesus' healing miracles may lead us to a significantly different perspective on these events and on the figure of Jesus himself. Although the historicity of the incident is impossible to establish, it is, perhaps, unsurprising to discover that in the earliest account of the story of the healing of the woman with the flow of blood it is she and not Jesus who brings the healing about. Although in Matthew's gospel it requires Jesus to discover who has touched him and to acknowledge her faith before the woman is healed (Matthew 9:22), in the earliest version found in Mark (5:29 and also Luke 8:44) the haemorrhage ceases as soon as the woman manages to touch Jesus – he has no conscious part to play in the matter. Perhaps this is not as odd as it sometimes appears, if we recognize that the place of the historical Jesus in his encounters with those who were healed or exorcised was not necessarily quite as central as often assumed. The agency may well have often resided with the sick rather than the healer – just as the crowds seek out Jesus rather than Jesus seeking out the sick for healing. If we take Moerman's perspective on board then the person healed ceases to be a passive recipient of healing *from* Jesus. Rather, through their 'meaning response' *to* the historical Jesus, those healed uncorked the powerful 'internal pharmacopoeia which all humans possess as a biologically programmed tool for self-healing' (Brody 1997, p. 90). At the very least, it takes two to make a 'miracle' – and often, when the complexity of the psychosocial context is properly addressed, considerably more than that.

CHAPTER 3

The theology of spiritual healing

Philip Clayton

In this chapter I will consider the question of spiritual healing from the perspective of a contemporary theologian. Theology inherited a very robust notion of spiritual healing, since the Christian scriptures provide multiple accounts of the healing of body, soul (psyche) and spirit. It likewise remained a crucial premise throughout most of the Christian tradition that God acts, and that among God's actions are sometimes acts of miraculous healing.

This theological approach is in accord with the opening chapter by Fraser Watts. In one sense the approach of this paper can be viewed as a direct response to Watts' invitation. He notes that theological and scientific approaches to spiritual healing are complementary, though his chapter is not primarily concerned with developing a theology of healing. In order to understand spiritual healing scientifically, he calls for an 'emancipated ontology', a broader understanding of reality than is provided by the natural sciences, and which includes the paranormal. I accept here the challenge of formulating this broader view of reality, though I do so as a theologian rather than as a student of paranormal phenomena. I am also happy to follow Watts in his attempt to construe spiritual healing in a non-dualistic fashion. He looks for 'a subtle interpenetration of the natural and the spiritual, rather than . . . a sharp disjunction between them'. Watts understands spiritual healing to be 'holistic', since it 'involves body, mind and spirit'. Finally, he describes spiritual healing as involving a 'resonance or attunement' between the healer, the healed, and the Spirit of God; those involved in the healing 'assume they can become channels of a healing energy that transcends themselves'.

At the same time, to be a *contemporary* theologian is to link traditional beliefs to a world in which very different structures of credibility and plausibility pertain. The fact that many theologians today no longer believe that God performs miraculous healings (i.e. direct healings that cannot be understood naturalistically) may be greeted with relief by some and with disdain by others. The goal of these few pages will be less about seeking to judge than to understand how it was that Christian theology traversed its route from New Testament practices and beliefs to those that predominate today.

In attempting to understand the conflict one could of course begin with the methods and assumptions of the sciences, subsequently exploring the question of what aspects of the traditional belief in spiritual healing might still be consistent with those assumptions. Proceeding in this way would assume that the thinking of most ordinary people in the West today seems to be primarily influenced by a scientific worldview and that they then use that worldview as the ground for differentiating between the traditional religious beliefs they will retain and those they will reject. In that case consistency with science or contradiction to it would serve as the operative criterion for evaluating all theological assertions. Another starting point, and the one used here, examines the history of the theology of spiritual healing *before* turning to the challenges raised by contemporary science. The advantage of this latter approach is that it allows the history of the theology of healing itself to help determine what are the forced trade-offs (if any) that believers today must accept. Given that the theological history is significantly different than most people imagine it to be, it seems doubly important not to neglect this second approach.

Of course, the possible disadvantage of this approach is that it might appear to exclude those individuals who come to the question of spiritual healing from different religious traditions, from parapsychological studies, or from a completely sceptical position. No such exclusions are intended, though certain readers will of course find the theological approach less central to their own interests. Still, non-theists may find an overview of the history of the theology of spiritual healing helpful, even if their concerns are more anthropological and cultural. Indeed, it may turn out in the end that there is more convergence of standpoints than one would have expected.

HISTORY OF THEOLOGICAL TREATMENTS OF HEALING

There is no question about miraculous healings in the New Testament.[1] 'And Jesus was going about in all Galilee, teaching in their synagogues,

---

[1] I am grateful for the research assistance of Simeon Zahl, a doctoral student in theology at the University of Cambridge, in compiling the sources for this historical section. I have been influenced by his perceptive work and by our discussions of this topic; where I use 'we' in the text, the reference is to our joint interpretation of the material. The responsibility for any omissions or misinterpretations is mine alone.

and proclaiming the gospel of the kingdom, and healing every kind of disease and every kind of sickness among the people' (Matthew 4:23).[2] 'Signs and wonders' were for the gospel writers an intrinsic part of the ministry of the 'son of man', a manifestation of his authority, and (especially for John) a sign of his divinity. The same powers of healing were transferred by Jesus to his disciples as a sign of their authority:

And He called the twelve together, and gave them power and authority over all the demons, and to heal diseases. And He sent them out to proclaim the kingdom of God, and to perform healing. (Luke 9:1–2)

And as you go, preach, saying, 'The kingdom of heaven is at hand.' Heal the sick, raise the dead, cleanse the lepers, cast out demons; freely you received, freely give. (Matthew 10:7–8)

In Acts the power to heal in the name of Jesus Christ was a part of the post-Pentecost ministry of Jesus' disciples (Acts 3:1–10, 9:34). Paul clearly believed that this power was one of the gifts (*charismata*) of the Spirit:

But to each one is given the manifestation of the Spirit for the common good. For to one is given the word of wisdom through the Spirit ... to another gifts of healing by the one Spirit, and to another the effecting of miracles, and to another prophecy. (1 Corinthians 12:7–10)

In several New Testament passages anointing the sick is associated with spiritual healing. 'And they [the Twelve] were casting out many demons and were anointing with oil many sick people and healing them' (Mark 6:13). By the time of the epistle of James this practice seems to be an established ritual, 'is anyone among you sick? Let him call for the elders of the church, and let them pray over him, anointing him with oil in the name of the Lord; and the prayer offered in faith will restore the one who is sick, and the Lord will raise him up, and if he has committed sins, they will be forgiven him' (James 5:14–15). As we will see, this ritual was gradually transformed as the expectation of healing progressively declined over the history of theology and church practice.

PATRISTIC THEOLOGY

Miraculous spiritual healings remain prominent in the literature of the early Church and the pre-Nicene fathers, and attestations to such healings continue at least to the time of Augustine.

---

[2] This and all subsequent biblical references are drawn from the New American Standard translation.

Augustine's early theological writings assume that miraculous healings were a sign of Jesus' ministry and the power of the Spirit in the early Church, but that they had died out in the centuries since that time. Interestingly however, his later work offers a more robust defence of such healings, which is apparently the result of having personally observed a number of miracles, including healings, and hearing reports of others. In the *Retractions* Augustine writes,

> But what I said should not be taken as understanding that no miracles are believed to happen today in the name of Christ. For at the very time I wrote this book I already knew that, by approaching the bodies of the two martyrs of Milan, a blind man in that same city was given back his sight; and so many other things of this kind have happened, even in this present time, that it is not possible for us either to know of all of them or to count up all of those that we do have knowledge of. (1.13.7)[3]

A TRANSFORMATION

A subtle transformation occurred in the period between Augustine and Thomas Aquinas, although historical theologians have rarely examined this history and the reasons for the switch are not well understood. Possibly the changes have their root in the rendering of the word 'heal' as 'save' in the Latin translation of the New Testament by St Jerome (*c.* 340–420), though it seems unlikely that this is the only reason. Whatever the causes, the transformation is manifested most acutely in the development of the sacrament of Extreme Unction.

This sacrament originally grew out of the anointing with oil as described in Mark and James; indeed, the passage from James (5:14–15) is still used by Roman Catholic theologians as the key biblical verse in its defence. In the period between Jerome and Aquinas, however, the practice gradually evolved from a ritual of healing to a sacrament for the dying. The goal was no longer that the sick person would be healed but rather that his or her soul would be prepared for death. According to Morton Kelsey,

> With the emphasis on the next life, a profound change took place in the sacrament of healing. Its meaning shifted gradually to healing of the soul in preparation. Unction for healing became unction for dying ... following

---

[3] Quoted in Kelsey 1973, p. 185. Kelsey continues to be one of the most insightful sources on the history of the theology of healing, and I gratefully acknowledge my indebtedness to his work. On Augustine and healing see also of *The City of God*, 22.8.

PHILIP CLAYTON

Jerome's translation of the word 'heal' as 'save,' the medieval church developed
its understanding of the sacrament of extreme unction, which remained until
Vatican II in 1962. (Kelsey 1973, p. 203)[4]

Those involved in the ritual apparently ceased to expect that healing
would result, focusing instead on the need for forgiveness of sin and an
individual's preparation for death and the life to come. Gradually, healing
came to be seen as a 'conditional and occasional effect' of Extreme
Unction, a rare by-product of the practice rather than its primary goal.
It's somewhat ironic then that the standard histories of theology still
attribute the movement away from a strong doctrine of miraculous
healing to the influence of the Enlightenment, almost a millennium later.

In the end it was Thomas Aquinas' advocacy of this new understanding
of Extreme Unction that solidified the *spiritual* interpretation of healing
and made it normative for Catholic practice. In the *Summa Theologica*
he argues, 'Extreme Unction is a spiritual remedy, since it avails for the
remission of sins ... now the effect of the sacraments is the healing of
the disease of sin' (III-Supp. 29.1). For Aquinas sin is the problem that
both pastors and theologians should stress, rather than physical sickness.
As a result, much of his discussion of healing focuses on spiritual, inward
healing, the healing of sin. In this treatment Jesus' healings and miracles
serve a primarily instructive purpose, either for validating Jesus' claims to
divinity or for helping people to have faith in him, whereas healing for its
own sake is downplayed. Aquinas writes

Now the confirmation of such things as are within reason rests upon arguments;
but the confirmation of what is above reason rests on what is proper to the
Divine power, and this in two ways; – first when the teacher of sacred doctrine
does what God alone can do, in miraculous deeds, whether with respect to bodily
health (and thus there is the grace of healing), or merely for the purpose of
manifesting the divine power ... The grace of healing is distinguished from
the general working of miracles because it has a special reason for inducing one to
the faith, since a man is all the more ready to believe when he has received the gift
of bodily health through the virtue of faith. (*Summa Theologica*, II-1.III.4)[5]

Like most other major theologians after him, Aquinas does not dispute
the *possibility* of miracles. In the *Summa contra Gentiles* (III, Qu. 100ff.) he
maintains that miracles are possible in all three senses: events that would

---

[4] The classic source for these developments is *L'Église en prière: introduction à la liturgie* (Martimort
1961, esp. pp. 580ff.) in English translation as *The Church at Prayer: An Introduction to the Liturgy*
(Martimort 1986, trans. O'Connell).
[5] Quotations from the *Summa Theologica* taken from the translation by L. Shapcote.

have occurred anyway but that reveal the nature of God; events that would not have occurred without God's direct divine influence, but that are nonetheless consistent with natural law; and events that are inconsistent with natural law. Elsewhere Aquinas leaves room for healing practices, though he sharply distinguishes them from the more important sacramental practices. In his discussion of penance he writes that the laying on of hands is useful for healing but is not sacramental and should never be part of the sacrament of penance:

That imposition of hands is not sacramental, but is intended for the working of miracles, namely that by the contact of a sanctified man's hand, even bodily infirmity might be removed; even as we read of Our Lord (Mark 6:5) that He cured the sick, *laying his hands upon them*, and (Matthew 8:3) that He cleansed a leper by touching him. (*Summa Theologica*, III.84.4)

The priorities set in Aquinas' writing remained dominant in Catholic theology through to Vatican II. The Council of Trent, for example, officially mandated that the rite of Extreme Unction be administered only to those in danger of death. (Note, however, that the listing for this sacrament in the post-Vatican II *Sacramentum Mundi* is as 'anointing the sick'; De Letter 1968, pp. 37–40.) In an interesting effort at retrospective harmonization, the article on 'Extreme Unction' in the *Catholic Encyclopedia* tries to make the case that the emphasis in this doctrine had *always* been on the forgiveness of sins in preparation for death (Toner 1909). (The exegetical argument that the passage on anointing in James was never intended to be primarily about healing the sick is equally as implausible.) Nonetheless, the article does reflect the majority position since Aquinas that, 'as a conditional and occasional effect of extreme unction, comes the restoration of bodily health, an effect which is vouched for by the witness of experience in past ages and in our own day'. On this matter the position in *Sacramentum Mundi* (and one presumes also Karl Rahner's position) is no different. 'The anointing of the sick may lead to the restoration of bodily health. But it does not replace medical care, nor produce health after the manner of the charism of healing. It operates for bodily healing in its own sacramental way.'

EXPLAINING THE SHIFT

Without having examined this portion of church history, one would probably not have predicted such an early shift away from the New Testament emphasis on healing. No single cause by itself suffices to explain the diminishing role of healing in the period between 400 and 1200 CE. But a collection of factors together helps to account for it. I suggest that the following four are particularly important.

1 Kelsey has correctly identified the major impetus as the shift from a Platonic to an Aristotelian philosophical framework for theology (1973, ch. 9). Admittedly, it is somewhat superficial merely to say that, as 'Aristotelian rationalism' took over from Platonism in theology, its mechanical worldview left no place for healing or the supernatural. Complex philosophical worldviews like these are much less black-and-white and much more subtle in their influence. Christian Platonism regarded all finite objects as participating in the divine, as permeated by its energies. Given this metaphysic, it was to be expected that the emphasis would be on influences from outside the finite world rather than on natural regularities or laws. If nothing exists except through participation in God, and all essential features of things come from their divine Source, then it's not surprising that they would sometimes manifest qualities and powers associated with their Source, such as healing. By contrast, Aristotelians emphasized the forms and essential properties that make all finite things what they are. Here the stress is on the essence of each particular thing, the *to ti ēn einai* or 'what it is to be' that particular thing rather than something else. Of course, in Christian Aristotelianism, things were *also* said to be dependent on God for their existence. But now God was understood to have created these natural regularities and hence to respect them in his interactions with them. As a result, it grew increasingly costly to maintain that God would disregard or overrule the very forms by which God had designed them in the first place. Thus Aquinas, deeply influenced by Aristotle, showed relatively little interest in supernatural healing and miracles, although he affirmed their possibility, especially at the hands of saints.

2 Tied up with this transformation over the centuries is the idea that sin and physical sickness are closely related. Sin is the real problem. When it has been dealt with, physical healing may result; but if it doesn't, it does not matter quite so much, since physical healing takes a clear second place to *spiritual* healing, the healing from sin and separation from God. Thus Extreme Unction came to concern healing the soul from sin more than (or even, rather than) healing the body.

3 One detects an inward-looking trend beginning around the time of Augustine, which provided an independent motive for the trend

described above in the second factor. Given this emphasis, it was natural that internal, spiritual problems – sin, guilt, and the like – would be viewed as far more serious than external, physical problems (see Thomas 2006, ch. 9). Doctors and natural philosophers could concern themselves with physical ailments; but the specific or 'proper' interest of theology, it was held, should lie with salvation. By the time of Aquinas it's clear that the spiritual state of the soul had become vastly more important than the physical state of the body.

4 Finally, one may speculate that one of the reasons why the church gradually spiritualized the ritual of 'anointing with oil' is that in many cases it didn't work as a means for bringing about physical healing – or at least it didn't work as frequently as the New Testament reports had led people to expect. When you expect that the laying on of hands and anointing with oil will heal the sick, then you practise the ritual with that end in mind; when your experience causes you to give up hope that healing will actually occur, you will inevitably begin to practise the ritual as a form of 'last rites'.

In the end, of course, the medieval Church never explicitly denied the possibility of miraculous healings. Presumably this is the reason why 'Enlightenment rationalism' and 'secular humanism' are so often associated with the church's changed stance towards miraculous healings. Nevertheless, the evidence shows that the most profound shift took place hundreds of years before the Enlightenment; in many respects the shift was essentially complete by the time of Aquinas. By then the role of physical healing had come to be radically downplayed within theology itself; it had come to be the exception rather than the norm.

THE REFORMATION

The Reformers seem to have been slightly divided on physical healing, but they more or less took over Aquinas' view. By abolishing the sacrament of Extreme Unction, however, they threw out the last traditional ecclesiological reserve for a theology of healing.[6]

John Calvin writes in the *Institutes of the Christian Religion* that 'the gift of healing disappeared with the other miraculous powers which the Lord was pleased to give for a time, that it might render the new preaching of the gospel for ever wonderful' (IV.19.18).[7] This view, which later came to be

---

[6] We follow Kelsey on this point, who makes a persuasive case for this conclusion (1973, pp. 220–3).
[7] Quotations from the *Institutes* taken from the translation by Henry Beveridge (Calvin 1989).

known as *dispensationalism*, holds that different gifts are given by the Spirit during different periods of salvation history in order to serve different functions. We should therefore not expect that all the charisms available to the church in New Testament times are still available today. It is no coincidence that this passage comes at the end of Calvin's argument against the sacrament of Extreme Unction. Calvin asserts, more emphatically than Aquinas does, that in the Bible anointing and other rituals of healing were 'not instruments of the cure, but only symbols to remind the ignorant whence this great virtue proceeded' (*Institutes*, IV.19.18). Since the dispensation of supernatural powers has passed, Calvin encourages his readers to focus no longer on spiritual healing.[8]

The situation in sixteenth-century Lutheran churches was not much different. One does not find the explicit dispensationalism of Calvin's theology. Still, miracles other than inward, spiritual miracles ('the miracle of faith', etc.) did not play a significant role in early Lutheran theology. There is no significant discussion of miracles, much less of healing, in the entire *Book of Concord*, except for the affirmation that Christ did indeed perform them (see *Book of Concord*, Formula of Concord, 'Solid Declaration', Article VIII.25).[9] Once again, the loss of the sacrament of Extreme Unction has removed the one locus where such affirmations had traditionally been preserved.

Luther's 'table talk' and some of his letters preserve hints of another position. In them, Luther tends to divide sicknesses into two categories: those that doctors can cure, and those that have a demonic or Satanic source and hence can only be cured by prayer. The latter is of more interest for our topic:

Physicians observe only the natural causes of illness and try to counteract these by means of their remedies. They do well to do this. But they do not understand that Satan is sometimes the instigator of the material cause of the disease; he can alter the causes and diseases at once, and he can turn fever into chills and health into illness. To deal with Satan there must be a higher medicine, namely, faith and prayer. (Luther, *Letters of Spiritual Counsel*, p. 46; cf. pp. 26–52)

In one of his later letters, Luther mentions a case in which 'a cabinetmaker here was similarly afflicted with madness and we cured him by prayer in Christ's name'. He even describes an impromptu service for this kind of

---

[8] According to Kelsey, natural healing is of so little theological interest to Calvin that it is never mentioned in *Institutes* (1973, pp. 220–3).

[9] The *Book of Concord*, published in 1580 contains the Lutheran Confessions – the definitive standard of what Lutherans believe.

healing, which functioned as a sort of substitute for the traditional anointing with oil (*Letters of Spiritual Counsel*, p. 52). Note, however, that the examples refer to what we would call mental illness rather than miraculous physical healings. It is true that Luther's letters to sick persons invariably affirm that he will pray for them. But his main concern is with their souls; he prays that they will be comforted by the gospel in the face of death, providing little or no sign that he put much hope in spiritual healing of physical infirmities. Where Luther does broach the topic in his correspondence, his comments are more pastorally orientated than theological.

MODERNITY

The modern, sceptical context provided the opening framework for this essay, and we shall shortly return to it again. The explosive rise of modern science in the seventeenth and eighteenth centuries brought growing scepticism about miraculous events, undercutting the belief that God sometimes acts directly as an agent to bring healing to human bodies that would not have occurred without that divine causal activity.[10] More emphatically than ever before, the rationalist thinkers of the Enlightenment viewed nature as a closed causal system with no room for non-natural forces.

As a result, the stance towards spiritual healing became more sceptical in modern theology than during earlier phases in the development of the doctrine. Still, the evidence suggests that the famous rationalism of the Enlightenment did not in fact constitute a radical break. Healings had already ceased to be a regular part of the church's practice by the time of Thomas Aquinas, and they played a minimal role in the thought and practice of the two major Reformation traditions. Modernity's contribution was to make this implicit scepticism into a matter of explicit principles and arguments. The *novum* was not that theologians began to have doubts about whether healings still took place – already Calvin seems to have doubted that they did – but that the doubts were now extended even to the miraculous healings ascribed to Jesus. The age of the miraculous had already been shoved back to Jesus and his early followers; now it began to be disputed even there (see Schleiermacher 1975; Strauss 2006; Schweitzer 2001; Dunn and McKnight 2005).

---

[10] The Enlightenment period was much richer and more diverse than the standard stereotypes suggest. For a sense of the full subtlety of this movement, see *The Enlightenment and the Intellectual Foundations of Modern Culture* (Dupré 2004).

TWENTIETH-CENTURY THEOLOGY

A full presentation of healing in twentieth-century theology lies beyond the scope of this paper. Nonetheless, a quick examination of the contrasts between two of the century's most influential theologians provides a fairly revealing picture of the main fault lines of the debate.

Christians can affirm miracles, Rudolf Bultmann believed, in a way that does not require actually contradicting the laws of nature. Miracles pertain to the language and life of faith, which by its very nature does not stand in tension with the scientific project. Many aspects of the worldview that dominated the New Testament are simply no longer live options for contemporary men and women.

The idea of wonder as miracle has become almost impossible for us today because we understand the processes of nature as governed by law. Wonder, as miracle, is therefore a violation of the conformity to law which governs all nature, and for us today this idea is no longer tenable. (Bultmann 1987, p. 257; cf. pp. 256–69)

Bultmann introduced a new sense of 'wonder'. A wonder in his sense is an event that is not in contradiction to the laws of nature but is seen, through the eyes of faith, to be an act of God. If we replace the out-of-date notion of miracles with the idea of wonders, 'it is really possible for the Christian *continually to see new wonders.* This world process, which to the unbeliever must appear as a sequence of events governed by law, has for the Christian become a world in which God acts' (Bultmann 1987, p. 267; emphasis original). Applied to our topic, this implies that Christians can believe in both physical and spiritual healings, and indeed in ways that are truly 'wondrous' (i.e., that utilize the language of divine action), yet without clashing with the laws of nature.

In his highly influential *Jesus and the Word*, Bultmann acknowledges the paradoxes in the notion of miracles, focusing explicitly on the question of miraculous healings:

Whoever affirms Jesus' thought accepts also the paradox that an event which from the observer's viewpoint must be regarded as a natural occurrence, as a part of the world process determined by law, is in reality something different, that is, a direct act of God. When he says 'miracle' he suspends the concept of nature. (Bultmann 1958, p. 179; cf. pp. 172–9)

Here Bultmann begins to nuance the position more carefully, however, 'to [Jesus'] mind and to the minds of his contemporaries . . . undoubtedly he healed the sick and cast out demons' (1958, p. 173) – with the implication that to *our* minds something rather different was going on. Perhaps for this reason Bultmann is careful to emphasize that miracles should never be understood as objective occurrences and should never be used as proof of anything. Instead, 'miracles *presuppose* belief in God' (1958, p. 173; my emphasis). Given Bultmann's existentialist perspective, deeply influenced by Martin Heidegger, it doesn't really matter whether healings actually occurred or occur today, much less *how* they occur; what matters to us today is seeing with 'the eyes of faith', which is a task for the existing subject before God. And no objective occurrence can either support or undercut the life of faith, since it is *sui generis* and as such distinct from all questions of fact.

Contrast this view to the position of Karl Barth. Barth is clearly less of a dispensationalist than Calvin. His classic statement of miracles occurs in volume IV.2 of the *Church Dogmatics*. There he writes:

> It is to be noted, however, that the astonishing or, in a general sense, extraordinary aspects of the traditional activities [Jesus' miracles] could not and cannot be called in question either by contemporary or modern analogies and approximations and the light which these throw on them. Over a wide range they could and can be found supremely credible even in their extraordinary character. (Barth 1975, p. 213; cf. pp. 211–47)

Barth's insistence that science and historiography cannot undercut the claims to miraculous healings might at first blush appear to be similar to Bultmann's. But the reason is in fact radically different: the miracle claims of the New Testament are eminently believable. So we have no reason to jettison them in the belief that the worldview of modern science is *more* plausible.

Barth is a true son of the Reformation in his emphasis that 'their significance [that is the significance of the New Testament miracles] is only as actualisations of His Word, as calls to repentance and faith' (1975, p. 217). But for him, unlike Bultmann, the centrality of faith does not substitute for objective truth. Because Christian faith is true, what it entails is also true; and because the revelation of God in Jesus Christ is trustworthy, the miracle claims are more to be trusted than what rests on the authority of science.

Barth recognizes that spiritual healings are not ends in themselves. Their purpose is not merely to improve someone's physical or bodily condition. 'His miracles followed a very definite line. But it was not the line of a welfare-programme executed with the assistance of supernatural powers' (Barth 1975, p. 217). They are invitations to repentance and faith.

Pace Bultmann, Barth makes this affirmation without in any way questioning the possibility of miraculous healings here and now. He writes in the context of a discussion of the freedom and power of the grace of God:

Therefore at the very heart of time, in restoration of the glory and peace of creation, and in anticipation of the glory and peace of the final revelation of the will and kingdom of God, [grace] is free to accomplish real deliverances here and now. That is to say, it is free to accomplish deliverances which obviously and powerfully concern the whole man: man in his totality as the soul of his body and together with his body; in the physical state in which he also exists, and is here and now subject to so many and varied afflictions and oppressions ... Is this only a future possibility? No, says God in His free grace. (Barth 1975, p. 246)

The free grace of God is the crux of Barth's doctrine of spiritual healing. God is free to do absolutely anything that is consistent with the nature of God and the character of God as revealed in Jesus Christ. No *a priori* conditions for what is possible may be imposed on the living Word of God. Because Barth wrote after the Enlightenment and the birth of modern science, he ended up taking this classic Reformation principle and applying it to the question of healing in a way that the Reformers never did.

THE CHARISMATIC MOVEMENT

Finally, the rise of Pentecostalism and the charismatic movement has brought the issue of spiritual healing back to the attention of theologians in a new way. Here the theological emphasis is no longer on the anointing with oil, as in Mark and James, but once again on the model of Jesus' actual practice, as well as on the Pauline teachings regarding spiritual gifts such as healings.

Of course, the lives of mystics and holy persons, movements of church reform and renewal, and the language (and practice) of popular piety had always included a more robust role for spiritual healing. In that sense, the contemporary charismatic movement is not a unique moment in church history. But it is the particular form in which the claim that miraculous healings still occur is being mediated to academic theology today.

Nonetheless, although the charismatic movement has spawned some theological reflection, it has not had a major impact on mainline Christian theology. Here and there one detects some signs of influence (e.g. Cox 1995; see also Anderson and Hollenweger 1999; Dempster *et al.* 1999) but most remain peripheral. For example, Vatican II recognized the Jesuanic/Pauline type of healing as potentially legitimate. According to the entry in *Sacramentum Mundi* on 'Charisms', after Vatican II the Roman Catholic Church became more open to 'charisms', including 'special gifts of healing'.[11] By and large, however, those who affirm and those who deny the possibility of miraculous healings today divide primarily along charismatic verses non-charismatic lines.

THEOLOGY, ANTHROPOLOGY, AND THE IMAGO DEI

To begin theologically is to begin by viewing all of reality as created by God, permeated by God, and directed ultimately towards God. To reflect theologically is to struggle with very different sorts of problems than modernity emphasizes. Whereas the contemporary worry is, 'Given the natural world, how is it possible to add in a god or gods?' the theological starting point inclines one to ask instead, 'Given God, how is it possible to add in a separate creation? How is it possible that independent beings or subjects could exist if everything stems from and is embraced by an omnipresent divine source?' The history of theology reflects the struggle to explain how it could be that persons and natural regularities would (appear to) function in relative independence from God. So theological essays on the problem of evil tend not to ask, '*could* God do anything to reduce evil and suffering?' but rather '*why* does God not act to do what God is capable of doing?' Theologians have described the movement, reflected in the Hebrew Bible, from polytheism through henotheism (the belief that, although other gods existed, Yahweh was the highest of the gods) to what H. Richard Niebuhr described as 'radical monotheism' (the claim that no other gods *could* exist alongside Yahweh; 1960, pp. 32, 37). The same movement has led some Christian mystics and theologians to wonder how *any* independent beings could exist outside the all-embracing divine presence and power.

   The Greek notion of multiple substances, each with its own essence, helped to block this thrust towards the all-pervasiveness of divine agency. If one begins with many independent substances, then their unity has to be established after the fact, as it were. Not surprisingly, one detects an inevitable tension between the Greek idea of a plurality of substances and the early definition of a substance as that which requires nothing outside of itself in order to exist. Descartes was perhaps the first to recognize this tension.

---

[11] See the treatment of charismatic gifts in *Sacramentum Mundi* (Bettencourt 1968, pp. 283–4).

By substance, we can understand nothing else than a thing which so exists that it needs no other thing in order to exist. And in fact only one single substance can be understood which clearly needs nothing else, namely, God. In the case of all other substances, we perceive that they can exist only with the help of God's concurrence. (Descartes, *Principles of Philosophy*, Pt. 1, Art. 51)[12]

Spinoza's pantheistic position stands out as the apparently inevitable outcome of this insight: there can only be one substance, which one might call God or nature (*deus siva natura*), and all else must exist as a mode or manifestation of that one ultimate substance.

How then is this unifying tendency in the concept of God to be integrated with the core belief of the three Abrahamic traditions that 'God created the heavens and the earth', that is, a rich and diverse reality that is distinct from God at least in its essential nature? One natural way to connect the two insights is to imagine creation as taking place *within* the being of God. The entire universe is like a foetus growing within the womb: permeated by the divine presence, sustained by divine nurture, enjoying a relative but not absolute independence.[13] This position – or rather whole series of positions – is known as *panentheism*, the view that the world is contained within the divine, although God is also more than the world. Panentheism radicalizes the doctrine of the immanence of God, attempting to give expression to the paradox that quasi-independent agents would exist at all. By understanding their agency *within* the very being of God, it holds their merely relative independence continually before our eyes. As a philosophical theology, panentheism is more Platonic than Aristotelian.

For a variety of theological positions it's true that *theology begets anthropology*. Theological views of human nature are guided by those powerful words in the opening chapter of the Hebrew Bible, 'And God created humanity in God's own image, in the image of God they were created; male and female God created them' (Genesis 1:27). The theologian is best guided by what we might call the *imago Dei* correlation. One looks to the 'image of God' to understand what humanity is, and – to the extent possible, and with appropriate caveats – one also reasons backwards from the distinctively personal nature of human existence to the often mysterious nature of our Origin and Source.

---

[12] Quoted from the translation by V. R. Miller (Descartes 1984).
[13] Note for example the use of this metaphor in Jürgen Moltmann and other contemporary panentheists (Moltmann 1985; Clayton and Peacocke 2004).

Biblically, one finds a variety of different categorizations of the human person. Most of the New Testament writers accept a tripartite anthropology, whereby humans consist of *soma, psychē* and *pneuma* (body, psyche or soul, and spirit). Yet Pauline anthropology also includes a dualism of *pneuma* and *sarx* (spirit and flesh), and the Hebrew Bible, at least in its earlier history, lacks the notion of an immortal soul altogether, focusing instead on the belly as the seat of the emotions. During much of the history of the church, the philosophy of Aristotle was dominant; as a result, *reason* tended to dominate as the defining characteristic of the human species – a view that is obviously not widely shared in the present.

So theologians must look for broader guiding principles for theological anthropology. I've suggested the *imago Dei* correlation: humans have those features that are appropriately seen as the reflection of God in humanity, as well as those features that are necessary for carrying out the function of 'cultivating the earth' and entering into a relationship with God. Panentheists are guided by a particular form of the *imago Dei* correlation that we might call the Panentheistic Analogy: God's relationship to the world is in some important respects analogous to our relation to our bodies. If the mental and the physical are as deeply and intimately correlated with one another as contemporary cognitive science (and related fields) seem to show, and if the causal relations between mind and body move in both directions, then the Panentheistic Analogy may offer a powerful way to capture God's intimate and mutual relation with all of creation at every moment.

STEPS TOWARDS A SACRAMENTAL THEOLOGY OF HEALING

What guidelines does our examination offer for a theology of healing? If one follows the method suggested in the opening paragraphs of this chapter – first providing a theological explication, and only subsequently asking how that view relates to the sciences – one finds that analogies with parapsychology and psychoneuroimmunology do not emerge as the first and defining features of a theology of healing. A different set of concepts, issues and problems dominates for the theologian. Here there is space to explore just four.

First, from a theological perspective, there is nothing surprising about a more-than-natural flow of energy through the human person. Of course God is capable of infusing such an energy, since God permeates all things and all created reality. In fact, the only real surprise, theologically speaking, is that there is *ever* normal human agency which is not at the same time a manifestation of divine agency. In other words, *human* agency, not divine agency, is the mystery for the theologian.

Second, one assumes that God is engaged in a long-term policy to enable persons to become agents who, as actors in their own right, freely emulate the divine nature and freely attempt to live according to the divine purposes (or against them), agents who are all the while participating in and within the One 'in whom we live and move and have our being' (Acts 17:29). Apparently God does not overwhelm finite agency, as one would expect, but works 'in, with, and through' it – although given divine infinity there is no *a priori* reason why this should be the case. As a result, *the doctrine of grace precedes the doctrine of healing*, as it also precedes theological anthropology. Humans owe their very existence to the unconstrained and unmerited favour of God, who allows us to exist as agents at all.

The third problem is not that God sometimes heals but that God so often does not heal. Theologically, one must assume that God *wants* always to heal, to reduce suffering, and to bring about wholeness, as well as that God is always *able* to heal. One assumes moreover that God is consistent and not arbitrary. When one thinks this problem through in its full depth and complexity, one discovers that no rational account can be given of why God would heal in some cases and allow such terrible, unmerited, and (as far as we can tell) unredemptive suffering in other cases.[14] Some, but not all, will be satisfied to speak here of the mystery of the Holy Spirit (John 3:8; Isaiah 55:8–9). I suggest that any adequate theology of healing will begin with and never lose sight of the so-called problem of evil – the fact that, for every apparent healing, thousands of other requests for healing go unanswered.

I suggest, finally, that all these various factors point towards a sacramental theology of healing. A sacrament is an outward, visible sign of an inward, spiritual grace; it's a present symbol and manifestation of the divine reality, one that serves as a promise of a fuller, completed state to come. The practice of Eucharist is both a remembering of Christ and a hopeful anticipation of a final celebration with him at the eschaton. So healing is likewise a memory of the one who came as Healer, but also a sign of that final state of wholeness (*salus* equals *Heil* equals health, salvation, wholeness). Therefore no individual healing can be interpreted theologically apart from God's overall salvific intent for humanity.

[14] The full argument is developed in 'Divine action and the "argument from neglect"' (Clayton and Knapp 2007, pp. 179–94).

Healing is never an end in itself, but always a means for revelation; and revelation is always subsumed under the final eschatological self-manifestation of God.

Those who are healed are healed sacramentally, that is, as a sign of hope and promise in a world in which many suffer and few are healed, a world characterized by sickness, pain, brokenness and a lack of wholeness. In my view, this fact suggests forms of church practice in which prayers for healing are treated analogously to the other sacraments.[15] Anointing with oil and the laying on of hands – and employing both of these practices in the context of the worship service – are means to emphasize the sacramental quality of the prayer of healing. It is no simple task to pray in faith and confidence, to seek to pray in a state of righteousness (for 'the prayer of a righteous [person] availeth much'), to pray in humility, and at the same time to view one's own practice sacramentally. The complexity of the sacramental stance is that it pertains as fully to the case in which healing is granted as to the cases where prayers for healing bring no visible response. One knows, even in the midst of praying, that one lives in a world in which healings are rarely granted. When the request for healing *is* granted, the healing is not the whole story; it must always serve also as a sign and promise for the vast number who never experience healing from brokenness. Any occasion of healing, and so healing of every type, serves as a ground for hoping in and longing for a state radically different from our own – that state where 'the tabernacle of God [will be] among men and women, and He shall dwell among them, and they shall be His people, and God Himself shall be among them, and He shall wipe away every tear from their eyes; and there shall no longer be any death; there shall no longer be any mourning, or crying, or pain' (Revelation 23:3–4).

CONTEMPORARY CONTEXTS OF PLAUSIBILITY

In this chapter we have examined spiritual healing both through its historical background and in its systematic theological form. We have noted interconnections between the theology of healing and other core doctrines of Christian belief. Unfortunately, in the midst of all the controversies surrounding healing claims, the theological richness of this notion is often overlooked. When one moves, in thought and belief, within the sphere of a

---

[15] I believe the same is true of other rituals, such as marriage, which Protestants no longer understand to be a sacrament.

complete Christian notion of healing, healing appears as part and parcel of a single worldview, a single network of beliefs.

It is tempting to stop there, underscoring the integral fashion in which the theology of healing fits in with other core theological beliefs. Indeed, many *are* able to stop at this point, since they experience no conflict between the world of traditional belief and the contemporary world with its standards of knowledge and acceptable knowledge claims. However two factors constrain many of us to emphasize the contemporary contexts of plausibility more strongly. One is the empirical fact that many Christian believers *do* experience a conflict between these two worlds. Theologians, in their service to the believing community and to the world, are required to struggle with these conflicts and to struggle towards answers. The second factor is the harder one, because it uses normative language; it is the claim that Christians not only do but *ought to* experience this struggle between the worlds of belief and unbelief and ought to work to find ways to bridge between them.

What should Christians (and other theists) do who experience the conflict? The options are easy to list: one could give up talk of supernatural healing because this notion is widely rejected in our culture; one could dismiss all one's doubts as unnecessary because supernatural healing is so deeply anchored in the Christian scriptures; or could seek to find some new, mediating position that seeks to do justice to as many of the insights from each world as possible.[16]

My own drive is to pursue the third option. Assuming that some mediating position is required, how might it be formulated? There are at least five different types of responses that can be developed, not all of which are mutually exclusive.

1 *Epistemological:* one could assert the existence of spiritual healings but nuance one's knowledge claims, accepting a fairly high level of uncertainty about specific claims to spiritual healing or even about spiritual healing as such.
2 *Ontological:* one could extend one's uncertainty to the question of precisely what occurs in spiritual healing. In this case, one might still believe that God plays a role in spiritual healing while also countenancing other competing explanations, including naturalistic and

[16] I have written extensively on these methodological questions elsewhere and will not repeat the arguments here (e.g. Clayton, 1989, 1997 and 2008).

psychological accounts. One may in fact be strongly attracted to some of the competing accounts.

3 *Agnostic:* however much one is drawn to the possibility of actual spiritual healing, a believer might in the end remain agnostic on the question, neither affirming nor denying, neither believing nor disbelieving.

4 *Symbolic:* one may be unable to assert spiritual healings as factual occurrences in the world but may still wish to retain healing language as an important symbolic resource. This sometimes leads believers to say that spiritual healings are symbolically or metaphorically true, though it's sometimes difficult to establish what exactly is being asserted in these cases. In other words, believers may continue to find an important role for the language of healing even in cases where they cannot assent to healing in the literal sense (e.g. Galipeau 1990; Epperly 2001).

5 *Practical:* A number of Christians engage in healing rituals and prayers for healings without a clearly formed theory or theology of healing. These activities function for them as a part of their religious practice and may even be partially determinative of their view of themselves as Christians. People may view healing rituals and liturgical language about healing as important, even indispensable, parts of their religious lives, without however forming a clear cognitive attitude about these practices or an unambiguous assessment of their implications for belief and practice.

These various cognitive, affective and pragmatic attitudes greatly multiply the complexity of debates about spiritual healing within Christianity. They also nuance the sacramental theology of healing, since such a theology can be developed within the context of any of the five approaches.

CHAPTER 4

Healing the spirit: mystical Judaism, religious texts and medicine

Simon Dein

Religion and medicine have always been close bed partners throughout history. Not only do religious systems offer some explanation for suffering in general and for sickness in particular, but illness presents a challenge to all concerned and it is not surprising that appeal is frequently made to supernatural entities for help, whether this be to provide an explanation to cope with the specific sickness or to offer cure, or something which we might term a 'miracle'. Religious systems seem to have little internal logical self-consistency. Episodes of sickness of any degree of intensity frequently occasion the question 'why me?' and raise concerns relating to theodicy, that is, attempts to reconcile the existence of evil or suffering in the world with the belief in an omniscient, omnipotent and benevolent God; in effect, the problem of evil. Consequently all religions offer a range of solutions to this problem, ranging from ideas that evil originates from mankind to the idea that suffering has educational value or the conclusion that we can never know God's ways, as exemplified in the book of Job, to list just a few.

The term 'healing' within religion is generally more holistic than that within biomedicine and encompasses body, psyche and soul. The mono-theistic religions deploy a plethora of techniques related to healing, both individual and collective; ranging from prayer, ritual, the recitation of myths and religious texts to the more empirical techniques of laying on of hands and the syncretic techniques deployed by religious healers in many parts of the world which combine prayer with the use of medicines. In each of these activities God plays a central role and it is generally recognized that doctors are only a vehicle of healing. It is through them that God acts to effect cure.

In this chapter I write from the perspective of an anthropologist with an interest in medicine. Anthropological perspectives offer advantages over other research methodologies in that they provide the opportunity to observe at close hand, through participant observation, what actually goes on in social contexts so providing 'experience-near' accounts of social phenomena. There are few ethnographic studies specifically devoted to healing within the Judeo-Christian traditions in Western cultures. This is not to deny that many ethnographic texts that focus on the anthropology of religion make some mention of healing. One of these is Thomas Csordas' *The Sacred Self* (1997), which provides a rich experiential analysis of ritual healing practices in the contemporary North American religious movement known as the Catholic Charismatic Renewal. His contribution demonstrates the importance of embodiment and sensory experience in the understanding of culture and self.

The focus in this chapter however is on Judaism and more specifically upon the use of religious texts for healing purposes among Hasidic Jews. It will examine the use of religious texts among Lubavitcher Hasidim in the context of sickness. This group draws heavily on ideas about language deriving from the Lurianic Kabbalah.[1] It is divided into different themes. First, it examines the 'creative' power of religious language. This theme is exemplified through an ethnographic account of the Lubavitch of Stamford Hill, London. This is followed by a discussion of the relation between popular healing, biomedicine and theology in Judaism.

RELIGIOUS TEXTS AND THE PHYSICAL WORLD

There is much anthropological and historical evidence suggesting that, among religious groups, appeal is often made to supernatural powers to influence some aspect of the physical world. Related to this fact is the commonplace finding that religious texts are deployed for their purely pragmatic (as opposed to their spiritual) effects. Such has been the case throughout the history of Judaism, especially in the Jewish mystical tradition, where the use of mystical texts has been used to attain material benefits as in the practical or theurgic Kabbalah. It is in these practices that the distinction between magic and religion becomes

---

[1] The term Kabbalah derives from the Hebrew root *Qof-Bet-Lamed*, meaning tradition. The classical Kabbalah was conceived in Provence, France in the thirteenth century. It spread into Spain where it was developed more extensively by the Spanish mystics. The primary work is the *Sefer ha-Zohar* (Book of Splendour), which consists of mystical commentaries and homilies on the Pentateuch. It was written by Moses de León (thirteenth century) but attributed by him to Simon ben Yohai, the great scholar of the second century. Kabbalah still has adherents, especially among Hasidic Jews, and the philosophy has recently become popularized by writers such as Rebbe Yehuda Berg. The *Zohar* describes God as *En-Sof* ('without end'). It contains a number of interrelated themes: God is unknowable beyond representation; He created the world out of himself; the chief aim of humankind is to achieve complete union with the Divine.

blurred.[2] The pragmatic use of religious texts has been appropriated among some groups of *Hasidim*, pious Jews deriving from Eastern Europe who originally followed the teachings of the Baal Shem Tov and whose spiritual devotion extends beyond the technical requirements of Jewish religious law.

HEBREW LANGUAGE AS CREATIVE

The use of 'religious' language for healing purposes appears to be common throughout the world's cultures. Prayer, spells, incantations, blessings and various other verbal forms are commonly deployed as essential parts of healing rituals. The Sri Lankan anthropologist Stanley Tambiah pointed out:

In most cases it would appear that ritual words are at least as important as other kinds of ritual act: but besides that, and this is the intriguing point, very often (but not always) if the ethnographer questions his informants 'why is this ritual effective?' the reply takes the form of a formally expressed belief that the power is in the 'words' even though the words only become effective if uttered in a very special context of other action. (Tambiah 1968, p. 168)

Indeed sacred words are held to possess a special kind of power not normally associated with ordinary language. This may result from the fact that the sacred language is exclusive and different from secular or profane language. In Hinduism, Islam, Buddhism and Judaism the sacred words recited at religious ceremonies are in the language of the authorized sacred texts. This differs from the practice in Catholicism where the service is recited in the vernacular rather than in Latin (although the Latin Tridentine rite was given the go-ahead, by Pope Benedict XVI in summer 2007, to be re-introduced alongside the vernacular).

The power of sacred words in ritual may derive from another aspect of religious language. These words function beyond the purely descriptive, they are creative in themselves. The idea that religious language was seminal in the process of cosmogeny is pertinent in many religious traditions where the universe is held to have been created through language. For instance in the Vedas, the gods ruled the world through the use

---

[2] The distinction between 'magic' and 'religion' has been a topic of longstanding debate among anthropologists (Tambiah 1990). Religious people worldwide rarely separate official theology from traditional practice, and the distinction between religion and magic is not always easy to make. One person's magic is another person's prayer. Neusner (1989) has argued that in Judaism the distinction is far from clear.

of magical formulae. In the Parsi religion it is asserted that chaos was transformed into cosmos through the spoken word. In a similar way the Gospel of St John speaks of the Logos: the word was in the beginning with God and the word was made flesh in Jesus Christ. In the Hebrew Bible divine speech called into being those entities whose names were pronounced at creation: 'And God called the light day and the darkness he called night' (Genesis 1:5). However, the first act of creation is mentioned in Genesis before any speech act of God is mentioned. After creation, it is unclear whether speech acts innovate the particular thing, they are created *ex-nihilo*, or cause a distinction in the chaotic mass. In the Midrashic and Talmudic literature there are several ways of understanding the biblical account. One portrays God as consulting the Torah and creating the world according to the same pattern. Creation, then, is an act of imposing the inner structure of the Torah on an undefined material.

LANGUAGE AND JEWISH MYSTICISM

Language plays a central creative role in Jewish mysticism. The Hebrew language was considered by mystics as performing a role far more important than the communicative one. The Torah (the five books of Moses, Genesis through to Deuteronomy) is seen as more than a holy book. It is a divine concept, an entity, an organism, which comes to humanity in the form of a narrative anyone can read and follow. For the Kabbalists it can be read at different levels that will ultimately reveal divine truths. According to Gershom Scholem, the great historian of Kabbalah,

The secret world of the godhead is a world of language, a world of divine names that unfold in accordance with a law of their own. The elements of the divine language appear as the letters of the Holy Scriptures. Letters and names are not only conventional means of communication. They are far more. Each one of them represents a concentration of energy and expresses a wealth of meaning which cannot be translated, or not fully at least, into human language. When the Kabbalists speak of divine names and letters, they necessarily operate with the twenty-two consonants of the Hebrew alphabet, in which the Torah is written, or as they would have said, in which its secret essence was made communicable. (Scholem 1965, p. 36)

Various combinations of the letters in God's Holy Name as it appears in the Torah were believed to possess power, and there was a belief that the Torah was, in its entirety, the Divine Name of God Himself. It was also believed that God had purposely given mankind the chapters of the Torah out of order, because, if the text were read in the correct order, mortals would be able to work miracles and raise the dead. In this respect Rabbi Meir, a Torah scribe of the second century, cautioned that Rabbi Ishmael 'said to me: My son, be careful in your work, for it is the work of God; lest by omitting one letter or adding one letter the whole world could be destroyed' (quoted by Levine 2001).

It is not surprising then that words, passages, names of God and prayers were key elements in both theoretical and practical Kabbalah. In the influential Kabbalistic text, the *Sefer Yezirah* (Book of Creation), the letters of the Hebrew alphabet were influential in the process of creation, not only as a creative force but as the elements of its material structure. Through this process Hebrew words maintain a close affinity with the material world such that manipulating words can influence in some ways different aspects of this world. As Idel (1992, p. 43) states, 'The letters are understood to constitute a mesocosmos that enables operations that can bridge the gap between the human or material and the divine.'

This idea was appropriated by Jewish mystics, who used the divine names as a way of influencing the material world, a form of Kabbalistic 'magic'. For example, Trachtenberg (1977) describes the use of divine names for magical purposes. Of great prominence was the recitation of the distinctive personal name of God YHWH, the Tetragrammaton that was understood to be equivalent to the divine presence. The pronunciation of the written name was only to be used by the priests in the Temple when blessing the people (Numbers 22–7). Outside this context they would use the title Adonai ('Lord').

There are many stories of humans being animated through using divine names. The famous story of the *Golem* refers to an artificial man made through Kabbalistic magic. He was animated by writing the Tetragrammaton on a piece of paper placed under his tongue or by engraving the Hebrew word on his forehead. This law of the combination of letters has a long history. According to the mystic Abraham Abulafia in *Sefer Ha Peliyeh*, it has been held that a Zaddik (see below) can combine letters into a favourable word. For instance, the letters of the Hebrew word for sore (*nega*) can be converted into the word meaning pleasure (*oneg*). The Bal Shem Tov, the founder of Hasidism, and a Kabbalist and Magician, speaks of *Hokhmat Serufei Haotiyot*, that is, knowledge of how to improve the fallen, or to purify the impure by manipulating the letters of the entity to be changed. In effect, changing the order of the letters which express a deleterious state in such a way that they form a noun and can transform reality in a positive way is a practice that is common in Hasidic thought. So a simple change in vocalization or accent can convert a curse into a blessing.

The use of spells, incantations, blessings and religious texts at times of misfortune has been popular throughout the history of Judaism and especially in Hasidism (Nigal 1994). Jewish magic is mentioned in the Bible as early as Deuteronomy 28:10–11 where various classes of diviners, astrologers and exorcists are named. Here the attitude towards magicians was one of fear and abhorrence. There is even more abundant mention of it in Talmudic literature, especially the Babylonian Talmud. Unlike witchcraft, which was prohibited, other forms of magic were accepted. Various forms of 'magic' were discussed, such as recitation of the Tetragrammaton and various magical words and formulae, with magical objects often used to avert the evil eye. The latter included amulets and talismans, copies of the Bible, phylacteries and slips of paper (*mezuzot*) attached to doorposts. In the medieval period Jews were often regarded as magicians. For instance at times of drought during the Middle Ages, people turned to the Jews because of the belief that they would be able to make it rain.

During this period practical Kabbalah came to the fore. There were many modifications and interpretations made of the Kabbalah through the centuries. In the tenth century the practical Kabbalah was introduced in Italy and then spread to Germany. It contained ecstatic practices, magic rituals but mainly techniques of prayer and contemplation. *Kabbalah ma'asit*, 'practical Kabbalah', seeks to alter the nature of existence and change the course of events via ritualistic techniques. Sometimes practical Kabbalah involves summoning spiritual forces, such as angels, and commanding them or causing them to swear to perform a certain act or function in reality. According to Gershom Scholem,

Historically speaking, a large part of the contents of practical Kabbalah predate those of the speculative Kabbalah and are not dependent on them. In effect, what came to be considered practical Kabbalah constituted an agglomeration of all the magical practices that developed in Judaism from the Talmudic period down through the Middle Ages. The doctrine of the Sefirot hardly ever played a decisive role in these practices. (Scholem 1974, p. 183)

LUBAVITCHER HASIDIM

Lubavitch is a worldwide movement of Hasidic Jews, whose main centre is in New York. Menachem Schneersom, known as 'the Rebbe' by his followers, led the movement until his death in 1994. This group attracted a great deal of controversy on account of their beliefs that the Rebbe was, and for many still is, the Messiah (Dein 2001). For many years prior to his death his followers spread messianic propaganda stating his messianic status and that the redemption was imminent.

Lubavitch communities exist throughout the world but the main centres are in Israel, Great Britain, the United States and Belgium. Unlike other Hasidic groups, Lubavitch emphasize the teaching of mystical concepts to all Jews. Another differentiating factor from other Hasidic groups is their emphasis on bringing back stray Jews to Judaism (Dein 1992, 2001, 2002). This movement is well known for its emissaries (*Schluchim*), who travel across the world, often to isolated communities, in an effort to teach Jews about Judaism in the hope that they will return to their heritage and perform *Mitzvot* (good deeds).

All Hasidic groups focus around their religious leader, the *zaddik* or *rebbe*, a perfectly righteous man who is the spiritual leader of the group and mediates between God and man. Rooted in Kabbalistic doctrines, the *zaddik* is a charismatic figure of extraordinary spiritual calibre. By devoting oneself to him, his adherents can benefit from his spiritual guidance and his ability to provide 'miracles'. The Rebbe, until his death in 1994, held regular mass meetings with his followers at his residence in Brooklyn, New York, called '770'. At these events about 6,000 people would congregate and wait in line to receive a blessing from the Rebbe and also a dollar that symbolized charity. Alternatively, his followers would fax or phone his secretary who would approach him with requests for intercession. He would write back requesting them to check their religious artefacts such as the *tefillin* (phylacteries) or *mezuzah* (scrolls of Torah encased in metal). At times of sickness informants often pointed to a one-to-one relation between defects in religious texts and bodily sickness.[3] Since his death his followers have persisted in e-mailing his tomb in the hope of receiving a response.[4]

[3] This form of textual healing is not unique to Judaism. Throughout the world the recitation of passages from religious texts is commonplace at times of misfortune. In Islam, *tibb al nabi*, reading of Qu'ranic verses or drinking water washed off Qu'ranic verses is a popular form of ritual healing.
[4] The Rebbe's followers fax or e-mail his secretary who reads their requests to the Rebbe at his tomb. The response is indirect and often signified by some sudden unexpected event that may have a bearing on the thing requested. For instance one man who was in severe debt e-mailed the Rebbe asking for help. He heard shortly afterwards that an aunt in Brazil had unexpectedly died leaving him a lot of money. Alternatively Lubavitchers will randomly open the page of a book of the Rebbe's teachings and find a passage directly relating to their predicament.

WORDS AND THE MATERIAL WORLD IN THE TANYA

According to the teachings of the *Tanya*, the mystical text of the Lubavitcher Hasidim, the Hebrew language is regarded as instrumental in the process of creation of the world and is a natural component of reality. This text, written by the founder of Lubavitch Rabbi Schneur Zalman (1745–1812) in 1796, states that the letters of the Hebrew alphabet were influential in the process of creating the world, not only as creative forces but as elements in its material structure. Language is an archetype of the world and also its very essence. It can be seen as immanent in the physical world. God combined the twenty-two letters of the alphabet as part of the creative process. Lubavitchers place great emphasis on the fact that language is the spiritual underpinning of reality and it bridges the gap between the human and divine planes.

According to Zalman, the words creating the material world

Stand upright forever, with the firmament of the heaven and are clothed with all firmaments forever in order to enliven them ... Because should the letter disappear for a second, God forfend, and return to their source (then), all the heavens would become naught and nil indeed and become as if they never existed at all ... and this is also [the case for] all the creatures that are in the world, high and lower, even this corporeal earth, and even the aspect of mineral. With the letters of the ten logoi disappear from it [the earth] for a second, God forfend, by means of which the earth was created ... who had returned to naught and nil, indeed, in the combination of letters in that form the name even [stone] is a vitality of the stone and this is the case for all the creatures of the world, [that] their names in the holy language are the letters of speech. They are emanated from one great gradation to another from the ten logoi in the Torah, by their substitutions and permutations of letters, according to the 231 gates until they arrive and close within that creature. (Zalman, *The Tanya*, book II)

Hence Zalman argues that Hebrew speech is the essence of all created reality. Without this speech there could be no material world. Disorder in the physical world reflects spiritual disorder. Among Lubavitchers, bodily sickness derives from aberrant religious texts. Healing can be obtained by the correction of such texts.

NARRATIVES OF HEALING

To give an example of this, Rabbi Nifield wrote to the Rebbe after suffering a small stroke, which left him paralysed in his left arm, although his walking or speech remained unimpaired. He had suffered from hypertension for some years but admitted he had not taken it as seriously as he should have, although he had been in hospital on several occasions with angina. Following the stroke, he spent a week in his local hospital, where he was given physiotherapy, which only slowly helped his weakness.[5]

Jacob Nifield was born in Poland but came to Britain in 1936 at the age of 4. He is the third of ten children. His father, a Rabbi, was a very learned man who spent all his time studying, and he had an ideal Jewish mother, a very quiet woman. Both parents died several years ago. Jacob grew up in an ultra-orthodox environment and carried out the prescribed rituals from a very young age. He spent a year in a Jewish seminary in northern England and became a Rabbi at the age of 26, and since then has been teaching in Lubavitcher schools (Dein 2002, p. 55).

The Rebbe responded to Rabbi Nifield's letter by offering a blessing and suggesting he check his *mezuzot*. His wife took all the *mezuzot* to a scribe, who thoroughly checked the scrolls and casing, only to find they were ritually pure. He could not understand this. Could the Rebbe be wrong? No the Rebbe is never wrong, if he says 'the *mezuzot* are not kosher', they are really not kosher. He sent a second letter to the Rebbe telling him about the scribe, but the Rebbe responded by suggesting the *mezuzot* were checked again. A second scribe was asked but he also found them to be kosher. A third letter to the Rebbe resulted in the same reply. The third scribe spent a long day examining the *mezuzot*, working until the early hours of the following morning. It was only then that, holding one scroll up to the light, he found there was a problem. A small beam of light shone through a hole in one of the letters of the word *lev* (heart) in the Shema. The hole rendered the *mezuzot* unkosher. Rabbi Nifield had the scroll replaced and immediately gained full movement in his left side and his angina also noticeably improved. Three months after his stroke he showed only some slight weakness in his left arm. He emphasized the relation between the physical (his heart) and the spiritual world (the word 'heart' in the religious text).

Rabbi Nifield pointed out the physical and spiritual worlds were interrelated, and his story exemplifies the point that there is a close relation between religious text and the physical body. The second instance provides a formal correspondence between the words of a text and the physical state of the body.

---

[5] Some of this material has appeared in Littlewood and Dein (1995), Dein (2002, 2004).

Earlier in the year, 41-year-old Mrs Halpern asked her daughter in Brooklyn to contact the Rebbe about the 'unbearable and unrelenting' back pain she had experienced since the birth of her eleventh child. Although the pain had started late in her pregnancy 'probably due to the baby pressing on my spine', it got much worse following the delivery. It was so bad that she could not sit still for longer than a few minutes. Lying down did not help either. She consulted the family doctor who 'after a very brief examination' recommended bed rest and analgesics. Mrs Halpern was not happy with this advice; for one thing, it prevented her giving her newborn son, Isaac, the care and attention a newborn baby required. Over the next couple of weeks the pain got worse. 'My legs felt weak and my feet were tingling.' She recounted that 'although it was the Shabbat, the pain was so bad that I asked my husband to phone for an ambulance' (it is permitted to use a phone on the Sabbath in the case of an emergency).

She was seen in the local hospital casualty department by an orthopaedic surgeon who told her she needed to be admitted for absolute bed rest and, if the pain did not settle in a few days, she would need an operation to remove a slipped disc. She reluctantly agreed to go into hospital but was perturbed by the thought of an operation. 'I had heard of someone having a similar operation who was permanently paralysed. I knew that these operations were not always successful.' As soon as the Sabbath was over, her husband phoned their daughter Sarah in New York and asked her to see the Rebbe's secretary and get a blessing for her mother.

Mrs Halpern is a short plump lady with a large blonde *sheitl* (wig) who looks somewhat older than her 41 years. She is very approachable with a 'motherly' personality. She was born locally, her parents being Orthodox Jews who had contact with the Lubavitch. An only child (unusually for an Orthodox family), she attended a Lubavitcher school in Stamford Hill where she did well and at the age of 18 went to a seminary in France for two years. 'Although I could have gone to "Sem" in Israel or America, my parents told me to ask the Rebbe's advice first. Whatever he says, you must do.' Following her return to England she was introduced to her husband Shmuel, himself a Lubavitcher who works as a printer. Mrs Halpern now works in a local group providing religious activities for children.

The Rebbe responded to her daughter's request by faxing a reply a few hours later. She was particularly keen to emphasize that 'he receives several hundred letters each day, yet he responded to mine so quickly because he knew it was important. Surely no ordinary man could do this.' The Rebbe suggested in his reply that all the household *mezuzot* were checked. He underlined the word all. This was done by a local scribe who found a crack across the words 'When you sit in your house' (Deuteronomy 6:7). Mrs Halpern pointed out that she had the greatest difficulty sitting for any length of time. The scroll was replaced and after a week in hospital she was almost pain free and did not require an operation. How did the Rebbe know about the *posul* (unkosher) *mezuzah*? According to Mrs Halpern

The Rebbe has a connection with Hashem [God]. He has a feeling for holiness because his soul is more spiritual than that of other men and the power of his prayer is greater. Because of this he can know these things. (Dein 2002, p. 54)

However, it is important to emphasis that Lubavitchers do not just depend upon spiritual healing. Understandings of sickness amongst Lubavitchers derive both from biomedicine through their interaction with GPs and the NHS generally and from Orthodox Jewish attitudes to illness and death and the Hasidic attitude towards suffering. Upon developing illness, their first thoughts are to consult their local doctor for biomedical help. Prayers are also said for the sick person and if the illness is judged to be serious *Tehillim* (psalms) are read. Prayer is always appropriate even if the person is terminally ill. Indeed, even if a sword is raised over a person's neck he must not refrain from asking for God's mercy (*Berakhot* 10a).

Orthodox Jewish teachings stress the importance of hope and express-ing one's faith in God at times of misfortune. It is expected that the sick person will always repent of his or her sins. In addition, among Luba-vitchers, when people become sick they should always try to find a religious explanation for their illness. This usually means checking their religious artefacts, such as the *mezuzot* or *teffilin*. Hence Lubavitchers see biomedical and spiritual healing as complementary.[6]

NATURALISTIC AND SPIRITUAL HEALING IN JUDAISM

Solomon (1999, pp. 166–86) points out that throughout the history of Judaism popular attitudes to sickness have coexisted with strictly scientific approaches and the two are linked by theology. The discussion below

---

[6] This form of religious healing utilizing the manipulation of religious texts was deployed when the Rebbe himself became ill. In 1992 the Rebbe had a stroke that rendered him speechless and paralysed. Despite incapacity, his followers persisted in approaching him for blessings. The fact that he had become ill justified their belief that he was the Messiah. They resorted to biblical justification, quoting Isaiah 53, which states that the Messiah will be someone acquainted with suffering and sickness. In order to heal him they wrote out a new *Sefer Torah* (Torah scroll) emphasizing that the 613 commandments in this scroll reflected the 613 parts of the Rebbe's body. The Rebbe died in June 1994 following a second massive stroke.

derives from him. Generally there has been no contradiction between using naturalistic (and latterly biomedical) approaches to healing alongside spiritual healing. The Babylonian Talmud, the main repository of ancient Jewish wisdom after the Bible, contains several collections of remedies introduced by the third-century teacher Abbaye. Many of these relate to the use of plants and herbs. Alongside this was a widespread belief in demons, spirit possession and the evil eye – invisible entities and forces which controlled or at least influenced a person's destiny. However, these ideas did not go without criticism. For instance, the medieval Jewish physician, Moses Maimonides (1135–1204) wrote that all these matters such as astrology and necromancy are clothed in deceit by means of which idolatrous priests in ancient times misled the people of the nation to follow them. However, Maimonides' views had little effect on the population generally and as late as the eighteenth century Elijah the Gaon of Vilna sharply criticized him for denying the existence of demons.

Beyond these popular views of sickness others held a more scientific attitude towards medicine. The Talmud is concerned with *Halakah* or law rather than the art of medicine. Much of what it discusses in relation to sickness refers to the legal details rather than the practical details of treatment. It is difficult to gain any understanding of the practice of medicine or its underlying theories by reading the Talmud (see Preuss 1978).

A more systematic approach emphasizing empirical treatment appeared only in the Middle Ages, and was heavily influenced by the Hippocratic school and Galen. Undoubtedly during the Renaissance Jews had played a significant role in the transformation of ancient Greek medical knowledge, even though they were largely excluded from the great European universities.

A third theological approach emphasizes the fact that God is all-powerful, merciful and compassionate and his providence extends to all creatures. Therefore, prayer is the way of dealing with sickness. 'For it is I the Lord who will heal you' (Exodus 15:26). The Torah is the antidote for sickness. As Rashi, the great eleventh-century biblical scholar, argued, 'God gave us the Torah and the Commandments so that we would be saved from the diseases he afflicted upon the Egyptians.' This theological position raises intriguing questions. For instance, if God gives us sickness, is it correct to seek medical help? Indeed there have been Jewish sects such as the Karaites who have denied the use of biomedicine. The Medieval scholar Nahmanides (1194–1270) held that God would protect from sickness any individual who served him in complete faith and ideally the sick person should turn to repentance not to doctors. However, the predominant Jewish view is not only that the practice of medicine is permissible but, in fact, it is virtuous. One should not depend on spiritual healing alone.

There is a positive obligation for those who are able to do so to use their skills and resources to heal. Orthodox Judaism does not expect everyone to be healed by prayer. According to the scholar David Ben Shmuel Ha Levi (1586–1667),

> True healing is through prayer, for healing is from heaven, as it is written 'I have smitten and I shall heal' (Deuteronomy 32:39). Not everyone however is worthy of this special divine intervention, so it is necessary to achieve healing by natural means. He, blessed be He, agreed to this and gave healing through natural cures: this is what is meant by 'he gave permission to heal.' Since human beings have got into the state of having to rely on natural cures, doctors are obliged to effect cures by natural means. (cited in Solomon 1999, p. 172)

The attitude of Talmudic teachers to medicine is ambivalent. On the one hand doctors are permitted to heal (*Baba Qamma* 85a). On the other hand King Hezekiah is praised for having hidden a book of cures, so that the sick would pray to God as opposed to relying on doctors. The justification for doctors being able to heal derives from Exodus 21:19, which states that anyone who has committed an assault must pay for their victim's enforced idleness from work and his cure (*ve rappo ye rappe*). So the practice of medicine becomes part of the spirituality of Judaism. Indeed it is an essential element of it, with Jews expected to seek medical help, not just to pray, in times of sickness.

CONCLUSION

The practice of medicine in Judaism persists alongside forms of healing which might be labelled as spiritual. It is common for the sick person and their family to seek help both from a biomedical practitioner and from a 'traditional healer', especially among some groups of Sephardim who make regular pilgrimages to the graves of 'saints' to make intercession and petition for miracles. The specific content of this 'spiritual' healing is greatly affected by cultural norms. To the author's knowledge the form of healing described among Lubavitchers is rare among other Hasidic groups and among Orthodox Jews generally.

CHAPTER 5

Conceptualizations of spiritual healing: Christian and secular

Charles Bourne and Fraser Watts

During the twentieth century there has been a marked revival of interest in spiritual healing within the Christian church. Initially this arose from an integration of liturgical and psychiatric elements, though more recently it has been given considerable further impetus by the charismatic revival. Alongside this, there has also been a marked development of interest in spiritual healing in more secular society, within what used to be called the 'New Age' movement (though that term is increasingly disowned). In this chapter we will compare how these two groups of healers understand spiritual healing. The focus will be on how spiritual healing is conceptualized and understood and we will compare expositions of healing in Christian and secular cultures.

Our methodology will examine and compare two sets of popular books about spiritual healing to see what assumptions about healing are made. On the one hand there are books written for Christians, embedding healing firmly in the tenets of the Christian faith and increasingly written from a charismatic viewpoint. Such books usually say little about healing outside the churches, though they may provide information about complementary medicine. There is a tendency to warn against techniques that employ mechanisms not understood by orthodox science. On the other hand, there are books about spiritual healing written from a non-Christian standpoint. These usually contain only a passing reference to healing that takes place in the Christian environment, though the tacit assumption is that Christian healing is a variant of other forms of spiritual healing.

There has been little attempt by either wing of the spiritual healing movement to really understand the other and the implicit assumption seems to be that they are concerned with very different forms of spiritual healing. However, we will show that there are in fact many common assumptions. Indeed, it seems that many of the apparent differences between how healing is understood in the secular environment and in the churches may arise from the context in which the healing is taking place rather than from fundamental differences in the form of healing that is undertaken.

The phrase 'Christian healing' will often be used when referring to healing that is taking place in a Christian environment and 'secular healing' when referring to healing that is taking place in a secular environment. This is not a judgement about the healing itself, rather a simple way of referring to the beliefs, practices and assumptions that surround that healing.

This chapter consists of four main sections. The first is concerned with the gift of healing, with how universal that is, and how the healing gift can be cultivated and developed. Next we will look at views about the source of healing power, and especially whether this is conceptualized in personal or impersonal terms. Thirdly, we will consider different approaches to healing, focusing particularly on the relatively active or passive approaches to healing identified by Lawrence LeShan. Finally, we will look at how the success and failure of healing are understood and interpreted.

THE HEALING GIFT

Most healers assume that the gift of healing is to some extent present in everyone, though there are divergences between Christian and secular healers about how far people can develop that gift through their own efforts. By 'gift' for healing, in this context, we mean how far a particular individual has an aptitude for being a channel of healing. Speaking of a gift for healing in this sense has no implications of how the ultimate source of healing power or energy is conceptualized.

Barbara Brennan, an internationally renowned secular healer, states that 'the gift of healing rests within everyone. It is not a gift given only to a few ... everyone can learn to heal' (Brennan 1993, p. 3). She sees evidence that the healing ability is universal in the act of a mother caressing her child when it is in pain. For Brennan, the difference between the healing that is taking place in this situation and the healing that flows between a professional healer and a patient is one of degree not type. A professional healer will have learnt to perceive and regulate that healing energy (Brennan 1993, p. 3) while it may remain unconscious in the relationship between a mother and her child.

Similarly, in Reiki, a healer is distinguished by his or her ability to regulate the healing energy. Reiki, meaning 'universal life-giving energy', is a specific form of spiritual healing which emerged in Japan in the nineteenth century. Reiki practitioners believe that, while anyone can be a channel of unconditional love, a Reiki practitioner 'can guarantee to give a transmission of this degree at any moment' (Keshava 2002, p. 4). So, though a parent may only be able to be a channel of healing towards his or her own child, a healer is able to do this at will with an unknown patient.

Within the Christian environment there is a similar assumption that healing is, to some extent, universal. Christian healing starts with prayer, which is something everyone can do (Maddocks 1992, p. 50). Agnes Sanford understands the healing gift as being like any other quality that has been given by God (Sanford 1966, p. 61). A recent report by the Church of England on the healing ministry talks of people who are 'particularly gifted' (Church of England 2000, p. 229), implying that healing powers can also be found to some extent in those who are not 'particularly gifted'.

Though many Christians may accept that the ability to heal is universal, there is widespread unease about the idea that the ability to heal can be developed by learning and practising a technique. Morris Maddocks sees the idea that Christians can become better healers as a result of practical instruction as a challenge to God's sovereignty. He believes that 'the essence of this ministry is that we expect but we do not presume' (Maddocks 1990, p. 233). Francis MacNutt is of a similar opinion, that 'God wants us to depend on Him – not upon a technique' (MacNutt 1989, p. 201). The implication is that some people may be unable to develop their healing skill, no matter what they do, because it is not what God has in store for them.

In contrast, it is more common in secular circles to assume that people can be trained to be healers. This is clearly assumed, for example, by those enrolling for three years at Brennan's School of Healing, or by LeShan, who spent a year and a half practising before he felt he could get into a state in which he could heal (LeShan 1980, p. 117). However, even in Christian circles, it is sometimes assumed that healing can be learned. Sanford found that, as she learned to heal, it was not just the gift of healing that she needed to pray for, but also the gifts of knowledge, wisdom and other things that she felt were required to use that gift of healing to the best effect. Her failure to heal at the start of her healing ministry did not contradict God's omnipotence, because whilst all things are possible with God, 'all things are not as yet possible with Agnes' (Sanford 1966, p. 64).

In Reiki, the ability to heal is acquired not through the learning of a technique, or through prayer, but through partaking in a mystical ceremony that 'facilitates the student's direct and perfect connection with the Source of Reiki' (Keshava 2002, p. 7). Although the acquisition of a healing ability may be rapid, it is seen as part of a larger process. The attunement is more often undertaken as the result of a conscious decision to follow the spiritual path, rather than in order that the person may become a healer. Attunement is not a substitute for growth and development but an integral part of it.

Though Christians are sceptical about the role of training in healing, they are more likely to accept that there is a place for personal and spiritual development. In this, Christian healing is quite close to Reiki. For example, Mark Pearson gives a list of the qualities that a Christian healer needs to develop. This list includes such qualities as a love of people, a spiritual life and the ability to take direction (Pearson 1996, pp. 226–7). Similarly, Maddocks talks of the importance of the healer placing his or her 'whole life at the disposal of God' (Maddocks 1990, p. 234). The healer needs first to experience being totally at the disposal of God, and healing is then seen as being dependent on this internal reaching for God.

Though the secular healer has a range of courses and models to follow in which the necessary inner change and development have been mapped out, there is little similar provision for Christian healers. This is partly because the Christian life itself is already one of spiritual development in which prayer and communion with God are encouraged. In Jesus Christ, Christians have perhaps the greatest example of a healer and studying his life through the gospels and trying to follow his example may be the best way of developing the healer inside each one of us. Moral and spiritual beliefs are also addressed very directly in the Christian environment. Christian healers already have a set of beliefs by which they are guided in contrast to the secular environment where a person who wants to develop his or her healing ability has to be guided in a much more specific way – leading to the need for courses on healing.

In addition, the training in healing that is offered in the secular environment may be a reflection of the commercial aspect of secular healing. Here there is a need for a product that can be clearly identified, a need that is not so prominent for those operating inside the Church. Equally, it is possible that there are few structured courses within the Christian environment simply because things are slow to change. It is only recently that classes where healing is taught have emerged in the secular environment (Meek 1977, p. 163) and it is possible that courses specifically for healing will emerge in the Christian environment.

There is both advantage and disadvantage in the development of the healing ability in the secular environment being structured through the use of classes. On the one hand it makes clear that the attainment of the healing ability is not achieved simply by asking God for this gift, without any contribution on the part of the person seeking it. The secular approach emphasizes that personal development is required for the receiving of the healing gift, even if the giving of the gift is beyond the control of the person concerned. On the other hand, a focus on the external source of the gift may lead to the misconception that participation in the ritual or completing of the course is all that is required (Brennan 1987, p. 13). This may lead to a neglect of the inner growth that virtually all healers seek, either as a result or as a cause of their ability to heal.

THE SOURCE OF HEALING

The vast majority of spiritual healers see themselves as channels for a healing power that comes from beyond them, rather than as the source of that power. However, there are considerable divergences over who or what is being channelled. Christian healers talk predominantly about the power of Jesus to heal, whereas secular healers usually talk about healing energy. LeShan could find no way of verifying the source of healing energy, and so explicitly decided to set aside these explanations (1980, p. 105).

Many secular healers have roots in Spiritualism and believe that they are in touch with discarnate entities when healing. Such 'mediumship' is anathema to the Church, which holds that Jesus is the only healing power who should be called upon. This is a major stumbling block to any reconciliation between the two groups. However, few secular healers would argue that these discarnate entities are the ultimate source of healing. Alan Young (1981, p. 24) claims that 'all genuine spiritual healers readily acknowledge that ... they merely act as a channel for the power of God, or the Divine Creator of the Universe'.

The difference arises because, while Christian healers may believe God is acting directly through them, those outside the Church often believe that the healer is simply the next to last link in a chain connecting God to the person in need. In this chain there might be a host of spirit doctors, healing angels and other beings (Young 1981, p. 22). Such a belief would lead to some recognition of the work being done by these beings, with a corresponding de-emphasis on the ultimate source. Though Young is probably right that there is a significant difference between Christian and secular healers, it is not clear that Christian healers need to call on the power of Jesus alone. It would be consistent with much Christian theology to call on the 'whole company of heaven' as well as Jesus himself. Nevertheless, most Christian thinkers would not consider that it was necessary to do so, and would not think that the power of Jesus needed to be mediated through any other discarnate spirits.

LeShan found that healers could be divided into three groups: those who believed that healing worked through the power of God, those who believed that it worked due to spirits, and those who explained it on the basis of energy (1980, pp. 103–4). These distinctions hide significant overlaps and parallels. Christian healers generally use more personal terms to talk about the agent of healing, and are less likely to talk about 'energy'. Nevertheless, where Christian healers do speak in terms of energy they hold views similar to those of secular healers about the role of the healer in relation to this energy. For example, Edgar Jackson, a Methodist Minister, takes an almost identical view to that taken in Reiki, describing the healer as 'a transformer of the energies that are God's nature into personalised forms that are more accessible to him or her' (Jackson 1989, p. 15).

Just as Christian healers can see God's action in healing as taking a variety of forms, ranging from the highly personal (Jesus) to the impersonal ('energies that are God's nature'), in the secular environment it is also possible to see the 'spirits' and 'energy' not as two distinct entities, but as different aspects of an underlying force for healing. There is certainly a difference in the predominant language used in Christian and secular healing circles, but a less absolute difference than might at first be supposed.

The blurring of distinctions between different sources of healing is particularly striking in an example described by Brennan. While she had often worked with a number of spirit guides, one time a being appeared to her that was very much more powerful than the others. This spirit guide she nicknamed 'the Goddess' because 'she appeared to be the feminine aspect of God' (Brennan 1993, p. 269). It was only later revealed to her that 'the healing energy that we call the Goddess' was in fact the Holy Spirit (1993, p. 269). She describes the spirit/force as both a 'being' and as an 'energy', which suggests that while it served her well to see this energy in a personalized form, it was not necessary to conceptualize this energy or aspect of God.

The activity of the Holy Spirit is the most common way in which Christians talk about God's ongoing action in the world. The role of the Spirit as the 'giver of life' encapsulates a source of vital energy, a Western analogue of concepts such as Chi, Ki and Prana. Reiki becomes a healing energy when it is channelled through the heart (Keshava 2002, p. 4). The Church is highly suspicious of any such energy (Church of England 2000, p. 188), calling Reiki an 'unqualified energy source', although it acknowledges that this label might be equally well applied to the Holy Spirit (2000, p. 197).

Brennan sometimes found that her spirit guides had different characteristics depending on what aspect of the person they were working on. At the lower levels the guides had quite clearly defined characteristics, but at the highest level 'they seem a bit impersonal' (Brennan 1987, p. 233). It is debatable how far one can make a distinction between personal spirit and impersonal force. In seeing the agent of healing as both a being and as energy, Brennan is pushing the meanings of words to their limits. Her language reflects the fathomless nature of a suprapersonal God, the description of whom (or which) must ultimately fall into terms that are either more or less personal. Some people experience the source of healing as a personal being, whether this might be an angel, a spirit doctor, Jesus, the Holy Spirit, or simply God. Others are more tuned in to the action that is going on, the force or energy that appears to be present, though the term God or Holy Spirit may still be used.

ACTIVE AND PASSIVE TYPES OF HEALING

We will now turn from the source of healing to how healers understand their own role in the healing process. Those involved in spiritual healing reveal a wide range of different views about this. Some envisage the healer as having a very active role and being largely responsible for the healing process; others see the healer as having a more passive role, attributing the main responsibility for healing to an ultimate source of healing power.

The work of Alice Bailey (1953) is of particular interest in relation to this because her understanding of spiritual healing is extreme. She looked forward to a new kind of healing in the future which would 'gradually supersede the more physical methods of the present art of healing' (Bailey 1953, p. 4). She found a model of how the spiritual healer should work in the example of the trained physician, and even suggested that a conventional medical training would be greatly beneficial to practitioners of spiritual healing. As she understands it, one of the qualities required of the healer is 'exact knowledge' (1953, p. 524).

The opposite end of the spectrum can be seen in approaches to spiritual healing that Bailey criticizes, including those which base their procedures 'on systems of affirmation, modes of prayer, stimulation of the will to live ... [they are] no true formula for an intelligent and expected cure, only the vague faith of the healer and of the patient' (1953, p. 644). She regards the claims of Christian Science to be 'a glamour and an illusion' (1953, p. 558). So at one end of the spectrum healers are characterized by action and knowledge, and at the other end by prayer, faith and affirmation.

Lawrence LeShan thought it more fruitful to focus on the distinction between active and passive approaches to healing than on where the ultimate source of healing power might reside. He looked at the range of activities engaged in by a number of established and prominent healers, and found that they conceptualized their healing in different ways, which he arranged into two categories, called Type 1 and Type 2. However, he found that individual healers did not necessarily use one or the other approach exclusively, and also that they did not always differentiate between the two approaches.

LeShan saw the heart of Type 1 healing as being 'a deeply intense caring and a viewing of the healee and oneself [the healer] as one' (LeShan 1980, p. 107). 'There is no attempt to do anything to the healee' (LeShan 1980, p. 106). LeShan noted several healers who exemplified this approach. Ambrose Worrall sought 'to become one with the patient', and Harry Edwards found that in the healing 'his being is merged ... into that of the patient, so that "both" are "one"' (LeShan 1980, pp. 106–7). Similarly, the Christian minister Edgar Jackson found that he moved beyond considerations of real or unreal, and subjective or objective. When this state was reached the patient was at one with the universe and therefore in 'an ideal organismic position' that enabled him to repair himself at a greatly accelerated rate.

In Type 2 healing the approach was quite different. The healer tried to heal, using a 'healing energy' that cured the sick area (LeShan 1980, p. 112). For Edwards, when operating in this fashion, all that mattered were his hands, through which the healing energy flowed (LeShan, 1980, p. 113). The difference between Type 1 and Type 2 can be seen in Bailey's views about healing. She endorses what LeShan calls Type 2 and criticizes what he calls Type 1. Healers who were Christian Scientists, for example, were found to use Type 1 exclusively (LeShan 1980, p. 106).

LeShan was not sure how Type 2 worked, but thought it possible either that it depended on some kind of energy process, or that Type 2 was simply a failed attempt to do Type 1 healing, arising because the healer and patient were uncomfortable with too much closeness (LeShan 1980, pp. 113–14). However, it is equally possible to take the opposite view and to suggest that Type 1 is actually a variant of Type 2, but one in which the healer is too closely identified with the patient for the passing of energy to be experienced.

A disadvantage of LeShan's approach is that it dichotomizes healing too sharply into two types. This can be seen in relation to Brennan's conceptualization of the healing process. Brennan (1993), having developed the ability to perceive subtle bodies in which there is less and less distinction between one person and another, came to the conclusion, held by Type 1 healers, that there are ultimately no boundaries between people. Yet she also believed that she was able to carry out healing only through manipulation of subtle bodies, which seems more like Type 2 healing. It would be unwise to imagine that there is such a sharp dichotomy between LeShan's two types. Another example of this is where LeShan would see distinct Type 1 and Type 2 processes going on, but where the healer views the healing as a single act.

Healing in secular settings often emphasizes the more active Type 2 healing, but in Christian settings there is often the opposite emphasis, with healing most commonly being conceptualized as a Type 1 process. No knowledge of the problem is required for prayer for healing. Edgar Jackson was found to only use Type 1. Jackson called prayer the 'subject–object bridge' (LeShan 1980, pp. 106–7). Other Christian writers have used similar Type 1 language to talk about healing through prayer. Maddocks talks of a positive aligning with the divine will (Maddocks 1990, pp. 234–5), while MacNutt speaks of the importance of focusing on the presence of God (MacNutt 1989, p. 208).

In the Christian environment the primary focus is on God: prayer and attunement to God give rise to the experience of oneness that characterizes Type 1 healing. In the secular environment it is possible that the healer may also focus on God (although not necessarily the Christian God). However, this focus, being a private matter, may not play an explicit role in either the training or the practice of healing. Though there is a difference of emphasis between secular and Christian environments concerning how far healers see their work in an active or passive way, it would not be appropriate to make the dichotomy too sharp.

The laying on of hands in church is more ambiguous in terms of LeShan's distinction. To the external observer, it is a clear example of active Type 2 healing, and phenomena associated with healing of that type do indeed occur in the Christian laying on of hands (Pearson 1996, pp. 238–9; MacNutt 1989, p. 207). Some Christian healers seem to understand the laying on of hands in that way, especially when it is used diagnostically to discern hot and cold areas, and when heat sensations accompany the physical action of touch. However, the laying on of hands is also sometimes seen purely as a symbol of the healing power of God being invoked (Church of England 2000, p. 242), and so is not critical to how God's healing power is mediated. In this view, it is prayer that is crucial, and the laying on of hands is only symbolic.

Reiki, to some extent, employs both Type 1 and Type 2 methods. While it involves the placing of the hands in various positions on the body, the position of the hands is not crucial for healing. The energy is intelligent and goes where it is needed. For beginners, the focus is on detachment: standing back and letting the Reiki do its work. This passive detached state is not dissimilar from that sought in Type 1. Also, the fact that Reiki can be done at a distance suggests it is not reliant on healing energy passing through the hands. It is only at a more advanced level of Reiki that there is a diagnosis of the nature of the disease and a greater intentionality is employed, indicative of a more Type 2 approach.

LeShan regarded Type 1 healing as the more important of the two types, and made it a rule in his own practice never to do a Type 2 healing without first using a strong Type 1 approach (LeShan 1980, p. 122). Most Christian healers would agree. It is significant that Bailey, who is one of the few to warn of the dangers of attempted 'healing' (Bailey 1953, p. 705), has little interest in the approaches associated with Type 1 healing, and focuses almost exclusively on the Type 2 approach. It seems likely that such possibility of harm as may arise from attempted healing is associated with Type 2 rather than Type 1 approaches.

INTERPRETATIONS OF SUCCESS AND FAILURE

In this section we explore how the results of a spiritual healing treatment are interpreted. We will focus first on why there might be no change at all, and then on why change might be only temporary.

Various reasons may be put forward for healing not occurring at all. The most common reason offered is that healing was not 'meant to be', or was not in God's purposes. This is true of healers in both secular and Christian environments. The possibility that the effectiveness of healing is limited by the proficiency of the healer is recognized not only among secular healers. Sanford, adopting a Christian approach, also saw her failures as being due to this (Sanford 1966, p. 64). The convergence between secular and Christian healers on this point indicates similar basic attitudes to the process of healing.

The possibility that a patient may resist healing has also often been considered (Meek 1977, p. 160). The general view is that in order to be healed, people need to have a desire to return to health even if they do not need faith in order to be healed. Having a desire to be healed implies that one should at least 'be prepared to give the healing power a reasonable chance to work' (Fricker 1977, p. 58). Worrall puts it the other way round, declaring that someone with a 'negative attitude' cannot be healed (Worrall and Worrall 1969, p. 167).

Most healers in both secular and Christian environments agree that healing means moving on, rather than returning to how things were before the patient felt a loss of health. Young believes the process of disease and healing is part of a person's spiritual path, and suggests that different responses to healing are the result of differences in 'people's progress towards learning the lesson which the disease was meant to teach them for the evolution of their soul' (Young 1981, p. 150). Brennan agrees that someone who has been through the process of ill health and healing is not only changed on a physical level, but also attains a new outlook on life and how it should be lived (Brennan 1993, pp. 82–3). She makes clear that this embracing of a new way of life is a necessary part of the healing process and is not just an optional extra (1993, p. 89). Similarly, Lawrence, writing about Christian healing, points out that healing brings both change and renewal (Lawrence 1997, p. 44).

Pearson (1996, p. 164) claims that New Age techniques neglect the moral aspect and treat just the symptoms, which is another potential reason why the benefits of healing might not be sustained. In fact, secular healers seem to fully understand the deeper significance of disease and healing, though they may be less inclined to press that aspect of healing on their patients. Brennan states that 'it is of utmost importance for the healer to accept whatever stage the patient is in and not try to pull them out of it' (1993, p. 84). If there is a lack of moral focus in secular healing it probably stems from the attitude of the patients rather than that of the healers themselves. The Christian environment, in which teaching already has a place, is a much more suitable environment in which to address the deeper moral aspects of health and disease. Differences between Christian and secular healers concerning the moral aspect of health and disease may focus not so much on how things are understood, but on how explicitly they are dealt with.

Let us now consider why the results of healing might be only temporary. First, it is possible that only superficial symptoms were treated in the healing, and the basic cause of the problem was not addressed. This possibility is addressed quite extensively in the secular literature but rarely in the Christian literature, suggesting either that such relapse is more widespread in the secular environment or that it is an issue that is not regarded by Christian healers as needing discussion. Second, the results of healing might only be temporary because even though the root problem was addressed, the patient was unwilling to make the necessary fundamental changes in his or her life, with the result that the root problem recurred.

Healing that is only temporary is particularly likely when the patient does not understand what true healing involves. This is an issue that is addressed in Worral's talk of emotional willing (Worrall and Worrall 1969, p. 166), and Arthur Guirdham's statement that 'the intrusion of will is a disaster in healing' (Guirdham 1964, p. 156). This seems to be a particular problem in healing in the secular environment. LeShan's Type 2 healing (which is more common in secular settings) is close to being a willed healing. LeShan himself found that Type 2 healing, when not accompanied by Type 1, tended to have more transient results (LeShan 1980, p. 122).

Another reason why willed healing is more likely to be employed in secular healing is that because of the product–consumer context, there is a strong desire for the healing to result in tangible benefit, especially if the healing session has been paid for. In the Christian environment the physical effects of healing are seen as secondary to a broader spiritual wholeness. There is not such a strong desire for tangible results because of an underlying hope that progress is being made towards that ultimate goal (Lawrence 1997, p. 67).

The variable results of healing may be due to a wide range of factors, related not only to the nature of the healing itself, but to the environment in which it takes place and the ability of the patient to understand and accept the healing process. The Christian environment is perhaps better equipped to deal with the mental and spiritual aspect of healing, and to set healing within the wider context of spiritual well-being. Though healers in the secular environment may have a similar understanding of what healing means, this understanding is not so readily communicated to the patient. Moreover, the pressures involved in conducting healing in the secular environment may be more likely to yield transient results.

CONCLUSION

There is much common ground between secular and Christian under-standings of healing, both in practices and assumptions. Christian and secular healers show broad agreement in assuming that the ability to heal is to some extent a natural part of everyone, but requires special develop-ment in those preparing to be healers. Though terms such as God, spirits and energy might seem very distinct and specific, the distinctions between them may not be as clear-cut as might at first appear.

A surprisingly wide range of terminology for the source of healing can be found in both Christian and secular healing circles, indicating that there is no complete consensus about healing in either group. There are various ways in which healing is conceptualized, some of which are emphasized in the Christian literature. Virtually all conceptualizations of healing that are found in the Christian environment have parallels in how healing is understood in the secular environment, even though some may receive greater emphasis in Christian circles.

Though Christian and secular healers often assume that they are conducting different forms of healing, it is at least possible that the differences are more technological than substantive. Apparent differences in how Christian and secular healing is conceptualized could be the result of the context in which healing is conducted, rather than reflecting a fundamental difference in how healing is understood.

It seems justifiable to suggest that Christian and secular forms of healing are part of the general family of spiritual healing rather than being two wholly distinct forms of healing. It is hoped that this chapter may encourage an appreciation of the parallel understandings of Christian and secular healers, and encourage a willingness to explore the possibility that they may have more in common than is often assumed.

CHAPTER 6

The psychodynamics of spiritual healing and the power of mother kissing it better

Bruce Kinsey

The role of psychoanalytic interpretation of almost anything to do with religion has a complex and difficult history, with arguments pulling in different directions and conclusions often preceding those arguments. While it is not the place of this essay to rehearse this well-trodden path of debate, it is important to remember that impartiality is a rare, if not impossible, stance.

Both spiritual and religious healing are complex areas, as this volume shows, and are open to a variety of interpretations. Some claim dramatic cures of terminal or chronic conditions while others prefer to talk of being healed and reconciled to their health issues in a more quiet and organic way. Not for them the spectacular dramatic intervening of a creator God, rather a more quiet and prayerful anointing with a still small voice of calm. Space needs to be created in our thinking to move us beyond the removal of symptoms or distress. In effect, understanding what the term 'healing' means requires a far broader terminology.

It is not my intention here to be reductionist or to explode the myth of spiritual healing. I intend to use case material from my own work and ongoing research in this area. Permission has been given to use this material, but the intention is that no one should be recognized from any of these cases. I have suitably disguised, amalgamated or generalized the material in line with current psychoanalytic practice to maintain the anonymity of those involved. Any similarity to anyone living or dead is coincidental and is likely to reflect the ordinary nature and the prevalence and frequency of similar cases.

My intention is to try to understand from a psychodynamic point of view what else might also be happening when someone claims to be healed; in other words, how psychoanalysis can shed light on this process. Although there is some acknowledgement of Object-Relations, Jungian and Person-Centred ideas within this essay, it stands broadly in the psychoanalytic tradition. This reflects my training background and research, rather than a denial or lack of interest in what other perspectives there are within the therapeutic world. Within this context, I will explore how some of the insights of psychoanalytic thought and theory can help us understand more fully the breadth of what it means to be human. If, as Ireneaus contended, 'the glory of God is a person fully alive', then surely both religion and psychoanalysis could be working together on this project. Indeed Sudhir Kakar (1985, pp. 841–53) writes from a Hindu perspective that both are involved in the attempt to restore and heal a person and it would therefore be better to see them as 'rivals rather than enemies who . . . use much of the same processes and mechanisms of the psyche as they go about their pivotal concern' (1985, p. 843). He prefers to refer to the relationship as one of siblings, with all the potential for love and hate that entails. More recently Black (2006) has suggested in the subtitle to his book *Psychoanalysis and Religion in the 21st Century* that the relationship of rivalry might be changing and be better seen nowadays as one of collaboration.

It is in that spirit of collaboration that I intend to explore some of the dynamics of healing and the healing process through an understanding of psychoanalytic ideas such as the meaning of illness and the relationship of the mind and the body, the place and role of placebo, the flight into illness and the flight into health, touch, conversion disorders and hysterical healing, the therapeutic alliance, the power of the group, transference to an institution and finally telepathy and being understood. In this way I hope to show that the borders between the worlds of psychoanalysis and religion need not be so hermetically sealed as to exclude their interrelationship. The model of collaborator might indeed be one that needs to be pursued further.

THE MEANING OF ILLNESS AND THE RELATIONSHIP OF MIND AND BODY

The meaning of illness is an intriguing and vast area of thought for psychoanalysis, and a lively area of writing and ideas (see Mainprice 1974; Kidel and Rowe-Leete 1988; Broom 2007). Exploration of the role an illness might have in the personal identity or family dynamic can produce some helpful therapeutic interventions. 'Illness' is in itself a vague and inclusive term covering a variety of conditions from the mild 'feeling poorly' to more chronic and life-threatening conditions. Understanding illness entails in part an understanding of the complex relationship of the body and the mind. These are broad and vast topics, but some engagement with them even in outline is important to comprehend where ideas of healing and recovery might fit. A fuller discussion of the relationship of mind and body and issues of causation are sadly beyond the limits of this chapter.

Although many have linked illness with meaning, it is important to bear in mind that some illnesses and problems with the body remind us of the unpredictable nature of existence. We might seek meaning whereas some illnesses might be meaningless; in life there are some things where it is difficult, if not impossible, to have control.

Much has been written about people who manifest somatic conditions because of psychological distress. George Groddeck has been seen as the founder of psychosomatic medicine and he saw no difference between organic and mental illness. In a short paper on the meaning of illness he wrote:

Sickness and health appear to be opposites. They are not, any more than heat or cold are, for instance. Just as the latter are effects of different wave-lengths, so illness and health are effects of one and the same life. Illness does not come from the outside; it is not an enemy, but a creation of the organism, the It. The It – or we may call it vital force, the self, the organism – this It, about which we know nothing and of which we shall never recognise more than some of its outward forms, tries to express something by illness; to be ill has to mean something . . . It is impossible to find a general and universal meaning, impossible because there is no definite boundary between sick and healthy. (Groddeck 1977, p. 197)

Many since Groddeck have tried to understand further the meaning and timing of illness and, if it is trying to 'say something' then to interpret the message it might bring. Groddeck saw a mystical link concerning a fear of death, which is also psychoanalytically a longing for it. He draws a parallel between Christ and the God of love dying, and the mother of Jesus and desire of all men to be reunited with the mother:

The truth is: man has a longing for death because he longs for love, and a longing for love because he craves death, the mother's womb. And illness, the meaning of illness, is this death wish and love fear, love wish and death fear. (Groddeck 1950, p. 201)

Although many might question the universality of this death wish, there can be a time when people give themselves over to an illness when they have lost hope or purpose, and seek death as an ultimate liberation from pain. On a more general level, the desire during an illness for comfort, love, attention, 'mothering' and the warmth of a duvet is strong. People retreat to a room or a bed for a time to get better. Many children sleep in their parents' bed when ill, loving the familiar smell and the engulfing sense it brings.

Sickness disrupts 'normal life', whose burdens may have become nearly intolerable, and causes people to live differently. Illness brings about a change in pace and often stops people 'in their tracks'. If we can adapt to these burdens and address them creatively then our health and well-being might indeed change.

Illness tends to be seen as only a negative thing, not as a type of communication, and to some extent this reflects aspects of our society, which tends to be highly competitive and achievement orientated. Illness interrupts this, and reminds us of our frailty, of ageing and of the inevitability of death. It is not seen as a helpful reminder, or as a means of gaining a different perspective. Rather, it brings to the fore the difficult area of the relationship we have with our bodies and our flesh. This can be particularly difficult in a society that is increasingly health conscious, which regards fitness as part of a purity code, with a regime of exercise and no junk food, and where any self-indulgence is seen as a sin. It is as if there is a dream, a myth of a perfect body and that perfect body is what has to be strived for and achieved. 'No pain, no gain' is the dictum of the gym culture, with the body an object to be sculptured. There is no place for illness, which is seen as failure, something people give in to and must seek to fight against.

Indeed this current relationship with our bodies is problematic, and creates a particular problem when it comes to illness. Despite a doctrine of incarnation (God becoming flesh), Christians often have a problem with flesh, which is seen as a place of temptation and weakness; something that needs to be trained and disciplined to prevent it giving itself up to wild, bestial animal instincts, or to weakness and vulnerability.

Illness might bring with it a message but it is one we are trying to avoid, and hence the potential for expression in bodily symptoms. So we can buy medication that will help us recover from a hangover sufficiently that we can go to work, we can buy drinks from the supermarket that will give us energy, and we can cover over numerous symptoms rather than listening to what they have to say.

A new teacher was telling a therapist about the terrible headaches she was having since she started teaching in a new school. 'I feel as if I have a brain tumour, I'm taking so many pills for migraines, and I fear I will overdose. I'm getting frightened. I've never had anything like this before, I never really get headaches. This must be something really bad.' The therapist started to ask about the new job, and soon discovered the tensions at work that needed to be addressed, and that preparation had to be done for lessons rather than ignored, medicated and hidden.

The teacher needed to listen to her head aching. When asked about the head teacher she added he 'was a pain' too. The pun on 'head' betrayed a deep sense of anger and disappointment in her own life and career. Soon after, the teacher found that the headaches reduced dramatically, as did her pill-taking, and her relationship with 'the head' improved much to her surprise. According to Kidel,

> Illness makes it possible for us to 'uncover' ourselves; to remove the masks that we wear on the stage of everyday life, but also to look within; to loosen the grip of our own repression. We speak of 'recovery' from illness, meaning we gain back our former strength and can return to normal life; but we also 're-cover', closing up again our wounds and our bared souls.' (Kidel and Rowe-Leete 1988, p. 14)

This idea is an important one. Therapy is about being able to uncover aspects of ourselves, to explore who we are in a safe environment. It is not about hiding or covering over. In her novels on the treatment of shell-shocked soldiers in the First World War, Pat Barker questions the morality of enabling officers to be fit enough to return to the horrendous conditions of the trenches. Their 'recovery' enabled them to return from the presenting symptoms to a life that was either going to break or kill them.

In *Theatres of the Body* (1989), Joyce McDougall writes about general bodily expressions of what is happening in the mind and its distress. Because this interrelationship between mind and body processes is ubiquitous, we are perhaps not as engaged with it as we might be. She writes of the 'psycho-somatic potentiality or part of every individual. We all tend to somatize at those moments when inner or outer circumstances overwhelm our habitual psychological ways of coping' (1989, p. 3). If we can understand what is going on beyond just a broad biochemical reaction/reduction then we might be able to acquire a broader understanding of the healing process.

The complexity of the mind–body interrelationship and the danger of the frequent splitting of an either/or approach has recently been explored by Leader and Corfield. They see this splitting as 'a defence mechanism against recognising how disturbing, excessive or unprocessable ideas affect us' (Leader and Corfield 2007, p. 323). They consider that

> Most illnesses are complex processes that involve many different contributing causal factors. In one case, psychological situation may be especially important, and even in the same case the factors that matter the most may change from one moment to the next. Likewise, the factors that predispose one to an illness will not necessarily be the same as those that sustain it or, indeed, those that initiate it. The presence of a whole cluster of predisposing factors may never result in illness in one person, yet be fatal in another. All of this moves us away

from simple single-cause models that are nonetheless so attractive to common sense thinking. (2007, p. 321)

So an illness might give a place, an identity, an excuse or a status that 'well-being' fails to afford. In some cases the illness of a child expresses a family tension and seeks an explanation beyond just the medical, according to Kraemer's work with young people.[1] For there to be healing, the tension within the family system has to be addressed, there has to be reparation or a replacement in some form. Phillips (1995) also writes about a child's experience of illness (in this case eczema) and the role it created in the family and in particular the relationship with mother. Mainprice's work explored the 'relationship between a certain kind of marital inter-action and the existence of a physical symptom in a sick child of the marriage' (Mainprice 1974, p. 13), looking in particular at encopresis and asthma. Brian Bloom's recent study (2007) highlights the meaningful nature of disease and the need for engagement through listening and responding in the healing process.

In the context of Christianity, illness and healing also have meaning (Porterfield 2005). Not only do the foundation myths recall Jesus using healing as a sign of the Kingdom, but also as a sign of faith. Suffering and distress have a theological legitimacy and meaning within Christianity and even God himself (in Christ) is seen to suffer. Indeed, to suffer is to be aligned with Christ in his suffering; it is part of a sought-after relationship with the divine. In the history of Christianity, some were healed because they believed, others believed and were healed. Illness has both a meaning and a potential. Healing is a sign of the Kingdom, not being healed is being aligned with Christ in his suffering. It could be said to be a win–win situation. The divine mission concerning illness led to missionaries, hospitals and more recently hospices witnessing to the saving power of God in both disease and in healing.

The complexity of the meaning of illness is wittily portrayed in the controversial 1979 Monty Python film *The Life of Brian*. At one stage in the story a former leper is begging for money after having been healed by Jesus. He is irate, for ironically in becoming healed he has lost his only source of income – begging. Previously when he was sick he had a meaning, a role, and a life: now he is cured all is lost.

A former priest explained the confusion of the role of illness in the parish where he worked:

---

[1] 'The doctor verses King Canute: from Georg Groddeck to family therapy' in Kidel and Rowe (1988).

There was a family which always seemed to have some illness in it. They got a lot of attention and concern from people. There was always something wrong. As they slowly got involved in the church some of the symptoms began to fade, and they lost their status and some of the attention they were getting. If I had been wiser I would have understood it more at the time, and found some way of raising their profile as a family of healing. Instead, I think I found it too confusing, demanding, disturbing and frightening ... we made a mess of it. They have now returned to how they were, except now they are sick and bitter: we failed them.

PLACEBO

Somewhat related to the idea of psychosomatic expression is the idea of placebo. Researchers are often trying to explore the extent of the placebo effect, not just in medical trials but also as an important part of healing itself. The complexity of the meaning of placebo suggests a strong link between the mind and the body's response. This is not surprising in psychoanalytic understanding as the unconscious communication between people is a powerful but intangible component, and things have meaning beyond and outside of themselves. Flowers or chocolates on Valentine's day are symbols of love, signifying the relationship between people – but clearly they are not the love itself. Small wonder that a placebo pill from 'someone who knows' should have a beneficial effect. Attempts have been made to try to find the percentage of the population who respond to placebo treatment, but there is no certainty in the result, nor confidence in the process of ascertaining a result (Harrington 1997). All of us are likely to respond favourably to love and care and so it is not surprising that the placebo effect does not lend itself to easy answers.

In the past some of this effect has been associated with the kindly bedside manner of the doctor and the blessing of their presence. Michael Balint (1964) referred to the doctor as being the most frequently used 'drug' in general practice medicine and encouraged doctors to take this broader aspect of their role seriously. Their impact was significant in patient recovery. Indeed, when people refer to how good a doctor is they seem to be referring to their personality rather than their efficiency. Roy Grinker (Grinker and Robbins 1954) suggested that an 'ill-advised sentence, a mistimed jocular remark, or a serious statement wrongly emphasised can damage the patients recovery process and result in a tragic outcome'. There can be a similarity in the power of a minister of religion:

the pastoral manner is often seen as more important than beliefs or organizational skills. There is an idealization that happens to both ministers and doctors that facilitates both trust and a positive transference. Used wisely, this is a gift that enables growth and development. The person who is offering the gift of healing has power and a role in someone's life that is extremely powerful and potentially life changing. If they are believed in, have a reputation for healing and are believed to have 'the gift', then it is hardly surprising that they will have an impact on someone's life. To dismiss such an impact as 'just a placebo' is to fail to understand the part such an effect has in so many parts of our existence, there is no 'just' to it. Small wonder therefore that a visit from a lay helper is not as special as one from the Vicar.

FLIGHT INTO ILLNESS

The psychodynamic notion of 'flight into illness' is related to the idea of 'gain from illness.' These broad and interrelated terms can be used to cover all direct and indirect satisfaction and meaning that a person might be able to draw from their condition. Many who have worked in health services have come across someone who revels in their sickness. 'I was a nobody before I became ill; now people are nice to me and care.' 'I'm a medical mystery.' 'I was running around caring for everybody before I became ill, and now people have to run around to care for me.' A further idea behind this is that a person seeks to avoid a conflictual tension by the formation of symptoms. Many a schoolchild has been genuinely ill on facing a test, declaring, 'no I really am ill', 'I'm not faking it' and indeed they have presenting symptoms.

To help clarify as well as indicate the broadness of this avoidance, Laplanche and Pontalis (1973) importantly distinguish the two potential types of gain. The primary gain has a hand in the actual motivation of a neurosis; such as the satisfaction obtained from the symptom, and thus a flight into illness can create a beneficial change in a person's relationship with their environment.

Secondary gain, on the other hand, may be distinguished from the primary kind by:

1 Its appearance after the fact, in the shape of an extra advantage derived from an already established illness, or a new use to which such an illness is put.
2 Its extraneous character relative to the illness's original determinants and to the meaning of the symptoms.

3 The fact that the 'satisfactions involved are narcissistic or associated with self preservation rather that directly libidinal' (Laplanche and Pontalis 1973, p. 182).

In a religious setting where, as one person described it, 'they have to love me, warts and all', the status that an illness brings, and the chance it gives for people to display their love, is a powerful gain. So both the sick and the well can benefit in their identity from the illness and there can be some sense in holding and maintaining the sickness. It would be difficult to give up the gain unless there was some replacement or gain from being healed. Any thought of healing has to deal with this. It could be that the testimony of someone who has been healed can bring its own reward. As the words of the hymn 'Amazing Grace' express, 'I once was lost but now I'm found, was blind but now I see.'

Freud wrote about a 'flight into psychosis' a 'flight into neurotic illness' and finally the broader 'flight into illness', and for him the person was seeking 'to evade a situation of conflict which is generating tension and to achieve a reduction of this tension through the formation of symptoms' (Laplanche and Pontalis 1973, p. 165).

THE FLIGHT INTO HEALTH

This idea of a flight into illness is readily linked in traditional psychoanalytic thought to 'the flight into health' that was developed within traditional analytic thinking by Greenson (1969). He writes of the therapist needing to maintain a state of abstinence, of privation, of not offering something to appease or to make the person simply feel better. Quoting Freud he opines that 'cruel though it may sound we must see to it that the patient's suffering, to a degree that is in some way or other effective, does not come to an end prematurely' (Greenson 1969, p. 275). In other words, substitute satisfaction or gratification will fail to deal with the underlying problem and through that the person is robbed of their motivation to continue treatment and avoid a more complete cure. For Greenson the striking feature of this flight is its defensive nature, it protects the inner self and, like most of our defences, it is there for very good reasons, but may no longer be appropriate.

Though symptom relief might be tempting, psychoanalysis has always been suspicious of seemingly easy answers. It prefers to address the underlying and persistent causes of a problem rather than seeking a temporary alleviation of it. The Church could be seen to be potentially guilty of this transference cure. Indeed, Greenson's description of some avoidant therapy as 'cheerful hours, great enthusiasm and prolonged elation indicate that something is being warded off – usually something of the opposite nature, some form of depression', could be seen as related to the more elated styles of some contemporary worship, where escape rather than encounter seems to be the intention. 'The flight into health, the premature loss of symptoms without insight, are signs of similar kinds of resistance and have to be handled as such' (Greenson 1969, p. 69). Christians need to be aware of the dangers of a simplistic and manic approach to the complexities of reality. These are problems and conditions that are profound, complex and not fully understood, and need to be handled as such.

However the viewpoint that the flight into health is negative (or wholly negative) has been contested. Frick (1999) argues that such flights could be interpreted as signs of 'emerging health' and the traditional pejorative interpretation of them may need to be challenged. He raises the issues of what a therapy cure actually is, and how one interprets what a sign of health might be, developing a theoretical framework dependent on Gestalt psychology and its view of the organization of self. His case material concerns psychological functioning, rather than being directly related to presenting physical conditions and how the well-functioning aspects of self might be enabled to become more prominent.

Frick points out that the origin of the term 'flight into health' is uncertain and therefore needs to be treated with more caution than is usually the case. Quoting Alexander and French (1946), he notes that the flight into health is traditionally linked to the psychic threat arising out of the psychoanalytic process. This phenomenon 'is observed in psychoanalysis when because of some clear and successful reconstruction of repressed tendencies, the patient reacts by losing his symptoms in order to save himself from further unpleasant truths' (Frick 1999, p. 62, quoting Alexander and French 1946, p. 153). It is therefore, within this paradigm, also a flight from insight (Wheelis 1949, pp. 915–19).

Frick suggests that this suspicious understanding of the flight into health is because it is interpreted as resistant, and as such is a threat to the 'wisdom and competence' of true psychoanalysis, which favours both long-term treatment as well as achieving insight. He draws on Oremland (1972) and the distinction between transference cures and flight into health. Although both are seen as superficial and temporary, occurring early in treatment, for Oremland flight into health involves a massive repression, whereas transference cures are more object related (that is, associated to a personal relationship). A further distinction is drawn between them suggesting that a flight into health is a response to the threat of neurotic symptoms, whilst a transference cure concerns the nature of the transference relationship. Indeed, Oremland suggest three types of transference cure (1) flight from the therapist, (2) identification with the therapist, and (3) desire to please or appease the therapist.

It might be helpful here to think about some spiritual healing which has a strong transference cure quality to it. One woman reported going to see her priest for confession and advice. She had been troubled with some of her actions in the past, and as she become older the concern over them had become worse. She had also developed irritable bowel syndrome, although she did not mention that to the priest at the time. She had liked what this new young priest had been saying in his preaching and had sought him out for further counselling. When he offered to hear her confession and anoint her it was exciting, intimate and frightening. Consenting she 'felt the weight of years fall away'. Not only did she find peace but her symptoms were significantly reduced.

Another story is not so happy. A middle-aged man in therapy reported that in his teenage years he had been confused and frightened by Christians who had tried to exorcise him. In their belief system he had the demon of homosexuality. After he was 'exorcised' by them he had indeed 'gone straight' and lost his homosexual desire. He had become a father but also suffered severe depression. In his desire as a teenager to leave the exorcism as well as his former way of life, he said that he faked spirits leaving him, he was frightened and anxious and he did not dare tell them 'the multiple complexity' of what he really felt. He was so keen to identify with the righteous, and to please the spiritual leaders, that at the time he genuinely felt 'healed'.[2]

Brief work that delivers results has always been regarded with suspicion. Indeed the current debate over the use of Cognitive Behavioural Therapy (CBT) could be a recent useful comparator. Sometimes brief interventions deliver what the person requires: symptom relief. The process that enables this is not always understood, but that is of little concern for the person who has been struggling. While the therapist may desire

[2] There is much discussion concerning the ex-gay movement. For recent articles about its relation to therapy see Tanya Erzen's chapter in Barnes and Sered (2005).

insight and long-term work, the person desires health and relief from symptoms.

The linking of 'flight into health' with 'flight into illness' suggests for Frick a false association; he sees them as entirely different mechanisms. He prefers to see the flight into health as an 'episode of health', when a person has their more healthy side dominant:

With few exceptions, they are not artificial, self-deceptive, pseudosuccesses, as traditionally interpreted. Rather than representing therapeutic failure ... they suggest therapeutic success; rather than threatening the goals of psychotherapy ... these forays into healthy states, in fact, enhance the goals of psychotherapy. (Frick 1999, pp. 71–2)

'Real healing' might be a chimera. Within the process of attending to themselves in a therapy or religious context people need to be offered the chance to address who they are. Through this journey of engagement and encounter they can find a change in identity. The creation of a space and an opportunity when all previously seemed closed can lead to the abandonment of illness. The new direction offered is healing.

Spiritual healing is as vulnerable as any healing to offering a limited recovery, a temporary relief of symptoms. There might be some attraction for the person concerned in achieving a break from the presenting ailments, but for psychoanalysis the return of the repressed is not to be considered lightly. In medical healing there can be a suppression of symptoms or an addressing of the condition. Spiritual healing also has the potential for similar pitfalls.

TOUCH

The role of touch and the laying on of hands is not part of current psychoanalytic practice, although it is frequent in both spiritual and religious circles. In that context, a physical ritual enables the divine and the human to work together. The human hands convey the divine process; the healer's body becomes a vehicle or conduit for divine expression, and contact with it brings healing. The traditional split between that which is earthly and that which is divine is transgressed, healed and restored. It is as if all is one and in that unity and re-creation further healings can happen. This is both deeply incarnational in its meaning as well as redemptive. It also models a healing of the split between mind and body. In faith healing the old dichotomies are challenged and this drive towards wholeness models a challenge in our traditional thinking. Mind and body, body and soul, earth and heaven are engaged with each other in a way that brings healing and peace.

Touch is not so happily received within psychoanalytic thought, and because of the power of the psychoanalytic relationship much attention is given to maintaining appropriate boundaries. In an important and much discussed case study Casement (1985) writes on the meaning of touch within a specific therapy and within the context of the analytic holding of a patient. He plays with the verbal concept of 'being in touch' in a therapeutic relationship rather than any physical expression of actually touching. The person in the study needed to feel literally held as a repairing recompense for an earlier childhood experience of a parent failing to keep hold of her hand. She put much pressure on the therapist to give into what seemed like an understandable request, in the light of her fear of abandonment. She demanded touch. It is a closely and carefully argued case study, where Casement manages to withstand the temptation to hold hands, which would have been too literal and not healing.

> She had been able to find the internal mother she had lost touch with, as distinct from the 'pretend' mother she had wanted me to become. We could now see that if I had agreed to hold her physically it would have been a way of shutting off what she was experiencing, not only for her but also for me, as if I really could not bear to be with her through this. (Casement 1985, p. 164)

Casement's work raises important issues for the understanding of intimacy and the misunderstandings of contact. By his carefully argued study he raises the issue of the pressure a therapist or a minister can be under when working with a regressed or damaged person. Although this person may seek touch and holding, these may not be the most therapeutic actions for them, and a deeper understanding of the processes might be more helpful. There are multiple meanings to touch and a simplistic understanding of the processes can be dangerous. Indeed it is probably because of a lack of understanding that some of the cases of inappropriate behaviour from both clergy and therapists have come about. This is not excusing them, rather it shows how such a response can compound a problem and fails to hear what is really being said.

In both religious and spiritual circles the problems over the boundaries of touch can be aided by the public nature of healing services and the distance created through ritual. Concern remains over the more private consultations where a different dynamic is often at play. Touch which is healing is very different from that which is abusive, manipulative or improper.

CONVERSION DISORDER AND HYSTERICAL HEALING

Healing is often associated with the dramatic culture of 'signs and wonders' where, in the context of a religious setting, full of fervour and drama, miraculous healings are reported. Weeping, crying, shouting, roaring and raging are highly charged emotional responses and may be deliberately created by some modern faith healers. The terminology for some of these healers has its own set of dilemmas: for some the importance is that they are divine healers, rather than depending on faith. This group often wants to differentiate itself from 'miracle healing', 'psychic healing' or 'spiritual healing' and make clear it is 'divine healing ... the direct intervention of the one and only true God, the living and personal God' (Wimber and Springer 1987, p. 26).

The sense of anticipation can have a powerful affect on those who attend and the contagious enthusiasm is palpable. The cathartic nature of such experiences can hardly be doubted. Indeed, even within more mainstream religious organizations visits on pilgrimages to shrines of healing can also have powerful effects.

The idea of a conversion disorder is little understood and for the medic diagnosis is notoriously difficult. In essence, according to Owens and Dein:

Conversion disorder is thought to occur primarily in societies with strict social systems that prevent individuals from directly expressing feelings and emotions towards others. Temporary somatic dysfunction is one possible mode of communication, particularly for those who are oppressed or underprivileged. The 'psychological mindedness' and ease of emotional expression typical of modern developed societies have led to the increasing rarity of conversion disorders in developed countries. (Owens and Dein 2006, pp. 152–7)

In psychoanalysis the classic paradigm of this theory reported by Josef Breuer and Sigmund Freud in 1891 was the case of Anna O. It was through this early case that the cathartic method was developed and explored with dramatic results. She presented some memory, reliving it emotionally in the session and her symptoms disappeared. She called it 'the talking cure' and 'chimney-sweeping' (Freud 1955, p. 30). Although there are some aspects of her progress which seem to be more like a transference cure, the technique was clear: the aim of her therapy was to move her to more mature defence mechanisms.

The relationships between hysteria, hypnosis and conversion disorder have been noted since the nineteenth century and certainly it seems to be the case that people with this disorder have a high hypnotizability. In a hypnotic state memories can be recalled, and with this recollection, the cause of the symptom can be discharged.

More broadly, other types of suggestion can carry a similar effect, for example in the action of an authoritative leader in the right setting. One middle-aged man reported that

I was praying in this Church and we had been singing and being lulled by the music. It was beautiful and then I started remembering some horrible things I had done and that had been done to me. I started to cry, and to shake; it was as if the deepest part of me was being touched. The minister came over to me and he knew what to do, he prayed. He put his hands very firmly on me and I felt I must be cleansed, because he touched me . . . and this was so powerful, it was as if I was ripped apart. But I knew that now I was safe, I was in the presence of Christ, and loved and not in danger anymore. It was after that that my back pain stopped. I was healed.

THERAPEUTIC ALLIANCE

It is well known that in therapy when a person speaks, the attitude and response of the therapist will have a significant effect on the therapy. Indeed the traditional blank screen (more of myth than complete practice) allowed for this confusion to be explored. Interestingly it is perhaps over two key areas of existence, those of sex and religion, where this silence can be experienced in a particularly powerful way. The response, or lack of it, from the therapist can have a big impact on the therapeutic alliance. Indeed it could lead to an overwhelming sense of shame and humiliation and disrupt or perhaps make impossible a working alliance. It is not surprising that a person might feel reticent when speaking of prayer, of a ritual or of healing. Indeed some who seek counselling or therapy often seek out a religious therapist so that this aspect of their lives is explicitly included. This is, however, not a neutral choice and can easily lead to avoidance or collusion, as indeed can any other such choice.

It might also be suggested that some people are reticent to speak of their experiences whilst at prayer or to speak of healing for fear that they will be dismissed or diminished. This of course may express some of their own ambivalence over such experiences, but generally the need for trust and acceptance is keen. Like other aspects of any personal history it is important that precious aspects of the self and experience will be accepted and explored, not ridiculed, rationalized or reduced. There is a delicate balance that is needed. One person explained,

I had gone to a Christian Counselling service because I knew they would understand me but then I found myself anxious over some of the doubts and questions I had. I started to mention these and the counsellor was really good and seemed to understand how I could have faith and doubt at the same time. She reminded me of a line in the Bible where a person said to Jesus, 'I believe; help thou mine unbelief.' I really appreciated that and it helped me feel free to think and explore. In my church I often felt I should have more faith and just shut up, with my counsellor there was a more honest approach, she was a real blessing.

Many therapists want to emphasize the importance of the relationship and being in tune with a person in the therapeutic process.[3] This working alliance of trust and security, where the person has a protected space and time to talk and reflect on their life with honesty, is not just a powerful tool in therapy, it is fundamental. Here issues that have formerly been avoided can be addressed. 'The patient experiences a relationship that is qualitatively different from early childhood relationships responsible for the maladaptive interpersonal patterns that ultimately led the patient to seek therapy' (Henry and Strupp 1994, p. 71).

Bringing in the ideas of Kohut (1977) Kakar writes, 'like the guru with his talk of rebirth for the disciple, the analyst too provides a kind of developmental second chance, the transmuting internalization of the analytic relationship building the core of a "new" and compensating structure of the self' (Kakar 1985, p. 85).

Andrew Samuel writes that 'the psychology of the soul turns out to be about people in relationship' (Samuel 1985, p. 21). Certainly within a religious setting relationships are all-important. Samuel later writes that 'If the analyst is moved by his patient, then the patient is more aware of the analyst as a healing presence' (1985, p. 189). Certainly within a religious setting the role a minister plays in healing is central.

In therapy, the transference relationship is an essential part of the analytic procedure. 'Classically, the transference is acknowledged to be the terrain on which all the basic problems of a given analysis play themselves out; the establishment, modalities, interpretation and resolution of the transference are in fact what define the cure' (Laplanche and Pontalis 1973, p. 445). For those who work in the classical tradition, the analysis consists of inviting the transference and gradually dissolving it by means of interpretation. It is about analysis first and foremost, not about cure. It is to do with seeking understanding and insight.

---

[3] The main change agent in psychotherapy is the relationship between therapist and client. See Howe (1999).

But there are historical and in practice other views, for example, the importance of the therapeutic relationship and the 'transference love' was central in the ideas of Sandor Ferenczi. He famously wrote that 'Psychoanalytic "cure" is in direct proportion to the cherishing love given by the psychoanalyst to the patient; the love which the psychoneurotic patient needs, not necessarily the love he thinks he needs and therefore demands' (De Forest 1954).

In life, relationships are an essential aspect of our growth and development. This is perhaps especially true when issues of vulnerability abound, such as in areas of faith, religion and therapy. Here, at the meeting-place of these ideas, the understanding of relationship is crucial. This relationship of course goes both ways and although it is easy to concentrate on the transference relationship the counter-transference relationship should not be ignored either. This counter-transference relationship has become quite central to the thinking of analysis and therapy in the past sixty years and in many ways it is seen as a keystone of interpretation. People who come to see a therapist arouse many strong feelings in the therapist including anger, sadness, despair as well as sexual feelings. Much of the therapeutic process is about how therapists allow themselves to have these feelings and how they feed them back to the person in a healing and helpful way, without attacking or dismissing them.

One person told their counsellor 'I felt so angry at my vicar, it was clear he didn't have time for me. I wanted to be noticed, but he didn't care. I was desperate; I was furious and tried to get him reported.' The anger was palpable in the session and the counsellor who brought it to supervision was quite scared by it, but was able to handle and engage with it. The counsellor's initial reaction in the session had been to try and ignore it, or dismiss it and get on with something else, only realizing as the session progressed that these feelings were part of a deeper process. It was clear from the rest of the work that much of the strength of this anger belonged to the person's parents who were regarded as more interested in the other 'more talented' siblings.

One of the tasks of a parent is to take the child's difficult emotions and help digest and metabolize them into something worthwhile. In Christianity, Christ takes in the violence of those around him, but does not return it to them. This idea of 'taking upon himself so we are free and don't have to' is central to the foundation texts of Christianity, but sadly lacking in parts of its history. Examples of this behaviour are held and admired in figures such as Desmond Tutu and Mahatma Gandhi, but it is a difficult and demanding message, and recognizable to many as clearly of divine origin. Perhaps an important aspect of this story in the Christian tradition is that the figure of Christ is not without anger, it is the expression of it that is important. In the story, in John 2:15–22, of the overturning of the money changers' tables in the Temple anger is expressed; there are strong emotions, but they are used to make a point not just to destroy. This wholeness in the person of Christ makes him a healthy, rather than pathological role model.

It is only when people are in touch with their own violence and anger that they can deal with someone else's. The alternative is denying their own anger and retaliating, taking revenge and projecting the rage onto other people and groups.

THE POWER OF THE GROUP

The power of any community gathering, and the desire to feel part of something larger and bigger than just oneself, is attractive, sometimes even more, it is seductive. It might also be said that needing to belong to something is fundamental to being human. Many join groups or clubs and this helps give a sense of identity. Common interest groups in particular reinforce a sense of identity and confidence. Divergence or individuality within the group can often be suppressed and this process does not always happen consciously. Clothing styles, language, mannerisms and general identity can become lost in this larger group experience. Mood changes within a group are well recorded with much evidence of the power of the group to address alcoholism, compulsive disorders or depression.

When this group is a religious one, the additional righteousness that this identity gives is a powerful supplement to the damaged sense of self that is generally part of the human condition. Paradoxically, many religions manage to foster both a sense of being a beloved child of God as well as being potentially outside of that family. This conditional love and acceptance, dependent on obedience, or right living or faith, can make being beloved feel fragile and tortured. The dependency can also be infantilizing and for some this is part of its attraction. Indeed many new religious movements have a cult-like quality to them requiring a giving up of independence in thought and decision making and handing over power and control to those who 'know better'. Initially this can be quite a relief for a person, giving a sense of freedom and a reduction in anxiety. There are some parts of this oceanic sense of infancy that are powerful, relaxing and liberating. Infants however tend to grow and mature and often those who at first welcomed such powerful parenting within a community can come to resent the intrusion and seek more independence and air. One person described the church they had loved and matured in as suffocating:

I had to leave to grow up. I still miss the overwhelming engulfing warmth of it ... at times it's what I feel I need, but I had to leave to live ... they (the community) showed me love in a way my family never could. I really felt this was God's family and I was part of it. I did a lot of repairing of myself within that place, there were some very good people there, who were very loving and caring, but now I feel as if I've seen behind some of that, like in the Wizard of Oz, I've seen things I shouldn't have, how some try to manipulate and control and that's not right. There was something very special and good, and there was something else too and somehow they couldn't be honest about that. It would have been better if they could have been. But they had to be All Right, and so I become someone who was All Wrong.

Interestingly this person records with affection that some parts of this community responded when healing clearly took place. The Church is one of the places people bring themselves for healing, and in this way it can be described as an alternative psychiatric out-patients department.

Potentially much of the activity of a church can be understood as a sort of group psychotherapy, with the church acting as some sort of therapeutic community. Indeed Yalom (1995) wrote of the instillation of hope in a group where it is also inevitable that some forms of healing and making whole will occur. Often difficult feelings will arise and if these can be properly handled then the Church as community can be a productive and creative space. Some of these ideas are related to Winnicott's (1953) notion of a holding environment and a transitional space. One church member reported:

I felt so good there, and really supported in a way that never happened in my so-called family. There was this great, really caring leader and I was really pleased when I was asked to help with the youth club. I began to speak more and offer to do things. I grew in confidence, whereas home used to crush me.

A religious community can be very supportive, after all they have to love you there. They have to take you in and accept you and this hospitality can protect many from hospitalisation. The numbers on your side willing for you, praying for you can be experienced as a 'corrective' experience. It is certainly a place where you are wanted. Within this community the people (as children) can be held and received by an accepting parent ... and this regression can also lead to maturing and new experiences that will help the person move on in a new way, re-addressing the past and going in a new direction.

Here in this context, I believe that the Jungian concept of the shadow is ironically illuminating. Alongside the ideals of goodness that religion embodies there is naturally a dark and sometimes more sinister side. As a collection of damaged individuals, a 'school for sinners', the group can feel helpless and there is potential for regressive behaviour. There can be a pretence that all is well, when behind the façade there is a different story of pain and hurt.

Many clergy also report how otherwise capable and efficient people suddenly become indecisive and lacking in confidence in a church meeting. 'They are like sheep without a shepherd, except most of them are graduate sheep' said one minister, 'and are shepherds and leaders in all other parts of their lives.' This regression, handled by thoughtful, reflective and caring ministers, can be a source of much that is good. If, by contrast, there is insufficient awareness of the multiple processes, there can be significant damage, and feelings of, if not actual, bullying and abuse.

TRANSFERENCE TO THE INSTITUTION

Related to this are ideas around transference to the institution. This can be a hugely positive thing as institutions are more powerful than individuals. If a person's formative experience of people has been disappointing and unreliable, it can be hard for them to trust a lone individual. Indeed they are often looking for something larger and stronger. How much better therefore to have a large institution or a school of thought to trump that earlier dysfunctional experience. The attraction of institutions is palpable and the trust handed over to them can be immense. People speak of 'The Church' as if it was something larger and bigger and more reliable than just the members they encounter. Indeed it is and Bowlby (1988) would have understood it as a secure base from which to explore themselves and their relationships. When it works well an institution can bring much holding, security and liberation. Sadly, the positive side of institutions can often be ignored as they are easy to malign and be seen as a source of only the bad.

TELEPATHY AND TRANSFERENCE

One final area of thought is more controversial and that is the area of how we communicate with each other. That there might be something 'out there' intervening or engaged with us here is often denied within our post-Enlightenment culture, and various research attempts to explore such encounters are met with derision and contempt. Paranormal activity and parapsychology have had an uncomfortable relationship with psychoanalysis. By its very nature psychoanalysis should have a powerful tolerance for the unknown, but when it comes to the area of psi or Ψ phenomena (to use J. B. Rhine's term), there is far more discomfort and disquiet. The area of parapsychology especially under investigation for therapists is that of telepathy and its relationship to transference phenomena and the thera-peutic relationship. It has been noted by Totton (2003, p. 2) that interest and engagement in this was more acceptable in the past than it is nowadays.

In 1953 a collection of essays, edited by George Devereux entitled *Psychoanalysis and the Occult* explored some of this material. It included papers from Freud, as well as other leading members of the analytic community such as Jule Eisenbud, Edward Hitschmann, Helene Deutsch, Dorothy Burlingham, Albert Ellis and others. Admittedly the meaning of the term 'occult' has changed since the 1950s, nonetheless this book is significant in that it explored the relationship we humans have with psychic forces. It quotes Freud who wrote:

It no longer seems possible to brush aside the study of so-called occult facts; of things which seem to vouchsafe the real existence of psychic forces other than the known forces of the human and animal psyche, or which reveal mental faculties in which, until now, we did not believe. The appeal of this kind of inquiry seems irresistible. (Devereux 1953, p. 56, quoting Freud 1941)

Totton writes of his difficulty in finding contemporary writers of similar distinction to enter this territory nowadays. For Totton the concept of telepathy in the therapeutic frame is a given. 'I have had frequent experi-ences of paranormal events which render the question of belief superflu-ous. Telepathy, in particular, seems to me so basic to human existence that it is hard to imagine society being possible without it (while at the same time certain aspects of social reality depend upon its denial)' (Totton 2003, pp. 12–13). For many therapists there is something that happens in the therapeutic encounter that can have a mystical quality to it (see Thorne 2002), and therapists have to be aware in case they are seen as gods knowing and seeing all, and, worst of all, able to do all. Such a projection is also often part of the process.

This powerful feeling of being understood and engaged with at this level can be a wonderful, if potentially dangerous, force in a therapeutic setting let alone within a religious one. One person spoke of their feelings on such a relationship:

I felt that he understood me and knew what I was going to say even before I said it. He seemed so in tune with me and what was going on in my heart. I knew I could trust him with my deepest darkest fears. It's as if he knew about them already. Just talking to him was like talking to God in a way: he knew, he accepted, he understood. This was unlike any friendship. Something flowed between us, it was like spirit force. This was an example of love, pure love.

Such an encounter handled well and wisely is healing. The potential for good is great, the dangers are obvious, and many find that whilst in such a position they are vulnerable for abuse and the misuse of power.

What is not so certain in this area is why this powerful means of communication gets called telepathy, as opposed to a more usual understanding of the depth of communication that there is within transference phenomena. As our understanding of the ways in which we communicate with each other expands, the former reductionist language of 'a talking cure' seems to fail to grasp the intensity of communication within a therapy setting. Perhaps our language prefers to use the metaphor of telepathy as a way of expressing something that seems to be 'out of this world' but only because our usual understanding of what is in this world is too limited.

CONCLUSION

I have tried to explore some of the ideas within psychoanalytic thought that might help contribute to an understanding of healing. This is not about explaining away, but rather about exploring what else is going on in the reported encounter a person might have with the divine. Shakespeare reminds us in *Hamlet* that there seem to be more things in heaven and earth than are dreamt of in our philosophy. It is clear that our preconceptions can cloud our insight. Whether or not we accept religious healing in all its manifestations as a biological phenomenon, there are enough witnesses to the experience at least to make us pause and wonder and ask better questions about it. It is certainly an area that has inevitably been the victim of pious exaggeration, but it also leaves many philosophies wanting – failing as they do to have a space for the unknown or the uncertain.

I was trying to explain some of the ideas of this chapter to a group of pupils I was teaching. They seemed to understand it well and contributed much to a lively discussion. One of them answered 'Is it like when you are young and you fall over and you want to cry and mummy kisses it better and suddenly it all stops hurting?' 'Yes', I replied, 'and a perfect idea as a subtitle for the chapter.' Most of us can recall the experience when young of being held and treasured when all seemed pain and hurt and feeling better: that kiss or that touch, that gift of love that healed and restored. At its best both religion and therapy give a loving touch which heals. To think we understand what brings healing in either might just be another example of our arrogance rather than our quest for truth.

CHAPTER 7

Spiritual healing in the context of the human need for safeness, connectedness and warmth: a biopsychosocial approach

Paul Gilbert and Hannah Gilbert

Healing is a term that captures the concepts of recovery or repair from dysfunction and/or injury. However, it only applies to 'living things' (we 'mend' or 'fix' rather than 'heal' the car), and refers to processes occurring in physical bodies, minds and relationships. The scientific study of healing is linked to theories and 'knowledge' of what causes dysfunction or injury, and the mechanisms underpinning recovery, repair and healing. Cultures vary greatly on both counts. For example, Nisbett *et al.* (2001) pointed out that collective societies focus on social relationships, and see the world in terms of patterns and the *interconnected* nature of things. Healing practices involve focusing on relationships between people, relationships of inner forces (for example yin and yang) and restoring inner balance in 'energies/processes' as a holistic approach. In contrast, in the more individualist and Western science-focused societies, there is concern to split and segregate things into individual categories and units, such as 'disease entities.' These are seen as having their own individual, autonomous characteristics, to be treated with the application of specific technologies (for example drugs and surgery), and evaluated in research trials.

A similar dichotomy was prevalent in early Greek medicine. The Hippocratic School focused on holistic medicine, the processes of becoming ill, personality and the contexts and life events and circumstances of the illness – a basic biopsychosocial approach. In contrast the Platonic school of medicine focused on the 'disease process' as an entity in itself that could be studied separately from the person who was suffering (Kendell 1975). However these dichotomies are gradually breaking down and Western approaches are increasingly focused on evidence that the body's own repair mechanisms can be activated in and through human relationships and psychological interventions (Martin 1997; Kiesler 1999; Sarafino 2003). These debates have relevance to the issue of 'spiritual' healing because such healing occurs against a backdrop of culture beliefs and social healing rituals. So although there are a variety of 'normal' and 'paranormal' explanations for spiritual healing, this chapter will focus on the interpersonal aspects of healing conducted in spiritual contexts (Aldridge 2000).

We will contextualize our approach within a biopsychosocial model (Gilbert 2005), as seen in Figure 7.1. It suggests that there are complex interactions between social relationships, the local ecologies in which they form and develop, the creation of people's beliefs and expectations and the regulation of physiological processes.

Social relationships are now known to have powerful physiological impacts which influence a hormonal and immune system involved in healing and mental states (Cacioppo *et al.* 2000). Disruptions to social bonds such as grief are well known to accentuate both the experience of dysfunction (for example, pain) and vulnerabilities to illness (via, for example, disruptions to the immune system, see Martin 1997). Having or developing social bonds has long been linked to reducing vulnerability to certain disorders and recovery (Sarafino 2003). Social relationships and personal beliefs are also contextualized in social and physical ecologies (Gilbert 2005).

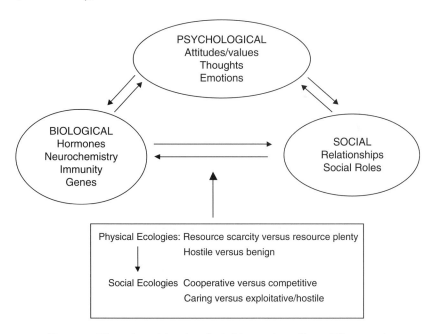

Figure 7.1 Biopsychosocial and ecological interactions (from Gilbert 2005)

With regard to internal psychological factors, altering people's beliefs about themselves, their relationships and how to cope with stressors or illnesses affects the recovery processes (Aldridge 2000; Sarafino 2003). Training one's mind in certain ways, such as with mindfulness training and compassion, has been shown to have major impacts on the immune system, symptomologies and brain organization (Davidson *et al.* 2003). The process by which social relationships, states of mind and psychological processes influence the body's ability for repair, recovery and healing is subject to increasing research from a biopsychosocial point of view.

THE SPIRITUAL DIMENSION

Explanations for suffering and illness differ greatly from group to group and can be viewed as: beliefs in the will of God, tests of faith, opportunities for spiritual growth, punishment, karma, personal inadequacies/deficiencies, bad luck or as having physical/biological explanations (such as certain viruses or certain genes – see Gilbert 1998). Spiritual healing refers to processes that operate via spiritual aspirations, beliefs and social practices of people. They operate through an individual's attunement to processes that may lie outside of the self (the relationship to spiritual beings or energies), and/or inside the self (restoring flows of energy within the self or giving new meanings). McClenon defines spiritual healing as, 'the restoration of physical, mental, emotional, or spiritual health ostensibly through occult, supernatural, or paranormal means. Examples include faith healing, prayer, shamanism, and some forms of folk healing' (McClenon 1997, p. 61). These, however, are contextualized in cultural discourses of social meaning.

Defining 'spiritual' healing and the processes by which it may exert effects is therefore not easy, but this does not preclude efforts at definition or efforts for its scientific study (for major reviews see Aldridge 2000; Miller and Thorsen 2003; Seeman *et al.* 2003). Increasingly, efforts are being made to link insights from spiritual traditions with western psychology and psychotherapy (Young-Eisendrath and Miller 2000; Goleman 2003), and medicine (Aldridge 2000). As Aldridge points out, spiritual healing is not just about repair or cure but can also be about finding hope and resolve in the face of suffering. Coping with pain, injury and loss of functions, or knowledge that one is dying, can be an intensely lonely and alienating experience. Such experiences not only increase suffering but influence physiological processes (for example, through stress). Spiritual beliefs and shared enactments of rituals can offer new

meanings and feelings of connectedness to others that can soften feelings
of despair and alter physiologies.

This chapter will not explore possible healing processes that lie outside
domains of explanations that current science allows, as these are addressed
by other authors. Rather we will address what is often a major subtext in
many healing processes: the notion of the healing qualities of a certain
type of *benevolent, supportive/loving connectedness.* We will first consider
why connectedness lies at the heart of evolution, how certain 'signals and
exchanges' between individuals have physiological effects, and how *social*
practices that are healing nearly always focus on connecting or reconnecting individuals to processes and relationships that are seen as
inclusive, accepting, forgiving, supportive and/or loving.

EVOLUTION

Forms of social relating evolved as the signals of one individual came to
be recognized and to have physiological impacts on another. For
example a sexual display can activate sexual interest in others, while a
threat display can activate fears. Importantly, however, the evolution of
parent–offspring attachment (Bowlby 1969, 1973; Cassidy and Shaver
1999; Mikulincer and Shaver, 2007) meant that signals of love and care
from a parent could calm an infant, deactivate threat/stress systems and
stimulate positive affects in the infant. Indeed it is now known that the
love and care an infant receives has major effects on the infant's developing brain, immune and other physiological systems (Schore 1994, 2001).
Moreover, there is now good evidence that human infants are exquisitely
sensitive to the expressions of the parent (such as voice tone, facial
expressions and holding). This means that the mind of the parent comes
to regulate the mind of the child (Trevarthen and Aitken 2001), with
major effects on the infant's brain maturation (Gerhardt 2004). In other
words, not only are humans born to be highly responsive to interpersonal
interactions, but their physical maturation, prosperity, health and interpersonal relating style are significantly influenced by love and affection
(Cozolino 2007; Mikulincer and Shaver 2007).

Signals that convey connectedness to safe and supportive others operate on and through safeness systems (Gilbert 1993, 2005, 2009a), which
can be both relaxing and stimulating of certain types of positive affect.
In fact we now know at least three key affect regulation systems that
have evolved – although these can be further subdivided (Panksepp
1998). Briefly, the first of these is the threat system which is the first

port of call for most incoming stimuli (to check out whether a stimulus is a threat or not). It gives rise to emotions such as fear, anxiety, and anger, and to behaviours such as fight, flight, and submission. A second system is more positive and gives rise to drive, excitement and seeking out resources and rewards. It is linked to the dopamine systems and gives an activated type of affect. If we have an inflow of resources – we win a lot of money or an important competitive game – we might feel excited and happy because of the dopamine effect. The third system, evolved from the contentment system, enables animals to be calm and quiescent when not needing to seek out things and when not under threat. This contentment soothing system has been the basis for the evolution of soothing via affection signals (Uväns-Morberg 1998; Carter 1998; Depue and Morrone-Strupinsky 2005). These systems are in constant interaction and co-regulate each other as depicted in Figure 7.2. We suggest that the relationship can heal via activating the soothing systems because when animals and humans feel safe and socially supported, physiological processes can be directed to healing rather than defending or seeking.

We are 'driven to' seek connectedness because it conveys safeness, stimulates positive affect and affiliation, and the psychobiological impact of safe-connectedness has far-reaching impacts on multiple healing

Figure 7.2 Types of affect regulation system (from Gilbert 2009b)

processes within the body, such as the immune system (Martin 1997). Indeed, the importance of social affiliation, its links to physiological systems, such as the opiate and oxytocin systems, and their health-promoting effects is now subject to intense research (Uväns-Morberg 1998; Carter 1998; Depue and Morrone-Strupinsky 2005). In contrast, feeling disconnected from others is strongly linked to health problems (Sarafino 2003). Cacioppo *et al.* (2005) in their report on the Chicago health and ageing studies suggest that there are different types of (dis)connectedness – isolation, relational connectedness, and collective connectedness. People who score low for social connectedness are more lonely, have higher depression scores, are physiologically more stressed, are more orientated to making threat interpretations and more vulnerable to a range of illnesses. As we will note below many spiritual healing rituals often operate to create feelings of safeness and connectedness to supportive others, so creating conditions conducive to healing. It is possible that when we feel in the compass of (say) the loving-kindness (warmth) of others, it is the opiate system(s) that give us the feelings of safeness/well-being that are conducive to healing (see Dupue and Morrone-Strupinsky 2005; Wang 2005). Feelings of safeness and content-ment turn off both seeking for achievements, things and possessions, and threat processing. We are, if you like, 'at peace' and this may stimulate healing processes. With regard to spiritual forms of relationships, there is increasing evidence that people can construct their experience of God through attachment (soothing) systems, perceiving him/her to be omni-present, omnipotent and loving, and a source of comfort and strength (Kirkpatrick 2005). Such beliefs may be conducive to health, coping with adversity and healing.

To receive signals of care and warmth from others that will impact on our physiologies, there must be others who are motivated to give it. Our sensitivities to recognize and respond to distress in others and to seek to ameliorate distress can be traced back to mammalian evolution of care-giving (Davidson and Harrington 2002; Gilbert 1989, 2005). Consoling behaviour has been noted in non-human primates (de Waal 1996). In humans, care-giving mentalities have evolved into a rich array of emotions, thoughts and behaviours that can loosely be called compassion (Gilbert 2005). These qualities include: (1) motives to help and feel concern; (2) being sensitive to others' distress; (3) being emotionally moved by the distress of others (sympathy); (4) the ability to tolerate distress in others without avoiding or turning away; (5) understanding the intentions and feelings of others (empathy), and in particular the sources for distress; (6) the capacity to be non-judgemental or blaming, and at times forgiving. For full compassion these qualities are all textured with feelings of warmth. Each of these qualities is important for the full engagement of compassion to another.

Spiritual healing often involves experiencing the compassion of others, and spiritual ideals often involve inspiration to develop our capacities for compassion (Gilbert 2005). When we experience deeply the compassion of others we may feel understood, accepted, safe and connected. The experience can be conveyed through verbal and non-verbal messages/signals and via our intuiting and sensing the feelings of others towards us.

There are a range of healing rituals that may involve actual body touching, or stroking, or using the hands (to direct energies) and where the voice of the healer is calming/soothing. Healing practices involving the 'laying on of hands' have been noted in ancient Egyptian, Greek and early Christian cultures (Wirth 1995; Field 2000). These rituals can involve beliefs in restoring balance or removing destructive energies, but can also be seen as offering types of connectedness (provided by a healer) that may stimulate conditions in the person that are conducive to healing. Touch is now known to have health-inducing effects (Field 2000), and healing by 'gentle touch' may help people with the stress caused by disorders such as cancer and their treatments (Weze *et al.* 2004). Although the role of touch in psychotherapy has always been controversial (Smith *et al.* 1998; Field 2000), for the most part *formal* psychotherapies do not offer such signals, but rely (to some extent) on non-verbal communication of facial expressions, voice tone and empathy. It is via empathy and empathic resonance (co-creating the same feelings in patient and therapist) that patients are believed to feel connected with, and understood by, their therapists (Gilbert 2005). Many spiritual healing rituals and practices however allow (give permission) for the patient to be *passive* and *a recipient*, rather than active and having to engage and explore painful memories or feelings, exposing the self to feared situations and the struggle of learning new coping behaviours. Some psychotherapists can be rather condemning of this passivity, but this is to undervalue the power of certain social signals and experiences, especially the importance of the experience of warmth, safeness and connectedness as a healing process. Some people may turn to alternative or complementary medicine because it can allow a certain type of passivity and 'receptivity'. One of Gilbert's psychotherapy patients also went for spiritual healing. She felt that it gave her a very different type of 'healing' experience, but that the two were not conflicting; she was able to understand the difference between both and what she needed to 'do' in both.

There are many elements of healing practices and rituals that are conducive to feeling connected, such as sharing pain, having 'an-other' take a healing interest in the self, and to acceptance of suffering. Csordas (1996) noted that healing rituals can involve 'ritual events' involving public behaviours, a focus for healing (e.g. mind, body and/or spirit), performative acts (e.g. laying on of hands, speaking in tongues) and rhetoric that creates a world of meaning in which such things can take place. His own work 'has shown how the rhetoric of transformation achieves its therapeutic purpose by creating a disposition to be healed, invoking experience of the sacred, elaborating previously unrecognised alternatives, and actualising change in incremental steps' (Csordas 1996, p. 94).

Some of these qualities for healing operate though the 'power of belief'. Others operate through creating states of mind within the individual, as in trance states or excited states through dance. McClenon (2001) suggested that humans have evolved abilities for altered states of consciousness, related to the regulation of attention via an-other (as in hypnosis), and these can be a medium through which shamanic healers can induce experiences (states of mind) conducive to healing (Krippner 2002). Although the healer's ability to create the conditions for such states is important, it also depends upon culturally shared beliefs. These ritual enactments can have profound effects on physiological processes, including the immune system (Money 2001). The way in which ritual facilitates physiological alteration within the person may play an important role within the healing properties of the ritual.

THE CULTURAL DYNAMICS OF HEALING RITUALS AND MEANS
FOR CONNECTEDNESS

Social and ecological aspects of spiritual healing are mediated through cultural beliefs, social values and rituals. Many cultures have a variety of rituals and practices that enable people to feel safe, (re)connected and healed. These rituals and practices work through the co-construction of relationships. With regard to spiritual relationships, our relationship to God or supernatural deities can be constructed as leader–(obedient) follower, father–child, or of co-operative participants or recipients of loving, healing energies (Jung 1998; Hinde 1999). Recent research has explored the brain patterns that are associated with mystical experiences related to feelings of union with God (Beauregard and Paquette 2006). It is unclear whether these brain patterns may also be conducive to internal healing processes, but if so, they would have a high adaptive value. Probably the most important relationships that can stimulate internal, healing processes are those conveying information that a powerful other(s) cares about us, and that we have some kind of kinship with them.

Bailey (2002) points out that kinship relationships can be of two kinds; one based on genuine *biological* kin relatedness, and the other on what he calls *psychological* kin relatedness, which is based upon sharing values, beliefs, and feeling a sense of belonging in a group. This distinction, between biological and psychological kinship, is mirrored in the types of healing rituals that take place in different cultures. Indeed, we will make a distinction between spiritual healing rituals, where individuals seek to connect to biological kinship groups (such as ancestors and dead relatives), and psychological kinship groups, where individuals seek to form relationships with those whom they may not be biologically related to, but to whom they wish to be linked or have a close relationship.

Spiritual healing and biological kinship

Relationships to spiritual beings or deities are often vocalized in kinship terms. For example, God may be described as a 'father', we are his 'children', and our relationships with each other termed those of 'brothers and sisters'. An earth-based spiritual energy may be described as '*Mother* Earth'. Mediums of the Temiar people – an indigenous group who live in the rainforest of Malaysia and who engage in spiritual healing – see their relationships with their spirit guides in kinship terms. For example, female spirit guides can be referred to as 'wives' (Roseman 2003).

There are a number of cultures who hold beliefs about survival after death, and in which those departed are able to relate to, help and support those still living. These beliefs are enacted through different social channels of communication than those used in everyday life. Communications with loved ones who have died can be based upon the use of imagery recall (imagining the smiling face of, or advice of, a deceased mother/relative). However, this kind of imagery can also be based upon images of ancestors, not personally encountered but characterized by social beliefs/ traditions. At times there can be sensory experiences (such as hearing the voice of one's departed relative), and research has suggested that a sense of the dead person's presence is not uncommon in the newly bereaved (Bennett and Bennett 2000).

Such relationships – between the living and the deceased – are often invoked in a ritual context, and are culturally supported by belief systems that legitimize such relating. However, many people may feel unable to have direct access – or a connection with their ancestors/relatives – and therefore require the mediation of a specialist to act on their behalf. In this instance, the purpose of healing can be concerned with easing the pain of bereavement by legitimizing the continuation of social bonds with deceased relatives. It is common to hear Spiritualist mediums emphasize to their clients that their 'loved ones' are still with them, surrounding them with love and affection (warmth). Indeed, ongoing research by Hannah Gilbert suggests that Western Spiritualist mediums often consider the importance of their work as a means of forming bridges and connections for people who have been bereaved. Consultation with a spirit medium can enable individuals to 'reconnect' and continue a bond with deceased loved ones (Walliss 2001).

Mediumship in other cultures operates on a similar system of reconnecting the living and the dead. Nabokov's (2000) ethnography of Tamil rituals explored the desirability of expanding the self by mingling and achieving continuity with others (i.e. spirits). While Tamil religious rituals often seek to dissociate people from an 'invasion' of spiritual influence, mediums – who are able to *control* such spiritual experiences and use them positively – are an exception. They offer evidential support for cultural beliefs in life after death and their 'localization of the afterworld at such a proximate distance also … [renders the] continuity of bonds quite feasible' (Nabokov 2000, p. 122). It is through *their* connectedness to a spirit world that they are able to 'reconnect' individuals with deceased kith and kin; they give 'visibility' and credibility to noncorporeal beings. It is also through this collective atmosphere that such 'reconnection' is validated and the non-corporeal can become visible; the potentially imagined is legitimized by a sensory, 'real' experience in a non-related individual (the spirit medium).

The impact of these practices on physiological systems, and on grief processes in particular, remains unclear. Moreover, insofar as they contextualize one's deceased loved ones as now being welcomed into a loving community of spirits, this experience of being part of a loving community will extend to the self, with the expectation that one will join that community (including seeing one's relatives again) after one's own death. There are three elements here: that your relative is (1) safe and happy, (2) continues to care about you, and (3) is part of a caring community to which you will one day be welcomed.

Spiritual healing and psychological kinship

Psychological kinship refers to creating bonds with those who may not be part of one's biological kin system (Bailey 2002) and is associated with feelings of belonging (Baumeister and Leary 1995). The basis for the relating is one of similarity with or some quality that is desired from the other, or can be created in the process of relating. In these forms of relating, healers may seek to link a person to 'higher deities' or 'higher powers' through their knowledge and their own relationship with these deities/powers. In this context healers may situate themselves within some hierarchical relationship between the more and the less powerful/knowledgeable. Healers may regard themselves as 'vehicles' for the channelling of powers from deities, and may believe themselves to be aided in this endeavour by helpers or spiritual guides. The healing aspects are manifested through the healer as a vessel to the 'higher more powerful other', rather than as an emphasis on facilitating reconnection to one's own kinship group.

Psychological kinships can also be formed between a healer and spiritual helpers. On occasion, spirit guides (those who aid the healer) may never have been in one's group. For example, many Western mediums believe they have Native Americans as spirit guides (Hess 1993). In some cases it may be that the relationship between healer and guide is seen as having been facilitated by the spirit guide, desiring to have a relationship with the living. Roseman's (2003) description of Temiar mediums points out that they often first encounter their spirit guides in dreams. In these dreams, the spirit guides are detached from a non-human source (e.g. a fruit tree) and 'humanized', expressing desires for a connection between the two. Spirits may interact with human 'hosts' or mediators to assist their living in their day-to-day lives, or to help them in their 'spiritual evolution', although they can also be unhelpful. The relationship between spirits and humans varies greatly from culture to culture, and even within cultures. What is key, when considering forms of spiritual healing, is *connectedness to benevolent forces*; others that will seek to alleviate injury or dysfunction in the patient by using their knowledge or powers for the patient's benefit. Again we can see how these experiences could link to activation of the soothing system.

Reconnecting within oneself

Fatigue, sleep difficulties, loss of interest and low mood feelings are common human experiences that can be very debilitating. Explanations for them, and means to recovery, reside in the culture. In the West the familiar concepts of 'viruses' or 'stress' are commonly used explanations, and people may seek out a variety of remedies to help them 'fight the virus' or 'de-stress'. In some ways the concept of a virus as an 'invading alien other' mirrors concepts of possession. If psychological explanations are used, Western psychotherapy may focus on stressful life events, unrealistic expectations or mis-attuned goals. Equally a therapist may explore repression and dissociation, acting to mediate for the patient between their conscious and unconscious, and in this way help a person reconnect with 'lost or denied parts of themselves' (Ellenberger 1970). In each aspect the experience of the patient to connect with, and feel understood and supported by the therapist (the therapeutic relationship) has a major influence on outcome. However, be it some unknown 'virus' or (known) psychological difficulty, healing seeks to help people stimulate and connect with their own internal self-healing processes: to strengthen their immune system, detoxify, de-stress, change their thinking, learn new coping behaviours or resolve an inner conflict. All focus shifts to helping the person connect with inner processes of mind and body to help him- or herself. What is sometimes missed in these contexts is people's spiritual desires for connectedness (Aldridge 2000; Cacioppo *et al.* 2005).

These approaches can be contrasted to those used when different explanations and meanings are given to symptoms, especially those that have supernatural causes. In some cultures such symptoms, as noted above, may be seen as the loss of self/soul. This is taken literally, and a shaman is required to visit the spirit lands in order to bring back part of the self (Ellenberger 1970). Desjarlais (1996) has described Yolmo (a community of Tibeto-Burman people) shamans, and their healing of *bla* (spirit) loss. The Yolmo believe that individuals have several 'life forces', and the absence of any of these forces is detrimental to an individual's health. It is believed that a person's *bla* can leave the body unexpectedly, when, for example, an individual is startled. Once separated, the *bla* is vulnerable to external supernatural dangers (such as ghosts or witches) that may carry it into the land of the dead. Without one's *bla*, 'the body feels "heavy," lacks energy or "passion," and the afflicted does not care to eat, talk, work, travel, or socialize: he or she has trouble sleeping, witnesses ominous dreams, and is prone to further illnesses' (Desjarlais 1996, p. 145). This is similar to symptoms of depression as perceived in the West, although Desjarlais points out that 'each incident presents a slightly different form and etiology' (p. 146).

The healing ritual involves a magical flight, in which the shaman journeys to the land of the dead in order to 'hook' the lost *bla* and return it to the patient.

> Yolmo healings involve the imagining of a symbolic ascent from weakness to strength, *fragmentation to integration*, disharmony to harmony, defilement to purity. The symbolic shift from illness to health here is not the method, but simply the scaffolding, of the rites (in fact, the shift often has more political that curative value). Generally, spirit calling for the Yolmo people is less like a mythic narrative, progressing from one stage to another, than an imagistic poem, evoking an array of tactile images which, through their cumulative effect, evoke a change of sensibility in the bodies of its participants – a change, that is, in the lasting mood or disposition that contribute to the sensory grounds of a person's experience. (Desjarlais 1996, pp. 150–1, my italics)

While these healings are not always successful, those that are see individuals reporting a reversal of their afflictions; the body now feels good. Harmony has been restored, life forces are reconnected and 'eyes brighten, the body electrifies, and the heart mind renews' (Desjarlais 1996, p. 149).

Based on complex systems of meaning and explanation for health and illness, individuals and groups are highly motivated to help others recover in ways that fit with their socially contextualized meanings. Rituals and procedures for healing may have emotional impacts on people by offering ways to reconnect to others, to feel helped and supported by others who put their knowledge and powers at their disposal, and to create states of mind conducive to healing.

With a healing relationship, be it focused on supernatural beliefs or Western medical ones, what matters to people is feeling cared for and about, and whether or not the healing efforts or the healer make sense to them and they can believe in them. Within this context, Western medicine is beginning to recognize that healing involves care and attentiveness to people's spiritual beliefs and feelings from which they can draw considerable emotional strength and comfort (Aldridge 2000).

COMPASSION AND HEALING

There are a range of spiritual beliefs which are focused on healing, but do not necessarily involve rituals. For example, Buddhist initiates are encouraged to focus on the idea that 'all life is suffering', and the way to alleviate suffering in self and others is with a process of compassionate mindfulness (Davidson and Harrington 2002; Goleman 2003). The whole philosophy of Buddhism is based on the notion of the inherent nature of suffering in biological beings. This is because we seek out resources and generate needs, wishes and desires (drive systems), and are easily threatened and so become defensive. A potential for reducing suffering is through proper 'mind training' that illuminates 'illusions of self'. These systems of thought are regarded both as a basic psychology, and as offering a basis for spiritual beliefs that orientate a person to their own inner selves, the essence of their 'being', and relationships to others. Recently, some mind-training practices such as 'mindfulness', that are embedded in a complex meta-psychology of mind and the spiritual nature of mind, have been stripped of this meta-psychology and used as healing processes in their own right (e.g., Segal *et al.* 2002; Davidson *et al.* 2003). This is not a denial of the importance of compassion in mind healing (Davidson and Harrington 2002), but a recognition that one can benefit from mindfulness without having to endorse other aspects of the philosophy such as reincarnation or notions of Karma.

In monotheistic religions, particularly in Christianity, two key themes for the alleviation of suffering are God's benevolence and the importance of forgiveness. The narratives of Christ mark a new archetypal relationship with God, a change from the relationships of the Old Testament, which had been building for some time and was crystallized and developed by Him and His followers (Armstrong 1993). While compassion is key to Buddhism, forgiveness is key to Christianity. Whether or not one seeks to be forgiven because this is linked to personal spiritual values or a self-identity, there is now growing evidence that individuals who can develop forgiveness, or feel forgiven, can be healed of emotional and possibly certain physical difficulties, and of difficulties in developing genuine affiliative relationships (Worthington *et al.* 2005). This is partly because vengeance and ruminating on vengeance can be physiologically deregulating. Forgiveness is hard when great harm has been done or when those that do harm or threaten us are seen as members of an out-group. In these circumstances, the ability to retaliate, get one's own back or make others suffer can be a pleasure (Leach *et al.* 2003). Forgiveness is easier when perpetrators display guilt and remorse (Worthington *et al.* 2005).

It is often suggested that developing care and compassion for others, and forgiveness, is related to a type of spiritual intelligence that operates inside individuals. However, for such potential to become actualized and manifest, it requires practices to value and legitimize such behaviours and link them to self-identities. 'Caring' and welfare-focused societies have lower rates of crime and ill-health than competitive and materialistic ones (Kasser 2002; Arrindell *et al.* 2003; Gilbert 2005). Although we often think about spiritual healing and development in terms of what we should do with *our own* minds and desires, focused on us as individuals (and there are now a vast range of New Age movements enticing us with various exercises and beliefs systems to achieve individual health, spiritual awakening and rejuvenation), the biopsychosocial approach also suggests that it is in the *collective* organization of values and practices that the healing properties of caring and compassionate behaviour can flourish. The 'individualization' of spiritualities and healing in the West can be troubling if it decontextualizes itself from the social and political. Whether or not we frame the working towards a fairer, more moral, just and compassionate society in spiritual or humanist terms, it is clear that the social and ecological environments in which we grow and live have major effects on the organization of our minds, for sickness and health, and we are collectively responsible for their creation.

With regard to the qualities of the healer, these will vary according to the nature of the task. In some societies they require mystical experience and courage, whereas Western therapeutic approaches have focused on the qualities of the relationship between patient and therapist. For the most part, what should be co-created between patient and therapist is a compassionate co-construction that enables the person to work with and accept painful material (Gilbert 2007).

CONCLUSION

We began this chapter by considering ideas of spiritual healing, and arguing that one aspect of it is focused on the process of connecting to benevolent others. We have taken an evolutionary view of the significance of social connectedness, and indicated the physiological power of such connectedness. We then suggested that, in the human mind, the experience of connectedness is mediated through a number of complex signal-sensitive systems (e.g., for warmth, acceptance) and cognitive processes such as belief formation (e.g. that others are working on our behalf, or that we are part of a loving, supportive community). These cognitive qualities offer new vehicles for the creation and experience of connectedness and healing practices. Spiritual processes utilize both sensory and cognitive abilities to create meanings that link people to a spiritual dimension. This spiritual dimension can be orientated towards biological kin relationships, 'higher powers', psychological kin relationships, or connecting to benevolent energies in the self or outside the self (e.g., universal). Different spiritual belief systems that create kinship systems for connectedness also provide a means through which individuals can engage in rituals that may themselves be physiologically potent.

Spiritual healing appears to be, at least partly, mediated through relationships and connectedness. We have suggested that any fully comprehensive engagement with such healing must engage with the evolved nature of our minds. So our minds and bodies have evolved to be highly influenced by the social and ecological contexts in which they exist. It is in our relationship with both real and imagined others that the experience of being care for, and cared about, can help us feel safe and connected and can stimulate healing processes, and the ability to find hope and meaning within us.

CHAPTER 8

Modelling the biomedical role of spirituality through breast cancer research

Michael J. Boivin and Burton Webb

In *City of God*, Augustine recounts the story of a woman he knew in Carthage named Innocentia. She was diagnosed with breast cancer and told by the physician that she could perhaps delay death through amputation, but that the disease was incurable. According to Augustine, she turned in prayer for help from God alone, and was told in a dream to wait at the baptistery for the first woman who came out after being baptized. She was then to ask for this woman to make the sign of Christ over the cancerous breast. When Innocentia did as she was told, she was completely cured. However, her physician was initially upset and disappointed at her account, thinking that such a cure might have perhaps enabled her to convey some great discovery to him in the healing arts (Shelley 2000, pp. 113–43).

Jones defines spirituality as 'the hope in something greater than ourselves' while 'religion is a community of shared spiritual values' (2006, pp. 26–7). We propose that spirituality can significantly enhance the likelihood of physical healing in the face of disease. In the following review, we share our own work and that of others in the field of breast cancer research. We do so in order to provide evidence in support of proposed biomedical pathways through which faith, such as that expressed by Innocentia, can lead to scientific discovery within the healing arts.

BREAST CANCER AS A NATURAL LABORATORY FOR THE STUDY OF SPIRITUALITY AND HEALTH

Breast cancer is one of the most significant disease threats to women today, especially in the high- and middle-income countries. According to the American Cancer Society, 211,240 women in the United States in 2005 were diagnosed with breast cancer – one every three minutes (American Cancer Society 2005). Each year more than 40,000 women die of this disease. The prevalence counts of women living with breast cancer in the United States number over two million, making it the single greatest public health threat facing American women following cardiovascular disease and stroke (American Cancer Society 2006). Breast cancer is of similar public health importance for women in Europe. In the European Union, roughly 270,000 women develop breast cancer each year and roughly 96,000 of these women die from the disease (European Union 2006).

When breast cancer is diagnosed, the impact on a woman can be existentially, emotionally and physically devastating. This is true even if the stage of the disease is very early and the initial prognosis is excellent. The effects of treatment for breast cancer (surgery, radiation, chemotherapy, hormonal medication and monoclonal antibody treatment) can greatly intensify the emotional and physical impact of the disease, potentially leading to lifelong disability. The psychological and emotional wounds can persist as well, since breast cancer affects the body image of a woman. Simply put, it is a disease of the whole person and must be conceptualized as such in order for a woman to feel that her medical treatment has been adequate in addressing her needs.

We believe that our own research is providing evidence that at the core of the disease is a spiritual dynamic that is vital in understanding the illness and treatment benefit from a holistic perspective. As such, this disease provides a strategic and powerful 'laboratory' within the human condition for exploring the interrelationships among the spiritual, social, emotional, neuropsychological and immunological domains. This natural laboratory can provide a rich and dynamic means by which medicine can evaluate the role of spirituality in healing and health outcomes.

THE CONSTRUCT OF SPIRITUALITY IN BIOMEDICAL RESEARCH

Researchers studying breast cancer have pioneered the role of spirituality in the biomedical study of disease during the 1980s and 1990s (Yates *et al.* 1981, pp. 121–8; Reed 1987, pp. 335–44; Highfield 1992, pp. 1–8; Jenkins and Pargament 1995, pp. 51–74; Kaczorowski 1990, pp. 105–17). Furthermore, the holistic approach to breast cancer over the past several decades is now serving as a model for similar holistic biomedical research specific to men, that of prostate cancer (Gall 2004a, pp. 454–61; Gall 2004b, pp. 1357–68; Krupski, Fink *et al.* 2005, pp. 375–90; Krupski, Sonn *et al.* 2005, pp. 461–8).

To illustrate this point, Figure 8.1 shows the number of 'spiritual' or 'religion' citations in the PubMed index of medical journals for each decade beginning with the 1960s. The number of citations dramatically

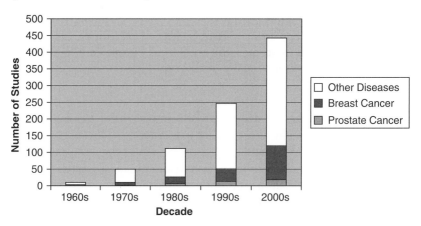

Figure 8.1 Studies relating spirituality to types of diseases

increased for each successive decade, with a significant proportion of these pertaining to breast cancer.

More recently, innovative treatments that have included psychosocial and spiritual components have emerged in clinical-trial research within the field of complementary medicine (Moye *et al.* 1995, pp. 34–9; Targ and Levine 2002, pp. 238–48; Barnes *et al.* 2004; Hernandez-Reif *et al.* 2004, pp. 45–52). Complementary medicine now has its own NIH center (http://nccam.nih.gov/). Other National Institutes of Health (NIH) have also begun sponsoring research which includes spirituality as a central construct (e.g., http://grants.nih.gov/grants/guide/pa-files/PA-07–181. html). Such developments at the NIH have allowed rigorous biomedical scientific evidence to complement the philosophical and theological dimensions of scholarly explorations on the nature of spirituality and healing.

A PARADIGM FOR A NEUROBIOLOGICAL APPROACH
IN STUDYING SPIRITUALITY

Despite the growing acceptance of spirituality as a construct in biomedical research, some have questioned the scientific legitimacy of this construct. For example, Sloan (2005, pp. 1–13) discourages scientists from the sort of neuroimaging studies of meditation conducted by Andrew Newberg (2004, pp. 1–18), because he believes that identifying areas of the brain that light up during prayer or meditation has little value and is not worth the cost of such studies. Sloan feels that identifying neurophysiological underpinnings of religious experience implies that religious experience is nothing more than increased brain activity of one sort or another.

I do not think his concerns are justified. More holistic models of the person such as the Hebraic model described by Boivin (1991, pp. 157–65; 2002, pp. 159–76; 2003a, pp. 17–22) conceptualize the various dimensions of personhood (spiritual and biological) as existing along a mutually interactive continuum. Within this continuum, the spiritual aspects of personhood can be related to a neurobiological substrate, and yet still be indicative of an ultimate reality that may cast a physical shadow, but originate from a domain beyond what our senses can now perceive.

Such theological approaches are part of a current movement referred to as 'nonreductive physicalism', and represent an important new paradigm in the scientific study of spirituality (Brown *et al.* 1998; Murphy 1998). Proponents of nonreductive physicalism believe that this approach allows us to better integrate neuroimaging science with a theological dimension of the human experience. It does so without compromising the importance of either biological science or the metaphysical dimensions of the human experience. Furthermore, it does so without having to maintain the legitimacy of the spiritual via an ambiguous Platonic dualism (mind/body/spirit compartments). Neither does nonreductive physicalism dismiss spiritual experiences as nothing more than their neurobiological underpinnings. It views these as emerging from the psychobiological, while at the same time supervenient in acting upon it. In other words, our spiritual experiences serve as both the orchestral director and musical outcome of a neurobiological symphony whose ultimate significance extends beyond the concert hall.

PROBLEMS WITH THE MEASUREMENT OF SPIRITUALITY IN HEALTH OUTCOMES RESEARCH

Sloan suggests that a lack of consistent findings between religion/spirituality predictors and health outcomes are perhaps the result of such methodological constraints as self-selection of study sample, confounding by factors related to religious demographics, measurement error for religious and spiritual variables, and data dredging within a wide array of religious predictors and health indicators. Furthermore, spirituality is a construct that is inherently subject to arbitrary and ambiguous definitions as theorists attempt to operationalize it.

Sloan has other concerns about attempts to scientifically study spirituality with respect to health outcomes. In terms of the overarching aims of research on religion and health, he asks the question 'What, precisely, is the larger objective of studies that seek to examine connections between religious practices and health?' (Sloan 2005, p. 7). He goes on to illustrate that if depression is found to be related to heart disease, a therapeutic intervention is plausible using pharmacotherapy and/or psychotherapy. However, he feels that it would be ethically problematic for a physician to propose a religious intervention even if researchers were able to conclusively document a relationship between that action and a beneficial health outcome.

This concern assumes that interventions meant to affect the religious or spiritual well-being of a patient, and interventions meant to affect emotional well-being (for example antidepressants), are clearly distinguishable in terms of their putative impact and medical credibility. What is needed is research that will allow us to understand better the degree of overlap between these two domains (spiritual and emotional) for women, for example, undergoing treatment for breast cancer. Such research may help us better appreciate the extent to which we are 'Finding God in Prozac or finding Prozac in God' when achieving 'spiritual' benefit from psychopharmacological treatment for the malaise and dysphoria that can accompany illnesses such as breast cancer.

PROPOSED PATHWAYS BETWEEN SPIRITUALITY AND HEALTH OUTCOMES

For the modern-day physician wishing to understand the role of faith in bringing about physical healing, a key area of biomedical research is likely to be psychoneuroimmunology (PNI). PNI is dedicated to the study of how the immune system is affected by environmental, social and cognitive/emotional processes as mediated by the brain. This only stands to reason, given the general recognition that lifestyle, personality, stress and emotions can affect our health through their influence on our immune system (Cohen *et al.* 1998, pp. 835–41). However, we present biomedical mechanisms and research evidence supporting this linkage between spirituality and healing as mediated by PNI.

The intersection between the immune and nervous systems can be found at several levels, but the best-known pathway involves neural signals that pass from the periphery to the brain through to the vagus nerve. These innervate regions of the body where the immune response occurs – the gut, spleen, thymus and lymph nodes (Maier and Watkins 1998, pp. 83–107). In fact, many of the vagus nerve fibres are actually sensory and send afferent messages from the innervated organs to the brain. Consequently, events in the environment perceived as stressors activate the same circuitry initiating the immune response in the body as is activated by systemic infectious agents.

The hormones that are viewed traditionally as stress hormones in mammals are thought to be heavily involved in this process, and this bi-directional immune-to-neural tissue communication is thought to have existed in biological evolution long before the fight/flight response so common in mammals. This pathway fostered the emergence of PNI as a separate scientific discipline, as it continues to consistently document a strong relationship between stress and sickness.

However, the role of spiritual and religious traits as they modify the physiological impact of stress within PNI is only just beginning to be systematically explored in this field of medicine. One recent example is the NIH-sponsored clinical-trials evaluation of T'ai Chi Training and Spiritual Growth Groups in comparison to a usual care control group of women with early breast cancer (McCain 2005, p. S121; McCain *et al.* 2005, pp. 320–32). In this study, outcomes of interest are psychosocial functioning, quality of life including spiritual well-being, and physical health including neuroendocrine mediators, immune status and disease progress. Such research is crucial in helping us better understand the interactive pathways between spirituality and health.

QUALITY OF LIFE (QOL) AND THE IMPORTANCE OF SPIRITUAL WELL-BEING (SWB) IN CANCER RESEARCH

Psychiatrist and cancer specialist Jimmie Holland and her colleagues published a thorough review of research literature pertaining to the effects of cancer on QoL. They observed that although QoL measures have become an increasingly important part of oncology research over the past two decades (Holland *et al.* 1998, pp. 460–9; Holland 2002, pp. 206–21; Holland 2006, pp. 445–59), these measures have rarely included a religious or spiritual beliefs domain. Larson *et al.* noted that in psychiatric research, spiritual or religious variables were mentioned in only 2.7 per cent of studies between 1978 and 1984 (Larson *et al.* 1986, pp. 329–34). This is problematic because of the clear importance of religion and faith as ordinary people cope with day-to-day stress, crises and trauma in their lives (Pargament *et al.* 1990, pp. 793–825; Pargament *et al.* 1997, pp. 347–61). Studies that have considered spiritual health in assessing outcomes for the care of cancer patients have found positive and significant results (Smith *et al.* 1993, pp. 89–103; Highfield 1997, pp. 237–41). This has led medical researchers such as Holland to advocate for the inclusion of a spiritual belief measure as part of a QoL assessment in any medical research pertaining to how people respond when faced with life-threatening disease. She and her colleagues have developed just such a measure and have used it in psycho-oncology research.

There is a good deal of overlap between psychological and spiritual well-being when QoL is assessed in breast cancer survivors. However, SWB is still distinguishable in terms of the unique variance it accounts for in the health outcomes for breast cancer survivors (Ferrell *et al.* 1998, pp. 887–95; Bauer-Wu and Farran 2005, pp. 172–90). SWB has also served as a strategic point of psychosocial intervention in holistic treatment (Coward and Kahn 2004, pp. E24–31). Furthermore, SWB is distinguishable from emotional well-being (EWB) in terms of those personality traits most important in effectively coping with breast cancer. Finally, SWB seems to be an especially potent predictor when it comes to more positive and effective strategies for coping with breast cancer and its aftermath (Gall and Cornblat 2002, pp. 524–35; Ramírez-Johnson *et al.* 2002, p. 1839).

EWB, SWB, AND THE IMMUNOLOGICAL EFFECTS OF ILLNESS

Aragona and colleagues observed that in comparison to women with benign breast tumours, breast cancer patients were significantly more likely to have psychiatric symptoms of depression and anxiety (1996, pp. 354–60). They were also more likely to have significantly higher stress hormone levels and lymphocyte levels of cells that result from tumour and infection. This was the case during periods of hospital admission, diagnostic uncertainty and preceding breast surgery. However, successful treatment of depression with Prozac raised the level of cells needed to fight tumours and infection (Natural Killer cell level response; Frank *et al.* 1999, pp. 18–24). Another study found that stronger spiritual expression in women with metastatic breast cancer was significantly related to both helper and cytotoxic T-cell counts after controlling for demographic, disease status and treatment variables (Sephton *et al.* 2001, pp. 345–53).

Studies document that diagnosis of breast cancer can severely diminish a woman's QoL, with subsequent disruption to immune function (Kootstra *et al.* 2008, pp. 2533–41). This is supported by the fact that individuals who are undergoing a stressful life event have shown similar reductions of natural cytotoxicity to those found in individuals suffering from a major depressive disorder (Irwin 1993, pp. 203–18; Irwin 1994, pp. 29–47; Irwin *et al.* 1997, pp. 83–90; Irwin 1999, pp. 1–24). In animal studies, both stress and surgical interventions can suppress natural killer (NK) cell activity and promote cancerous tumour growth (Ben-Eliyahu 2003, pp. S27–36).

THE RELATIONSHIP BETWEEN SWB AND EWB IN CANCER PATIENTS

Boivin and his students evaluate men and women cancer patients representing a broad range of tumour sites and disease stages. These patients completed a quality-of-life assessment packet at one of several outpatient treatment centres. We observed in this sample that EWB was significantly related to SWB. Jarrett and Boivin went on to more thoroughly assess SWB, EWB and QoL in a subgroup of fifteen men and seventeen women, twenty-six of whom were currently undergoing cancer treatment (Jarrett *et al.* 1999; Jarrett and Boivin 2000). For these patients, depression, anxiety, spiritual belief and social support were the most critical components of overall QoL. Furthermore, it was found that depression was related to anxiety and predictive of poorer sleep quality. Poor sleep quality can compromise immunological response in the face of illness.

We subsequently evaluated twenty women newly diagnosed with breast cancer and about to undergo radiation therapy along with twenty-six comparison-group women who had completed treatment for breast cancer at least a year earlier. Women in active treatment reported poorer sleep, more symptoms of fatigue, greater anxiety, greater depression and poorer QoL. They also exhibited poorer performance on delayed memory and concentration, and greater distractibility during neuropsychological assessment. In these women, less depression and better QoL were correlated with stronger social support and SBW.

In the active treatment group, women undergoing chemotherapy during the treatment phase also had a significant decline in an important immunological marker for fighting disease (CD8+ counts). This seemed to be especially related to their overall level of fatigue and stress, and was statistically mediated by their level of SWB. In Figure 8.2, we have attempted to model the place of spiritual and emotional well-being amidst the effects of illness on overall QoL and subsequent immunological and neuropsychological response, based on the study findings previously summarized (Boivin and Webb 2005).

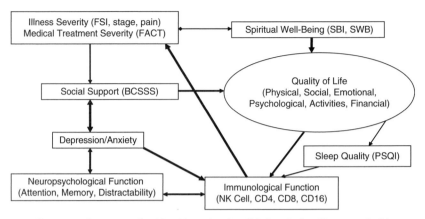

Figure 8.2 Summary of spiritual/emotional well-being during illness on QoL/ immunological and neuropsychological response (from Boivin and Webb 2005) BCSSS – Bottomley Cancer Social Support Scale; FACT – Functional Assessment of Cancer Therapy; FSI – Functional Status Index; PSQI – Pittsburgh Sleep Quality Index

BRAIN IMAGING RESEARCH AS A MEANS OF MEASURING SPIRITUALITY

When a person experiences a happy mood, fMRI (functional magnetic resonance imaging – an imaging technology for measuring brain activation) signal is heightened in the middle frontal gyrus of the frontal lobe (Symonds *et al.* 2006, pp. 3823–30). Similarly, several groups have suggested a key role for frontal regions based on neuroimaging studies of meditation (Herzog *et al.* 1990, pp. 182–7; Lazar *et al.* 2000, pp. 1581–5; Newberg *et al.* 2001, pp. 113–22; Newberg *et al.* 2003, pp. 625–30). Increased prefrontal activation, followed closely by cingulate activation, was specifically tied to regional cerebral blood flow effects in 'expert' meditators such as Tibetan Buddhist monks (Newberg and Iversen 2003, pp. 282–91).

We believe that fMRI and other brain imaging technologies can help clarify the causal pathways between SWB and immunological response as affected by chemotherapy for breast cancer patients, and we are presently exploring that link in our research programme. Our fMRI preliminary data show that we can measure brain activation response reliably in the prefrontal and cingulate brain areas. These are regions of the brain that have been implicated by Newberg and others in the mediation of heightened spiritual response. We are presently evaluating in breast cancer and control patients whether greater fMRI activation response in the frontal and cingulate cortical areas is specifically related to the presentation of spiritual pictures to our patients.

Recent fMRI studies have revealed some of the brain regions which are commonly active during induced emotional states. For example, induced sadness reliably activates areas in the obitofrontal prefrontal cortex, the subgenual cingulate cortex and the anterior insular cortex (Mayberg *et al.* 1988, pp. 937–43; Mayberg *et al.* 1999, pp. 675–82; Damasio *et al.* 2000, pp. 1049–56; Phan *et al.* 2004, pp. 258–66). In contrast, both induced disgust and fear are more likely to activate the amygdalae, though the subgenual cingulate area also appears to be involved, particularly in women (Butler *et al.* 2005, pp. 1233–6; Butler *et al.* 2007, pp. 1–7). Our goal is to see whether spiritual pictures have a distinct pattern of brain activation. Also, we hope to evaluate whether chemotherapy in breast cancer patients diminishes brain activation response to spiritual pictures. Finally, we plan to evaluate how well brain activation to spiritual pictures correlates with SWB and EWB assessed by questionnaire response, as well as the extent to which spiritual themes emerge from the narrative interviews of our patients described below.

CANCER STORIES, SPIRITUALITY AND HEALING

Hufford (2005, pp. 1–72) discusses QoL and health outcomes research, and observes that there is a distinct lack of qualitative assessment of religious belief or assessment, even though QoL almost by definition requires a combination of the quantitative and qualitative. Using structured interviews to allow a breast cancer patient to tell her story, we are presently relating those cancer scripts to the degree of brain activation from spiritual pictures before and after completing the full course of chemotherapy. We are also relating degree of activation to SWB and EWB scores as assessed by questionnaires. Finally, we plan to relate our brain activation, questionnaire and cancer script measures of spirituality to the changes that take place in the immunity system of our patients from diagnosis to the completion of chemotherapy treatment.

Figure 8.3 depicts the hypothesized role of SWB within the broader context of disease, treatment and health outcomes for breast cancer. The 'Medical Interface' (e.g., Medical Care Accessibility and other forms of life stress) between the severity of the disease and the subsequent impact on brain processes (neuropsychological integrity) is important to note. The impact of care and stress on brain function set

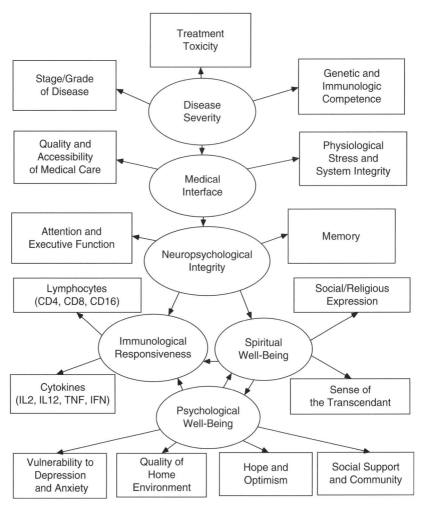

Figure 8.3 Summary model for the integration of the spiritual, emotional, neuropsychological and immunological in health outcomes

the stage for immunological resilience in the face of disease and treatment by chemotherapy, as modified by social support. We feel that psychological and spiritual well-being is closely coupled with health outcomes from disease through psychoneuroimmunological processes that are measurable. Furthermore, spirituality has an important mediating role in this process, as it determines emotional and psychological well-being.

Finally, the spiritual dimension in our model can be represented by a social/religious variable, which represents the way in which a person might think about and respond in giving expression to the spiritual in her life. However, it is also encompassed by a separate more universal and foundational 'sense of the transcendent' dimension. It is that aspect of spirituality which we believe is hard-wired within and unique to the human genome and subsequent brain. It is also that aspect of the genome which has compelled humankind to seek religious expression since the dawn of the species, and that aspect that we believe provides a key link for a transcendent source of spiritually derived healing within what otherwise would be an entirely closed physiological system. 'Fundamental to our lives as sentient beings is a quest for our origins that must conclude where human consciousness ultimately can be said to have begun; with early hominids that buried flowers and ornaments with their dead in a longing or recognition of purpose derived from a sense of the transcendent' (Boivin 2003b, pp. 609–11).

ACKNOWLEDGEMENTS

Work on this chapter was supported by a Templeton Advanced Research Program (TARP) grant to Michael Boivin administered through the Metanexus Institute (www.metanexus.net/tarp), and by a grant from the Council of Christian Colleges and Universities (CCCU) programme of Initiative Grants to Network Christian Scholars. The expertise in the field of immunology provided to this chapter by Dr Burton Webb, Indiana Wesleyan University, is also gratefully acknowledged. Research findings summarized in this chapter are based on the work of a number of former students; including Beth Bonkoski, Heidi Walker, Kerri Burton, Ryan Rhoads, Sarah Schumacher, Ryan Bence, Gwenda Jarrett, Connie Harmon, Melanie Mingus, Susan Browne, Shelly Shockley, Faith Watkins, Cindi Harnish, Rebecca Marcotte, Geoffrey Aaron, and Nathan Felt. Stephanie Smith, Research Assistant with the Spirituality, Emotional Well-Being, and Quality of Life (SEQL) Breast Cancer Research Program at Michigan State University assisted in the preparation of this chapter.

CHAPTER 9

Spirituality and health: assessing the evidence

Marilyn Schlitz

A fresh breeze is blowing through many corridors of medicine today. Patients and professionals are demanding that the heart and soul of healing be reinstated, alongside the best of modern technology. Many people acknowledge the multiple dimensions of living, healing, and curing, dimensions that were overlooked in our exclusive courtship with the bio-scientific-technological model of medicine.

This breeze is a new model of medicine for the twenty-first century. It is an integral model that is, at its very core, a dynamic, holistic and lifelong process. In fact an integral practice that exists in widening and deepening relationships with yourself, your family, your culture, your connection to the natural world and with the great mystery of life (Schlitz *et al.* 2005).

An integral perspective honours multiple ways of knowing, represented by different viewpoints, belief systems and worldviews. It moves beyond cultural competence, in which we consider different worldviews in the course of living and working with diverse ethnic and cultural groups, to a deep appreciation for the divergent systems of healthcare that coexist in a modern medical context. Chinese medicine, curanderismo, Spiritism, Christian Science, evidence-based medicine – each offers insights into healing. In this way, the integral model is inclusive of both conventional and alternative approaches, but always with a sense of discernment for what is right and true within the various healing systems (Schlitz 2007, p. 58).

An integral perspective is as much about healing as it is about curing. It involves harnessing our desire for health, as well as our will to live. These qualitative domains are as significant to an integral perspective as the role of scientific information and advanced technology. In addition to the science of diagnosing, treating or preventing disease and damage of the body or mind, an integral approach is one that *heals* – even in the face of potential death and dying.

One area where we can see the value of an integral approach is in the reintegration of spirituality into modern healthcare. This is happening through a meeting of the best of spiritual care with the rigour and discernment of science. As we hold a deep appreciation for psychology and culture, we may move into a vision for a more effective and life-enhancing personal and socio-political model of medicine. Through such a lens of perception, new breakthroughs are possible that can expand our sense of hope for the future.

In this chapter I consider this new integral model within an evidence-based approach to spirituality and health. In particular, I review the different domains of evidence for the health benefits of spirituality in healthcare. These include different cultural, social, psycho-biological and transpersonal studies. I will then take these findings and consider the implications of spirituality and health for a more expanded model of medicine, in which meaning and purpose are as important as facts and rational argument to the promotion of human flourishing.

An integral approach to evidence involves a multidisciplinary lens. There are five primary areas of data or evidence that support the health benefits of spirituality and religious practice. These are cross-cultural data, survey studies, public health research, basic science related to mind–body medicine, and basic science and clinical studies of distant healing. Because most of these areas are covered in greater depth in other essays in this volume, my goal will be to overview these various data sets while focusing on distant healing, given that this provides the strongest support for the transpersonal dimension in spirituality and health.

Throughout history, and in every reported culture, spirituality has played a role in different models of health and healing. Indigenous cultures hold no separation between healing and a connection to the sacred. If you examine various traditions, it is only within the Western materialist culture that we make a demarcation between reason and mystery. Some individuals, such as Carmelite nuns, spend their lives in contemplative prayer devoted to healing intentions, and some monks and nuns devote a substantial proportion of their prayers to requests for healing. For example, the Unity Church has offered prayers on behalf of anyone who requests it, 24 hours a day and 365 days a year, for over a century. In Jerusalem, an internet prayer service allows people around the globe to request prayer at the Wailing Wall. During the holy month of Ramadan, millions of Muslims gather at Mecca to engage in group prayer several times each day.

In contemporary Western culture it is difficult to determine the precise prevalence of the use of spirituality as a complementary and alternative medicine (CAM) therapy, not because it is rarely used but because it is so popular that surveys have had to focus on finding the exceptions. We do know that prayer is the most common healing practice used outside conventional medicine in the United States. In a recent survey of adult Americans, conducted by the Center for Disease Control and Prevention's National Center for Health Statistics, of the top five most popular CAM healing practices, three involved prayer and spirituality (Barnes *et al.* 2004, pp. 1–19). The most popular CAM practice was prayer for self, and the third most popular was prayer for others.

In a poll of 1,004 adults in 1996 conducted by Time/CNN, 73 per cent of adults in the United States believed praying for someone else could help cure their illness (Ameling 2000, pp. 40–8); 50 per cent of patients wanted physicians to pray with them. This says something about what people are calling for, how people will feel happier and more contented, and how they feel satisfied in terms of the therapeutic encounter.

An earlier national survey found that 82 per cent of Americans believed in the healing power of prayer, and 64 per cent felt that physicians should pray with patients who request it (Wallis 1996). Another survey found that 19 per cent of cancer patients reported that they augmented their conventional medical care with prayer or spiritual healing (Cassileth 1984). A survey of American Cancer Society support groups for women with breast cancer showed that 88 per cent found spiritual or religious practice to be important in coping with their illness (Johnson and Spilka 1991, pp. 21–33), although the extent to which specific prayers or intentions of healing were part of their activities was not clear. In acute illnesses, such as cardiac events, these numbers are higher. For example, Saudia *et al.* (1991, pp. 60–5) found that 96 per cent of patients stated that they prayed for their health before undergoing surgery. Some 33 per cent of Hispanic patients with AIDS reportedly sought such prayer assistance (Suarez *et al.* 1996, pp. 685–90). And in the UK there are more spiritual healers (approximately 14,000) than therapists from any other branch of CAM (Astin *et al.* 2000, pp. 903–10), indicating the widespread practice and use of spirituality in healing.

Among medical professionals, the concepts of spiritual healing, energy healing and prayer are slowly gaining acceptance as well. In a 1996 survey of northern California physicians (Wallis 1996b, pp. 58–64), 13 per cent of practitioners reported using or recommending prayer or religious healing as an adjunct to conventional interventions. Therapeutic touch, which can be performed at a distance, is used by nurses in at least eighty hospitals in the United States (Maxwell 1996, pp. 96–9) and has been taught to more than 43,000 healthcare professionals (Krieger 1979). Among the lay public, Reiki International, the largest training organization for 'subtle-energy healing', reports to having certified more than 500,000 practitioners worldwide. While Reiki healing is frequently performed through physical contact, it is also regularly practised over distances of thousands of miles (Schlitz and Braud 1985, pp. 100–23).

Another area of support comes from the field of public health. Making use of epidemiological methods and tools, we are beginning to understand the correlations between spiritual and religious practice and physical outcomes. Jeff Levin, a social epidemiologist, noted that more than 1,600 studies have been conducted examining the correlation between religious and spiritual participation and health (Schlitz *et al.* 2005). He believed the evidence to be compelling. High levels of religiosity correlate with lower morbidity and mortality, enhanced well-being and quality of life, lower cardiovascular-related mortality, and lower levels of depression and psychological stress. According to Levin, the findings persist regardless of religious affiliation, diseases or health conditions, age, sex, race, ethnicity or nationality of those studied. This finding is positively correlated with education. People who have a strong educational background believe that these kinds of practices and principles are important for health and well-being. There are many possible explanations for these correlations, including lifestyle, diet, social support, as well as a greater sense of meaning and purpose in their lives.

BASIC SCIENCE ON MIND–BODY MEDICINE

From a psychological perspective, all forms of spiritually based therapy may be thought of as employing a simple coping mechanism in the face of uncertainty or dire need. In addition, the concept that prayer for self promotes healing is no longer considered radical because of the growing literature on the salutary effects of positive emotions, meditation and placebo. More importantly, there is the plausibility of psychoneuroimmunological models of self-regulation that demonstrate a clear link between mind and body (Kiecolt-Glaser *et al.* 2002, pp. 15–28).

While there are many examples to draw from, one recent study followed a group of patients with a high probably of Alzheimer disease (Kaufman *et al.* 2007, pp. 1509–14). Religiosity and spirituality were measured using standardized scales that now exist due to the proliferation of studies over the past ten years. After controlling for baseline levels of cognition, age, sex and education, the researchers found a slower rate of decline associated with higher levels of spirituality.

Critics suggest that the effect of this study, and scores of others like it, is due to suggestion, expectancy or the 'infamous' placebo effect. But as Harris Dienstfrey, former editor of *Advances in Mind–Body Medicine* – a journal dedicated to this field of study – has noted, 'The mind as a source of medicine is waiting to be explored' (Schlitz *et al.* 2005, p. 60). Indeed, it is interesting to note that the placebo effect is something researchers tend to put aside. It is the control condition in clinical trials. Yet if we really want to understand the innate capacities of the body to heal, it is here that we should focus. How is it that we can take an inert substance and produce a physiological change? Moreover, this inert substance appears to know the specific cascade of responses that are necessary to lead to a particular kind of outcome. How does this happen? These are mysteries that remain to be answered as various disciplines converge in efforts to document the role of spirituality in health.

In my own current research with Harriet Hopf and Cassandra Vieten, conducted at California Pacific Medical Center, we have been looking at the effects of prayer and spirituality on wound healing. This is a three-arm clinical trial with 100 women, primarily breast cancer patients, who are undergoing reconstructive surgery after a mastectomy. We have recruited spiritual and energy healers from across the country to participate in this study – people who believe they can use their minds, their prayers and their intentions to heal other people at a distance.

Such healers include Chi Gong masters, Johrei practitioners, Reiki practitioners, Carmelite nuns, Buddhist monks and Christian groups. All the healers in our research study keep a daily log that describes their practice and their experience. People report making use of techniques such as directing healing energy towards the distant person, using some kind of focusing tool, such as a photograph to direct their attention to the distant person, or making use of petitionary prayer to call on divine help from supernatural forces. The sample used is broad.

The women who come into the surgery unit are randomized into two blinded arms. Either they receive distant healing or they do not. In the third arm of a distant healing or prayer-and-intention healing group, patients are called every day and are told that they are getting healing. The outcome in this study is the rate of wound healing, gained by measuring collagen deposition in a small GORE-TEX patch inserted in the groin area, a standardized location. A variety of psychosocial measures are also observed. This is an example of bringing spiritual and religious practices, so-called 'compassionate intention', into a laboratory setting and looking at the role of expectancy and placebo as it relates to the particular outcome measure. We are framing the possibility that our intention can actually influence the physical well-being of another person, even if that person is unaware of that intention.

DISTANT PRAYER AND HEALING RESEARCH

Of course when people pray or send loving intention to another person, they are not always thinking that they are generating a mind–body effect. It is more that they think they are generating a mind to mind–body effect. In areas such as intercessory prayer or other forms of spiritual healing, there is a belief that the intention of the prayer has an affect on another person, even at a distance and under conditions that preclude conventional sensory interactions. This moves us into the area of distant healing intention (DHI).

DHI has been defined as 'a compassionate mental act intended to improve the health and well-being of another person at a distance' (Sicher *et al.* 1998). The fundamental assumption in DHI is that the intentions of one person can affect the physiological state of another person who is distant from the healer. Such a possibility provides yet another source of data to support the efficacy of spirituality in health and healing (Schlitz and Radin 2007).

Over the past half-century researchers have developed techniques for measuring possible distant healing effects on living systems (Braud and Schlitz 1983; Solfvin 1984, pp. 31–63; Benor 1993; Dossey 1993; May and Vilenskaya 1994, pp. 1–24; Schlitz *et al.* 2003, pp. A31–A43; Schmidt *et al.* 2004, pp. 235–47). The goal of these experiments has been to see whether an individual's intentions can produce a measurable response in a distant living system. The best experiments have employed rigorously controlled designs that rule out all known conventional sources of influence, including environmental factors, physical manipulations, suggestion and expectancy (Schlitz *et al.* 2003).

This relatively small but compelling body of experimental literature supports the DHI effect in organisms ranging from bacteria (Nash 1982, pp. 374–7) to laboratory animals (Snel *et al.* 1995, pp. 251–7) to human patients in randomized clinical trials (Byrd 1988, pp. 826–9; Sicher *et al.* 1998, pp. 356–63). As of 1992, at least 131 controlled DHI studies had been published, of which 56 found a statistically significant effect (Benor 1993). More recent reviews of subsets of these experiments continue to show positive trends (Astin *et al.* 2000, pp. 903–10; Schmidt *et al.* 2004, pp. 235–47). We will review a few of these experiments to illustrate the research and its relevance to assessing the plausibility that there may be some non-sensory dimension to spiritual healing.

Numerous studies have addressed the question of whether physiological measures – specifically autonomic nervous system activity in humans – might be susceptible to distant intentions. In the majority of these experiments, electrodermal activity (EDA) was used as the physiological measure. EDA provides a sensitive, non-invasive measure of the degree of activation in the autonomic nervous system.

Beginning in the 1970s, William Braud and I conducted a series of experiments in which skin conductance was measured in the target person (a 'receiver'), while in an isolated, distant room a 'sender' attempted to interact with him or her by means of calming or activating thoughts, images or intentions (Braud and Schlitz 1983, pp. 95–119; Schlitz and Braud 1997; Schlitz and LaBerge 1997, pp. 185–96). In these studies, the sender's intentions were not necessarily aimed towards distant healing, but the experimental task was consistent with a distant mental influence as proposed by DHI.

In 2004, psychologist Stefan Schmidt and his colleagues from the University of Freiburg Hospital, Germany, published a meta-analysis of these EDA-based experiments in the *British Journal of Psychology* (Schmidt *et al.* 2004). Schmidt's team found forty experiments conducted between 1977 and 2000. Overall the results were in favour of replicable DHI-like interactions ($p < 0.001$, Cohen's d-weighted effect size d = 0.11). The possibility of inflated statistical results due to selective reporting practices was investigated, and no such bias found. In addition, no significant relationship was found between experimental methods and the resulting outcomes, so the results were not explicable as design flaws.

In a second set of EDA-based experiments focusing on an effect conceptually similar to distant intention, namely 'the sense of being stared at', albeit over closed circuit television to avoid sensory interactions, Schmidt's team found fifteen experiments conducted between 1989 and 1998. The meta-analysis again found a significant overall effect ($p = 0.01$, Cohen's d = 0.13), no evidence of selective reporting biases, and no relationship between study quality and outcome.

With decades of repeatable, statistically significant findings reported from different laboratories, confidence is increasing that DHI effects are real. The absolute magnitude of the effects observed in the laboratory is small, but this is true for many other medically relevant effects.

For example, a major clinical study on the use of aspirin to prevent second heart attacks was stopped early because researchers decided it was unethical to withhold the drug from the control group given its observed positive effects. The effect size for the aspirin effect was 0.03, nearly four times smaller than the equivalent distant intention effect size of 0.11 (Schlitz and Braud 1997).

A recent experiment attempted to build a bridge between basic science investigations of distant healing using healthy volunteers and clinical studies on distant healing under conditions of genuine need (Radin *et al.* in press). The study investigated what would happen when the powerful motivations associated with clinical trials of DHI were combined with the controlled context and objective measures offered by laboratory protocols. It also explored the role of training in potentially modulating DHI effects. In the 'trained group', the sender of distant healing (the healthy partner) attended a day-long training programme involving discussion and practice of a secular DHI technique based on the Tibetan Buddhism practice of Tonglen meditation, Judeo-Christian forms of meditation and therapeutic touch.

After attending the training session and practising the DHI meditation daily for three months, each healthy partner and his or her spouse or friend who was undergoing treatment for cancer were tested in the laboratory. In a wait-group condition, the couple was tested before the healthy partner attended the training. A third control group condition consisted of healthy couples who received no training. The results of this experiment showed that the overall effect size for the motivated condition was 0.74, nearly seven times larger than the earlier DHI meta-analytic estimate of 0.11, and over twenty-four times larger than the aspirin study mentioned above. This suggests that distant healing practised with very high motivation and training may be far more robust than previously observed in laboratory studies.

CLINICAL STUDIES OF DISTANT HEALING

Although there appears to be evidence to support proof for the hypothesis that the intentions of one person have a measurable effect on the biology of another living system, we are still left with the question: does DHI have clinical relevance? Can focused intention affect the course of healing within real patient populations? To date, only a small number of scientific studies have directly addressed this important question. So far, these clinical studies provide conflicting evidence that DHI can improve medically relevant outcomes in people suffering from conditions including arthritis, cardiac problems, hernia surgery and AIDS. Interpretation of these clinical studies is complicated by a lack of homogeneity in patient populations, a lack of control and documentation of current medications, a lack of consistency in healer background and intervention (Sicher *et al.* 1998), and uncertainty about the role of patient expectancies and belief in DHI outcomes.

However, this is not to say that there is no evidence. The majority of randomized, double-blind investigations to date support the clinical efficacy of DHI (Schlitz and Lewis 1996, pp. 29–33; Roberts *et al.* 2000). In a systematic review published in the *Annals of Internal Medicine* (2000), John Astin and colleagues found that 57 per cent (thirteen out of twenty-three) of the published randomized, controlled clinical trials (RCTs) on DHI showed a positive treatment effect in a wide range of human populations, including both genders and a wide range of ages and ethnicities.

After the systematic review by Astin *et al.* was completed, an additional three DHI RCTs have been published; none has found significant evidence for a DHI effect (Schlitz 2007). In the first, an NIH-funded clinical trial initiated by Elisabeth Targ and others at California Pacific Medical Center (later completed by John Astin), distant prayer had no effect on outcomes for AIDS patients. However, there was a surprising outcome. The treated patients correctly guessed that they were assigned to the treatment group to a highly statistically significant degree, unlike the control patients, who guessed at chance. This suggests that the treated patients accurately sensed the healers' distant intentions, but those perceptions did not correlate with medically relevant outcomes. This finding is consistent with laboratory DHI studies, which also indicate that one person's intentions can influence the nervous system of a distant person, without implying a healing effect.

The second DHI study was conducted under the direction of cardiologist Mitchell Krucoff of Duke University Medical Center. Earlier in his career, Dr Krucoff was a volunteer in a spiritually based hospital in an ashram in rural India. There he observed that despite sometimes primitive facilities (it was the only place he had ever seen bare feet in an operating room) and poor prognoses, patients appeared relaxed and calm and filled with a sense of well-being. He wondered what created the 'healing space' he had experienced. Could the same atmosphere in the ashram's hospital be translated into a state-of-the-art hospital in the United States, and would the combination of modern medical care and attention to spiritual well-being help patients more than standard medical care alone?

To test these questions, Krucoff conducted a pilot project on 150 cardiology patients scheduled for angioplasty at the Durham Veterans Affairs Medical Center from April 1997 to April 1998. Before the procedure, each patient was randomly assigned either to standard care or to an intervention involving guided imagery, stress relaxation and healing touch, which were all performed at patients' bedsides, or to intercessory prayer, which was distributed among prayer groups including Buddhists, Roman Catholics, Moravians, Jews, Baptists and the Unity School of Christianity. The results showed that all of the interventions were helpful, and patients in the prayer group did the best (Krucoff *et al.* 2001, pp. 760–7). However, a larger and more recent follow-up study involving 748 cardiac patients (Krucoff *et al.* 2005, pp. 211–17) found no overall result on the primary study outcome. A surprisingly strong effect was observed in one condition in which a group of people were assigned to pray for those undertaking the prayer. This potential additive or 'booster' effect leaves researchers intrigued despite the failure of the primary outcome to support the DHI hypothesis.

In the third recent clinical study involving cardiac patients, conducted by Herbert Benson and his colleagues (Benson *et al.* 2006, pp. 934–42) at Harvard Medical School, a group who received intercessory prayer without knowing that they were in the treatment group showed no improvement. But the group who did know that they were the object of distant prayer showed results that were significantly worse than the control group. This new experimental condition, which combines expectation plus DHI, had not been studied before, and it implies that, under some conditions, knowledge of receiving prayer may have a detrimental effect. Some researchers speculate that this might have occurred because patients with such knowledge may have feared that they were receiving prayer because their health had a particularly poor prognosis.

Based on all clinical trials conducted so far, we are left with more questions than answers. Should we conclude that DHI does not influence healing based on recent experiments that failed to show an effect? Or should the weight of all published clinical and experimental studies influence our decision in a more positive direction? Should we conclude from the Harvard study that knowing someone is praying for us might cause harm? Does it make sense that DHI can be effective independent of any personal relationship between the person who prays and the person who is prayed for?

Researchers are faced with these and other challenges in designing and establishing scientific protocols to objectively measure whether prayer or intention may help a particular medical problem. Some of the most significant and still unresolved experimental questions include what type of prayer to use, how often to pray, how to describe what healers did so that others may reproduce the results and how to match the belief systems of the patient with those of the healer. Investigators also face sociological constraints from some scientists and some theists who do not want this research to take place at all. The former assert that prayer is non-scientific, and the latter maintain that testing prayer is blasphemous.

None of the clinical trials conducted so far has made use of what scientists call 'ecological validity'. This means the trials were not designed to model what happens in real life, where people often know the person for whom they are praying and with whom they have a meaningful relationship. In the Harvard study, for example, prayer groups were instructed for the sake of standardization to use a pre-scripted prayer that was different from prayers used in their normal practice. So the Harvard experiment did not really test what the healers claimed works for them. In addition, in most of the clinical studies, the investigators were tightly focused on medical outcomes, and hardly any attention was paid to the inner experiences of the healers and the patients.

APPLYING AN INTEGRAL APPROACH TO SPIRITUALITY AND HEALTH

Whether a person is dealing with heart disease, cancer, an immune disorder or some type of stress related condition, there is a place for an integral approach that embraces the search for meaning and purpose that is reflected in spirituality. Medicine has emphasized the objective aspects of care, such as: What are the best forms of diagnosis? Which medications are best? Is surgery needed? What is the nature of the scientific evidence for a particular cure with a particular disease? And yet, it is abundantly clear that it is often more than just the physical that needs to be addressed. Indeed, the experience of illness involves a heartfelt search for meaning, in which all the dimensions of our being are called upon to grow and change (Dossey 2007).

The integral perspective calls for an expanded view of the person. Each of us is composed of biological, phenomenological, cultural and transpersonal dimensions, which can come together in meaningful synergy in the context of healthcare. There is data to support the efficacy from all these domains. Any disease can be seen from a variety of perspectives. Diabetes, for example, can be treated strictly as a biological condition. In order to understand the disease fully, it is important to take into consideration the psychology of the patient (what does the disease mean to the person in terms of their identity, their sense of purpose and locus of control in their lives?), cultural dimensions (what types of food does the patient eat, how do they understand their condition within a cultural framework?), and socio-economic dimensions which impact on compliance as well as access to the resources needed for the patient to gain and maintain optimal health, as well as the spiritual and cosmological framework in which the person is holding their life.

Central to a spiritual calling, the integral perspective calls on us to touch base with our own inner experience. Healthcare for the twenty-first century must include little practices to assist us find our centre, to encourage meditation and deep listening to sources of inspiration and simply taking time to smell the roses. We need to feed our bodies, souls and psyches, giving ourselves resources to deal effectively with the many complex issues, emotions and interactions that occur in the course of health and healing. More and more studies are showing that this is helpful. Through various means, ranging from art therapy to guided imagery, writing a journal and prayer, we help create a place for ourselves to explore the meaning of health and illness, and perhaps to discover new pathways to healing.

Ultimately, an integral perspective requires a deep examination of our core assumptions about reality and our place in it. Standard science holds that objective truth is arrived at through discovery of causal laws of the natural world that exist independently for all time, and for all human beings. When it comes to the human condition, an integral perspective suggests that so-called objectivity may need to be fundamentally transformed. In fact, no science and no medicine is possible independent of consciousness and the awareness that we bring to our life experiences.

INTEGRAL TRANSFORMATION

As we open ourselves to pain and suffering, as well as joy and human flourishing, we begin to see these experiences as catalysts for transformation – of ourselves, our families, broader society, the institutions that serve us and ultimately of our relationship to the sacredness of life. Holding this view of transformation can liberate suffering into a vehicle for healing. We are meaning-making creatures. We can choose how to ascribe meaning to any aspect of our experience, and to help others in this search to make sense of what they are coping with in their treatment.

Ultimately, an integral healing philosophy is a call to action for health professionals and patients alike. Medicine is in trouble. Each of us carries the responsibility to help craft a new, more fitting model. As Roger Walsh in his article 'The Practices of Essential Spirituality' (2005, pp. 294–303), writes so beautifully, 'our world is in grave trouble, we all know this. Our world is in grave, grave trouble. But our world also rests in good hands, because, actually, it rests in yours.' Simply by taking the time to consider an integral perspective, you serve as a hospice worker for a dying paradigm. In so doing, you must be gentle with yourself, with others, and with a system of medicine that is struggling with its very existence. Change can be hard. But it is also revitalizing and ultimately transformative.

Relating spiritual healing and science: some critical reflections

David Leech

In the opening chapter of this volume Fraser Watts advocates an approach to understanding spiritual healing in which both theological and scientific perspectives play a role. He claims that spiritual healing can become intelligible if current scientific assumptions are broadened sufficiently, though he does not suggest that even such a broadened scientific account of healing will be complete and says that there will always be a place for a theological account of spiritual healing alongside a scientific one.

This position, which I shall call (3), is implicitly contrasted with two alternative views: (1) the 'reductionist' position that what appears to be spiritual healing can be explained completely in terms of currently understood scientific processes and requires no additional assumptions; and (2) the view that spiritual healing defies any scientific explanation and can only be understood in supernatural terms. The first, appealing to the authority of current science, infers that spiritual healing in a strong sense does not actually occur and seeks to accommodate to science by demythologizing religious accounts of spiritual healing or reinterpreting them psychosomatically. The second defends a traditional strong account of spiritual healing as actually occurring, without attempting to accommodate to current science.

Watts' position presupposes the accumulation of inconvenient facts that defy incorporation within current science. That leads him to call for an 'emancipated' version of science, and he seeks to defend a strong account of spiritual healing while accommodating to such a projected future science. As Watts notes, calling for an 'emancipated' or enlarged version of the current paradigm implies a readiness to expand science to account for currently highly controversial phenomena such as biopsychokinesis (the evidence for which is reviewed in this volume by Marilyn Schlitz, in Chapter 9), should they prove to be well attested and inexplicable within current interpretative frameworks.

For the purposes of this chapter let us call approaches (1), (2) and (3) the theologically liberal, conservative and liberal-conservative approaches to relating spiritual healing and science.[1] In what follows I will offer some critical reflections on relating spiritual healing and science with a particular focus on this third minority 'liberal-conservative' contribution to the conversation.[2] My primary interest here is not in evaluating the relative merits or demerits of this third approach[3] but in suggesting that it can be a useful vantage point for throwing into relief certain issues concerning how to relate spiritual healing and science which are generally not made thematic. Reflecting critically on this theological position both brings to light difficulties proper to this position and exposes latent presuppositions (and difficulties) of the liberal and conservative positions concerning how to relate spiritual healing and science.

In what follows I suggest that although the liberal-conservative approach might seem to offer prima facie support for something like a traditional (literal) theological understanding of spiritual healing (its apparent conservative moment), this support is probably best regarded as ambiguous. This is for two principle reasons: firstly, because the purported parapsychological findings about spiritual healing, even were one to assume that they were genuine, seem to suggest that spiritual healing phenomena take place in various religious and non-religious traditions/contexts, and therefore cannot count as evidence for any particular religious tradition (for example Christianity or Hinduism). Secondly, parapsychology standardly strives to be methodologically naturalist, therefore the bare findings (if they are such) unembellished by additional extra-scientific premises cannot be assumed to count as evidence for religious supernaturalism. An enlarged science probably should only be regarded as compatible with something like a traditional

---

[1] I label the third approach 'liberal-conservative' because in its effort to defend something like a strong account of spiritual healing it can be seen as having a conservative moment, while in its effort to accommodate to a future enlarged science (and in its tendency to avoid appeals to special divine action) it can be seen as having liberal moments. 'Liberal', 'conservative' and 'liberal-conservative' are of course far from ideal as labels for these approaches since they also have other theological connotations; in what follows it should be understood that I am using these terms in the more restricted senses stipulated above.

[2] For other proponents of this type of theological approach see, for example Griffin (1988), Benz (1983).

[3] The assumption by proponents of a liberal-conservative approach of the genuineness of parapsychological phenomena is of course deeply controversial. For the present purposes this difficulty can be bracketed aside since the issues discussed in this chapter are chiefly concerned with generic issues about how to relate spiritual healing and science and can (and should) fruitfully be discussed irrespective of claims about whether spiritual healing actually occurs in the strong sense.

religious/theological understanding of spiritual healing in a carefully qualified sense, namely, as not ruling out the reality of (parapsychological) healing processes, as in the case of the liberal approach, but granting that these may be purely natural phenomena (in a suitably expanded but not supernaturalistic sense of 'natural') and then interpreting them as an aspect of God's general providence, just as, for example, natural selection can be so interpreted. Any stronger theological claim than this implying that the purported evidence for spiritual healing pointed to the reality of special divine action or something similar would require the addition of further extra-scientific (such as, in this case, extra-parapsychological) premises.

BENZ: A LIBERAL-CONSERVATIVE APPROACH

I will start by taking the Marburg theologian Ernst Benz' reflections on how to relate spiritual healing and an enlarged science in the above defined sense as a jumping-off point for a broader consideration of issues surrounding the question of how to relate the two. Benz, unusual among theologians, recognized parapsychology as a legitimate science investigating phenomena which fell outside the explanatory frameworks of contemporary physics, biology and psychology, and anticipated that its data would one day become part of the conventional scientific outlook. As such he regarded it (and by extension a future enlarged science) as a possible dialogue partner for theology, even where in practice the dialogue has been very sporadic.

Benz was of the opinion that Christian theology could learn from parapsychology and vice versa. In his posthumously published *Parapsychologie und Religion* (1983), Benz claims that in the New Testament and throughout the history of the Christian Church one finds numerous accounts of various experiences and phenomena which bear immediate analogies to phenomena studied by parapsychology. According to Benz, the latter discipline can enable Christianity to return to a more robust traditional understanding of the charisms (including the gift of healing) which it prematurely abandoned in early modernity out of a mistaken awe for the new mechanistic science and the philosophies to which it gave rise. Conversely, Benz considered that parapsychology could perhaps learn from the holistic Christian doctrine of the person that a more holistic explanation of parapsychological processes may prove more adequate than some of the reductionistic theories proffered by current parapsychologists (Benz 1983, pp. 42–4). Benz regrets the historical reduction of the numerous charisms in Western Christianity to those chiefly making use of ordinary cognitive processes, namely, the gifts of preaching and interpretation. He traces the cause of this development to the acceptance by enlightened scholars of the gospels and of church history, such as Reimarus and Strauss, of a 'scientific' attitude that nothing can exist which contradicts the physical laws as established by the contemporary materialists. This led them, in his view, to recategorize all biblically recorded events that seemed to be inconsistent with the physical laws thus defined by their contemporaries as myth, that is, as stories which contain or communicate important truth but which are not literally true. In Benz's opinion, this subsequently became *the* dogma of liberal theological and biblical criticism, that charisms such as the gift of healing were myths, and a myth, although communicating truth, does not record a literal event but is ultimately a creation of the human imagination. Benz regards Strauss' interpretation of charisms as myths as a symptom of his intellectual captivation with the positivist, materialist assumptions of his time, and Bultmann's demythologization programme (and its successors) as the contemporary form of this approach.

According to Benz, the theologians' preoccupation with accommodating themselves to the assumptions of a narrow materialism was mistaken in the first place and is now anachronistic. According to him, while contemporary natural scientists (especially physicists) were showing an ever greater degree of openness to a more 'emancipated' ontology and increasingly abandoning a narrow physicalism, theologians were running scared of the latter and demythologizing the charisms in the belief that this was the only intellectually respectable option.

It is firstly to be noted that Benz's liberal-conservative approach represents a sort of middle way between typically conservative and liberal theological approaches. On the one hand, in his belief that a (purported) science, in this instance parapsychology, ought to be influenced by Christian theology – not just at the problem-setting level but also at the level of theory construction and interpretation – and in his defence of what he sees as the traditional literal reading of the healing charisms against a demythologizing approach, his position has conservative moments and partially overlaps with the position of more conservative Christian thinkers like Alvin Plantinga. On the other hand, in his stress on Christian theology's ability to learn from and seek integration with parapsychology/enlarged science, his position has liberal moments and overlaps with much standard liberal engagement in the conversation between theology and secular culture.

However, although Benz' 'middle way' would appear to have something appealing to a certain theological sensibility in avoiding the Scylla of conservative anti-scientism/religious expansionism[4] and the Charybdis of excessive liberal *Anpassung* or resort to unsatisfactory NOMA-like positions, it is not clear (even setting aside the issue of the genuineness of the parapsychological data) that it can solve as many theological difficulties as it may hope to do. Benz' position can be criticized on at least the following two grounds: firstly – and this is an objection to religious expansionism in general – even were the parapsychological findings to be genuine, it is not clear that Christian theological assumptions about the nature of spiritual healing phenomena should be allowed to dictate, or even suggest, what sort of explanations – natural or supernatural – parapsychologists should adopt. It is argued by some more conservative theological voices (see Sardar 1989; Plantinga 1996; Marsden 1997) that the only form of science we can have is a worldview-partisan one. However, as Stenmark has pointed out, this appears to lead to the view that we should have a proliferation of sciences – naturalist, theistic, feminist, left-wing, etc. – rather than one common science, with no obvious and uncontentious criteria for choosing between the worldviews which should inform science (2004). This does not seem to be a desirable direction, but since this religious expansionist position is not always endorsed by sympathizers of the liberal-conservative position, I will not consider it further here. Secondly, an emancipated science incorporating the purported data of parapsychology cannot be construed as directly supporting the claims of any specific religious tradition, since the purported parapsychological findings relating to spiritual healing point if anything to the universality or near universality of these phenomena (they are found not only in a variety of very different religious contexts but also in New Age and secular contexts). The fact that no one religious tradition appears to have a monopoly on spiritual healing phenomena deprives them of their traditional role in witnessing as signs to the truth of one tradition in particular (a role they traditionally served in Christianity for example).[5] Indeed,

---

[4] I borrow the term 'religious expansionism' from Mikael Stenmark, who defines it as the view that the idea of a religiously neutral science must be rejected and it ought instead to be accepted that 'worldviews (religions or ideologies) always shape science and that therefore the only form of science we reasonably can have is a worldview-partisan science [in which] religion shapes science' (Stenmark 2004, pp. 183–4).

[5] Documented cases of purported spiritual healing outside the Christian context (the cases could easily be multiplied) include, for example, claims of supernatural healing events by the South Indian guru and religious leader Sai Baba and non-religiously affiliated British healer Matthew Manning.

not only do spiritual healing phenomena fail to support specific religious traditions, they need not be construed as evidence for supernaturalism in general, since the ideas of paranormal processes and supernaturalism are not logically related. As a matter of fact many parapsychologists assume at least methodological (and a significant proportion even metaphysical) naturalism; claims about parapsychological phenomena being evidence of the *super*natural therefore require the addition of some extra-scientific premises.

Benz is thus only in a qualified sense correct in assuming that the findings of parapsychology can support a more traditional understanding of charisms and contemporary spiritual healing. Certainly, they legitimize a stronger account of healing phenomena than the demythologizing one. In turning to parapsychology, however, Benz could arguably be construed as supposing the Enlightenment presuppositions he ostensibly rejects, since the latter discipline, as a would-be respectable contemporary science, characteristically seeks to find *natural* explanations for the phenomena (including spiritual healing) which it investigates, and this can be seen as having important implications for liberal-conservatives who attempt to integrate theology and enlarged science.

PLANTINGA: A CONSERVATIVE APPROACH

To better appreciate what sort of issues are at stake here with the liberal-conservative move (and to what degree it might be construed as defending a weaker account of spiritual healing than it intends to), let us turn by contrast to the work of Alvin Plantinga who represents a more conservative theological position regarding the relationship between religion and science. Plantinga's *Warranted Christian Belief* (2000), which examines germane issues but with quite a different set of theological assumptions, also implicitly agrees with Benz that the difficulties set in with the Enlightenment project of historical biblical criticism, which relies on reason alone and in principle brackets any theological presuppositions in order to proceed 'scientifically' (Plantinga 2000, p. 390). Similarly to Benz, Plantinga sets out to expose the liberal presuppositions of historical biblical criticism and subject them to critique. As he notes, one basic principle of this form of Enlightenment biblical criticism is the 'principle of analogy' which supposes that historical knowledge is only a possibility because all events are basically similar, so that the same natural laws that operate now also operated in first-century Palestine (Collins 1990, cited in Plantinga 2000, p. 391).

As Plantinga points out, aside from assuming that there are such things as natural laws – not an uncontroversial thesis in contemporary discussions – the main intention of this methodological principle seems to *rule out direct divine action in the world* (Plantinga 2000, p. 393). Plantinga traces this assumption through the work of Strauss, Bultmann and more contemporary theologians such as John Macquarrie.

> The way of understanding miracles that appeals to breaks in the natural order and to supernatural interventions belongs to the mythological outlook and cannot commend itself in a post-mythological climate of thought . . .
>
> The traditional conception of miracle is irreconcilable with our modern understanding of both science and history. Science proceeds on the assumption that whatever events occur in the world can be accounted for in terms of other events that also belong within the world; and if on some occasions we are unable to give a complete account of some happening . . . the scientific conviction is that further research will bring to light further factors in the situation, but factors that will turn out to be just as immanent and this-worldly as those already known. (Macquarrie 1977, cited Plantinga 2000, p. 394)

But, unlike Benz, Plantinga criticizes historical biblical criticism in order to establish the legitimacy of still believing in the possibility of special divine action. He argues that theologians who adopt the Enlightenment presuppositions are precluding the possibility of miracles (including healing miracles) and special divine action generally, but according to him this exclusion has no warrant. As he ironically observes, such theologians generally simply assume that God will not act specially in the world.

> The . . . [assumption behind historical biblical criticism] is that there is a certain way in which things ordinarily go; there are certain regularities, whether or not due to natural law, and God can be counted on to act in such a way as not to abrogate those regularities. Of course God *could*, if he chose, abrogate those regularities (after all, even those natural laws, if there are any, are his creatures); but we can be sure, somehow, that he will not. (Plantinga 2000, p. 395)

Against this pervasive assumption that contemporary persons 'simply can't help' accepting a worldview that excludes special divine action,[6] Plantinga alludes to the fact that we are not *forced* to assume that the world as revealed to us by the mainstream natural sciences exhausts the real. Most people in the world presently *don't* believe this anyway; and

---

[6] Plantinga cites Bultmann's celebrated remark 'it is impossible to use electrical light and the wireless and to avail ourselves of modern medical and surgical discoveries, and at the same time to believe in the New Testament world of spirits and miracles' as a characteristic expression of this attitude (Bultmann 1961, p. 5, cited in Plantinga 2000, p. 403).

even if (as Plantinga suggests) the real point of this presupposition is that everybody *in the know* must assume this, it is not clear who belongs to this group. If the point is that educated Westerners can't believe anything other than this, this is also not true (Plantinga 2000, p. 404).[7]

Plantinga further points out that it is not an argument to say that the practice of science assumes the prior rejection of the idea of miracles or special divine action, since when actually spelled out it amounts to a very dubious reasoning,

If X were true, it would be inconvenient for science; therefore, X is false. (Plantinga 2000, p. 406)

He notes that it is not necessary for the religious person to accept a form of deism rather than classical theism in order to accept or do science. One only needs to assume that God is not 'often or usually' acting specially in the world in order to do science, because the latter does presuppose a certain amount of predictability about the world; provided that God is not constantly acting specially, the practice of science is not jeopardized.

The important point here is that although Plantinga agrees with Benz' historical thesis about modern biblical criticism assuming narrowly materialist presuppositions, he does not appeal to parapsychology but rather is ready to appeal traditionally to the special action of the Holy Spirit in effecting miracles, including healing miracles. In other words, he would be happy to talk about *spiritual* healing in a strict etymological sense (i.e., as proceeding from the (Holy) Spirit), and supplies arguments for why this is not a ridiculous thing to do, even today. This is a straightforward conservative defence of classical supernaturalism and the possibility of special divine action.

By contrast, Benz appeals to parapsychology as *scientific evidence* for healing 'miracles', employing a different strategy to Plantinga in order to defend the possibility of spiritual healing in some non-demythologized (or similar) sense. However, parapsychology, in its efforts to find natural explanations for the phenomena it studies, characteristically imports many of the same presuppositions that Benz and Plantinga agree in rejecting, which means that Benz cannot infer from the bare parapsychological evidence for genuine spiritual healing that God acts either

---

[7] 'Many physicists and engineers, for example, understand "electrical light and the wireless" vastly better than Bultmann or his contemporary followers, but nonetheless hold precisely those New Testament beliefs Bultmann thinks incompatible with using electric lights and radios' (Plantinga 2000, p. 405).

generally or specially in the world. The Enlightenment presupposition that we should bracket aside beliefs which arise from faith and only assume those things on which general agreement can be reached implies that any form of study striving to be scientific should adopt methodological naturalism. However, if parapsychology devises exclusively natural explanations for these phenomena, this could be construed as rendering superfluous explanations of spiritual healing which appeal to supernatural factors.

MESMER: A NATURALISTIC APPROACH

Because parapsychology is often assumed by sympathizers and critics alike to provide evidence (genuine or otherwise) for supernaturalism, it is as well to be clear about the type of claims parapsychology makes about the phenomena it studies. Modern parapsychological research has from its beginnings with the German physician and astrologist Franz Mesmer (1734–1815) in the eighteenth century tended to explain anomalous healing phenomena in purely naturalistic terms and avoided reference to transcendent agency in principle.[8] The phenomenon of mesmerism or 'animal magnetism' – namely, hypnotism or suggestion – was discovered by Mesmer in 1775 and enjoyed much public attention even into the 1840s. Mesmer drew his patients into a somnambulistic state through his technique of 'magnetizing', claiming that this method had profound healing effects. During these sessions various forms of extrasensory perception such as clairvoyance and thought transference were also reported to have occurred.

Healing and so-called psi phenomena had been reported earlier in European history. However, the significance of Mesmer is that for the first time an attempt was made to investigate such psi phenomena experimentally. Mesmer understood himself as a scientist in the service of Enlightenment principles (Kropf 1999, p. 19). On the basis of his experimental work he built up what he regarded as natural scientific theories to explain the phenomena with which he became associated. During the years 1774–8, for example, Mesmer entered into controversy with the exorcist Johann Joseph Gassner, and his theories were received as an enlightened alternative to the traditional Christian notion of exorcism. He refused to describe the phenomena as miraculous or in terms of spirits,

[8] In what follows I follow Andrea Kropf's account of the development of parapsychology in Europe (1999, p. 20).

but offered physical/physiological explanations in terms of hyperaesthesia of the sense organs or in terms of his fluid theory.[9]

The important point here is that Mesmer's naturalistic explanations represented a rupture with theology. Previous to this, it had fallen to the Church to explain healing phenomena (mental and physical) in terms of special acts of God's grace or demon possession.[10] With Mesmer, an enlightened attempt was made to explain such phenomena without recourse to theological categories. A brief perusal of the literature shows that something like this set of naturalistic assumptions also informs the later attempts of Charles Richet (1850–1935; originator of the 'ectoplasm' theory), Johann Zöllner (1834–82) and William Crookes (1832–1919) to investigate spiritualistic phenomena, and anticipates the professionalization of parapsychology through J. B. Rhine's (1895–1980) experiments in Duke University in the United States of America from the 1930s onwards.

This naturalistic approach in parapsychology remains dominant today. Contemporary parapsychologists typically prefer to explain healing and other phenomena they study either in terms of as yet unknown physical mechanisms or in terms of properties of natural (evolved) human minds.[11] If we survey in a cursory way the views of many modern parapsychologists it is evident that a turn from explanations appealing to a transcendent source to purely naturalistic explanations has largely become the norm. Kornwachs, for example, says the following of modern parapsychology:

In my view the decisive factor in the development of a methodically practiced parapsychology resides in the interdisciplinary attempt to develop a theory of the phenomena in question which, *avoiding any appeal to transcendent explanations*, seeks to deduce testable predictions on the basis of physicalist models, and to render these falsifiable through controlled test conditions in the laboratory. (in Kropf 1999, p. 28, my italics)

In this sense Mesmerism can be regarded as the genuine forerunner of the modern discipline of parapsychology.[12] An important upshot of this is

---

[9] According to the latter theory, invisible fluids from outside the body stood in a close relation with the person's nervous system and exercised an effect on it.

[10] Admittedly the Church had always had a challenger in the form of magical traditions, but Mesmer can be taken as representing the first attempt by modern science (or an unorthodox offshoot thereof) to wrest these phenomena from the Church and explain them in natural categories.

[11] See, for example, a recent (popularizing) attempt to offer an account of a non-supernaturalist explanation of the mechanism of spiritual healing in terms of human minds by Targ and Katra (1999).

[12] The 'Mesmerist' approach has not of course always had an explanatory monopoly – another forerunner of modern parapsychology was scientific spiritualism, which often imported straightforwardly supernaturalist presuppositions into the theory-building of some

that a potential future enlarged science which accounted amongst other things for parapsychological phenomena would not be able to supply the liberal-conservative approach to spiritual healing with any direct evidence for supernatural agency.

Since most of the best contemporary theory-building of the parapsychologists characteristically makes no reference to transcendent agency, it is not immediately obvious what import a future enlarged science incorporating and explaining parapsychological healing phenomena naturalistically would have for theology. As we have seen, it appears that any liberal-conservative attempt to relate theology and an enlarged science should probably accept the following two premises:

1 Parapsychology (like any form of study with pretensions to scientific status) is characteristically naturalizing: it explains naturally what has traditionally been explained supernaturally.

2 The parapsychological evidence for genuine healing (assuming for the sake of argument that it is genuine) suggests that healing phenomena are found near universally, both across religious traditions and also in secular contexts. They lend no special support to one religious tradition any more than another.

If these two premises are granted, it would seem that any simple claim that religious healing claims would gain strength if parapsychological healing phenomena really occurred is – in this simple form – unsupported.

However, there is a more modest sense in which the parapsychological phenomena, if genuine, might support some traditional religious claims about spiritual healing. It could of course be argued by proponents of a liberal-conservative approach against more classically liberal theological positions that an enlarged science is *indirectly* useful to (Christian) theology in justifying a robust rather than watered down (and thus verging on vacuous) notion of spiritual healing. However, the counter-objection could come that this does not go so far as making the stronger claim that

---

parapsychologists. Nevertheless, the Mesmer tradition of theory-building within modern parapsychology seems to have now largely displaced the spiritualism-influenced one, and there are presently a considerably larger number of parapsychologists who explain almost all parapsychological phenomena in terms of so-called superpsi and psychokinesis, that is in purely naturalistic (although presupposing an enlarged sense of 'natural') terms.

the broadening of contemporary science to include such phenomena would in any sense provide compelling evidence for the truth of a religious interpretation of spiritual healing. An enlarged science would not necessarily strengthen this view – for example the Christian theist's claim that transcendent agency is at work in such healing. The proponent of a liberal-conservative position could, however, perhaps make the weaker, but nevertheless still significant, claim that an enlarged science, by undermining a narrow sort of materialism, shows that the more literal theist interpretation of spiritual healing (and other phenomena which escape current scientific explanation) is not straightforwardly false, as is often assumed by the religious liberal and the non-religious person. H. H. Price, one of the most eminent philosophers of the last century to have taken a sympathetic interest in the data of parapsychology, makes a strong case for this weak claim:

> The support which psychical research gives to the religious outlook is only indirect. Psychical research does [however] remove, or at any rate it undermines, the greatest *obstacle* to religious belief. That obstacle, at least in these days, is nothing more nor less than the Materialistic conception of human nature, which is accepted as a matter of course by a large majority of Western educated people. So long as this conception prevails and determines our whole outlook on human experience, the claims of religious people are simply not taken seriously ... But if there are empirical facts which show that there is something seriously wrong with the Materialistic conception of human nature, and if these facts come to be widely known (which they are not at present), the situation is likely to alter a good deal. The claims which religious people make will at least get a hearing. *It will not have been shown that they are true, but at least it will have been shown that they are not demonstrably false, as they are widely assumed to be at present.* (in Dilley 1995, pp. 13–14, my italics)

This might be regarded as describing the proper extent of an enlarged science's potential attractiveness to theology, were it eventually to gain the kind of recognition the liberal-conservative anticipates. It would not be able to provide direct evidence for a religious interpretation of spiritual healing, but it could be indirectly helpful to the theologian in removing what Price calls the greatest obstacle to a robust notion of spiritual healing – a narrow materialism – and make sure that it 'gets a hearing'. It could do no more, but (some might want to add) also no less, than this. In this sense – Benz (liberal-conservative) and Plantinga (conservative) could agree here – it would undermine the rationale for demythologizing scriptural accounts of healing, and for the effective dismissal, whether by liberal theologians of the Straussian persuasion, or by many non-believers, of past and contemporary cases of spiritual healing.

CONCLUSION

In conclusion, one possibility for the liberal-conservative who wishes to integrate his or her religious position and an enlarged science in the sense we have discussed could be to acknowledge with the parapsychologists the naturalness of spiritual healing phenomena and to reinterpret it theologically as God's action on human persons through secondary causes. This would be consistent with the above-mentioned premises, and some might also see this as mitigating certain theodical difficulties. Clayton, in his contribution earlier in this volume (Chapter 3), makes the important point that although from a theological perspective there is nothing surprising about God directly intervening to heal human persons (God, being omnipotent, can do this if He wants), there is nevertheless a serious 'argument from neglect' problem, namely, why does God heal some but not others? On the more conservative assumption that spiritual healing is a case of God's special action in the world it has to be assumed that God does not choose to heal all who ask for healing, and representatives of this more conservative position (such as Plantinga) must confront the theodical problem in this form. However, on the alternative supposition that God's general providence has provided for (natural) healing mechanisms in the world which the current scientific paradigm has not yet enlarged itself to explain, it could be argued that this difficult theodicy problem is somewhat mitigated. Also, because an enlarged science would entail an expanded understanding of 'natural', an attempted integration of this sort between theology and such a projected future science could avoid the idea of healing involving a divine suspension of the laws of nature which the proponent of a liberal-conservative approach may recoil from (see, for example, Watts' contribution in Chapter 1 of this volume, but see also Plantinga's above-mentioned critique). With such an approach, appeal to an enlarged science may be seen as indirectly helpful in the ways outlined above.

The liberal-conservative might in this sense argue that emancipated science could legitimize a stronger account of spiritual healing in religious and non-religious contexts. Were the relevant phenomena to turn out to be genuine, this approach could claim that spiritual healing, whatever it is, does occur and that it is not mere illusion, malobservation or fraud.

This would leave open the possibility that a theistic, or some other supernaturalist account of what is going on might be the correct one. In the Christian case, for example, this might suggest that Christians need not demythologize their understanding of the charisms, although they may have to modify their understanding of the manner of God's healing action, namely, as happening through the Holy Spirit's indirect rather than direct action.[13] On the other hand, they might also have to grant that such a future science could not provide any sort of direct evidence for Christian beliefs about the healing work of the Holy Spirit. Parapsychologists' standard accounts of spiritual healing are generally couched in terms of the person's own psychokinetic effects on their own body, or through a combination of the extra-sensory perception (ESP) and psychokinesis (PK) of others on the person receiving healing. If parapsychology characteristically naturalizes spiritual healing in terms of ESP and PK, Christians who subscribe to a liberal-conservative approach might have to re-describe what happens in Christian healing in terms of an indirect working of the Holy Spirit through human persons exercising natural capacities.

For the reasons discussed in this chapter, appeal to an enlarged science without the further addition of extra-scientific premises cannot as such lend weight to a supernaturalist over a naturalist worldview. Should the relevant phenomena turn out to be genuine, it would presumably establish with respect to spiritual healing that 'something is going on', and, for reasons H. H. Price noted, this would ensure that a theological interpretation of what that was could at least expect to get a hearing. However, any broader claim than this – whether supernaturalist *or* metaphysically naturalist (in an enlarged sense of 'natural') – would appear to require the prior acceptance of extra-scientific assumptions, regardless of whether the science in question to which such claims appeal is the current one which we know today or a future enlarged science of the above-defined sort.

---

[13] The proponent of a liberal-conservative approach need not hold that the enlarged science and demythologizing approaches are entirely incompatible – they could, for example, hold that scripture contains *both* myths (in the Straussian sense) *and* literal reports of supernatural phenomena; for example, they may decide that the miracle of the loaves and fish is to be interpreted mythically, whereas the healing miracles of Christ are to be interpreted in a strong sense as actually having occurred.

CHAPTER 11

Concluding integration

Fraser Watts

It will be helpful to begin this final chapter by restating and developing some of the assumptions set out in the first chapter.

1 Healings can be spiritual in various senses. Spiritual healing can (a) be facilitated by spiritual practices; (b) involve spiritual aspects of the person; (c) depend on a spiritual explanation in terms of transcendent resources. These different concepts of spiritual healing are increasingly radical, in the sense of involving increasingly controversial assumptions.
2 'Spiritual' healing should always be approached within a framework that is holistic rather than dualistic and sees the spiritual as one facet of an integrated human nature. The spiritual aspects of human nature can be distinguished from the physical and psychological, but are not separate from them.
3 I assume that it will be possible to offer some kind of scientific account of spiritual healing, though it may be limited. In order to rise to the challenge of doing so, it may be necessary to draw on areas of radical science, such as parapsychology, as well as on conventional medical science. The scientific account that can be offered of spiritual healing is likely to include processes that radical science is still attempting to conceptualize and investigate, but which are not yet well understood.
4 Whatever scientific account of healing is offered will, I believe, be insufficient because a theological account will always be needed as well. That is true of all kinds of healing, 'spiritual' or otherwise. From a theological point of view, I assume that all healing is the work of God, however it is mediated. Much healing proceeds without invoking God explicitly, whereas some spiritual healing occurs in religious contexts and makes explicit use of a religious framework.

In this final chapter I will first draw threads together from the preceding chapters about a scientific approach to spiritual healing. Then I will try to put current issues about spiritual healing in broad historical context.

DOES SPIRITUAL HEALING ACTUALLY OCCUR?

There are always both outcome and process questions about any kind of therapeutic or healing activity. I will consider outcome questions first, that is, whether spiritual healing actually occurs. I am particularly concerned here with healing in the strong sense (1c above), healing that is seen as explicable only in terms of transcendent or supernatural resources.

There is little doubt that spiritual practices can at least facilitate healing, though it is an empirical question whether spiritual healing in a strong sense actually occurs. My impression is that it really does, though the supporting evidence is admittedly of poor quality. However, poor evidence for a particular phenomenon is often due to it being difficult to investigate, rather than to the phenomenon not occurring.

There is an initial problem about what criteria should be used to assess healing. Healing is not the same as cure, and does not necessarily involve cure. It can be based on a change in perceptions or attitudes of the 'ill' person or in how they are treated by society, or on a better adjustment to the illness. There are many medical conditions that cannot be cured, but for which rehabilitation is possible (Watts and Bennett 1983). Religion may have a particular interest in improved adjustment where no cure is possible, but that is not the unique preserve of religion. Health services are also, in that sense, in the business of adjustment or healing.

Some might want to suggest that all religious healing is based on adjustment rather than cure. That is, in effect, what John Pilch (2000) proposes for the healings of Jesus (see Chapter 2 in this book). However, I am not persuaded that it is necessary to go so far as to say that religious healing has no interest in cure, and has no way of bringing it about. I want to leave open the possibility that religious healing may bring about cure, while also emphasizing the important contribution that religion and spirituality can make to improved adjustment. It is at the heart of the religious mind-set to look for ways in which problems that cannot be simply eliminated can nevertheless become a source of blessing, through God's grace and growth in spirituality.

It is hard to take a balanced view of the question of whether spiritual healing in a strong sense actually occurs. There is a risk of being too gullible and accepting inconclusive evidence too easily. On the other hand, there is also a risk of being too sceptical, and dismissing suggestive evidence too quickly and dogmatically. A modernist assumption that religious cure is impossible can lead to an over-sceptical view of the available evidence. No one should be in favour of either gullibility or prejudice; what is required is an approach that steers a path between them. Science is, or should be, an open-minded investigation of all reliable, demonstrable phenomena. There is an urgent need for better investigation of alternative methods of healing that there is prima facie reason to think might be effective. If they are proved effective, modern medical science needs to be prepared to revise its assumptions in order to make sense of how they work.

My judgement in favour of the reality of spiritual healing is based partly on the anecdotal reports of spiritual healing that can be found in many traditions. However, there is also collateral evidence that needs to be weighed. For example, as Marilyn Schlitz has indicated here, there seems reasonably good evidence for biopsychokinesis – that is, control through mind and will of specific aspects of the bodily processes of others. If biopsychokinesis is a real and demonstrable phenomenon, it is not difficult to believe that spiritual healing also occurs. Hans Eysenck and Carl Sargent (1982) have also set out a helpful summary of the evidence for biopsychokinesis in *Explaining the Unexplained.* Eysenck took a very rigorous approach to evidence, so it is no little compliment when Eysenck and Sargent say that Braud's research programme on biopsychokinesis was 'a remarkable, sustained body of excellent work ... as a body of findings this remarkable research is without peer. Given that there is support for key findings within it from other experiments, it represents a formidable challenge to the sceptic' (1982, p. 119). If the evidence for biopsychokinesis is as strong as they claim, it is not difficult to believe that spiritual healing might also be efficacious.

Like others, I have mixed feelings about the use of scientific evidence in connection with spiritual healing. I detect ambivalent attitudes, and recognize them in myself. It is interesting to note two rather different attitudes that can often be found jostling alongside one another. On the one hand it is tempting to complain, on theological grounds, about the attempt to provide evidence at all. The healing work of God, one is inclined to say, is not open to human measurement. On the other hand, it is tempting to take the evidence seriously but to complain, on scientific grounds, about the poor quality of the evidence produced. There is something contradictory about these attitudes. If scientific evidence were not appropriate in principle in connection with spiritual healing, the quality of the evidence that had resulted from misplaced attempts to collect it would be irrelevant.

Though it is understandable that there should be theological reserve about 'putting God to the test' in the way that scientific evaluation of religious healing does, it is not attractive to go to the other extreme and assert that there are no detectable benefits of religious healing. It is worth noting that practitioners of secular forms of spiritual healing do not generally have the same reserve about evaluation as religious healers do. Objections to the collection of scientific evidence seem to arise from a failure to recognize that there is a place for a scientific approach to healing alongside a theological one.

Though the evidence for healing itself may be poor, the evidence for biopsychokinesis actually appears to be reasonably strong, though it is still widely dismissed. Scientific scepticism often reflects double standards. Higher standards of evidence are set for research that leads to controversial conclusions. Many of the studies that are relevant here are open to methodological criticisms, but that is true of virtually every scientific study in the human sciences. The perfect study is a mirage. Every piece of research, with hindsight, has problems that were not anticipated, and that render the research inconclusive; there is always more research to be done. However, on any particular topic, one has to make a judgement about what is probable, given the currently available evidence. My judgement, on the basis of the evidence available, is that spiritual healing is more likely than not to be a real phenomenon. Of course, that doesn't involve accepting every claim in a gullible fashion.

It is a methodological problem that spiritual healing is a somewhat unpredictable phenomenon. That creates difficulties for scientific methods that are wedded to the concept of repeatable observations. However, with chaos theory and other current scientific developments, science is beginning to grapple with the problems of studying unpredictable phenomena scientifically, and I assume that this is a methodological challenge with which the human sciences will be able to deal in due course.

BACKGROUND FACTORS THAT CONTRIBUTE TO SPIRITUAL HEALING

Let us now turn to process questions, to the task of giving some kind of scientific account of how spiritual healing might work. It is important here to make a distinction between long-term background factors that contribute to healing, and specific actions or events that occur at a particular time or place, and which may help to bring about healing.

This is a familiar kind of distinction in psychology. For example, the development of depression arises from background factors that increase vulnerability to depression, and which then interact with specific events that trigger an episode of the illness. For example, it is well established that a lack of adequate social support makes people vulnerable, and that this interacts with particular stressful events that are likely to trigger depression. It is the combination that is particularly closely associated with the onset of the illness. Lack of background social support may not lead to such a predicament, provided there is no acute stress. Equally, particular acute stresses may not lead to depression provided background social support is good. In a similar way, healing is likely to occur when there is combination of background and triggering factors. The combination is likely to be more powerful in producing spiritual healing than either alone.

The background factors that contribute to spiritual healing are probably fairly uncontroversial, in that they can be understood without resorting to either an expanded metaphysics of the human person or an expanded scientific paradigm. It also seems likely that the background factors that contribute to spiritual healing will enhance any kind of healing, including conventional medical and surgical treatment. However, my hypothesis (and it is one that lends itself to empirical investigation) is that there is a particularly strong interaction between these background factors and specific actions designed to bring about spiritual healing.

So, for example, I would predict that conventional medicine and surgery can work without any background spiritual factors, though they may be enhanced by them. In contrast, it seems likely that actions designed to bring about healing, such as the laying on of hands, will have little effect unless they occur with people who have the relevant background predisposing factors. So healing actions might only be much more effective in people of faith, whereas a broad range of medical treatments might be enhanced by faith only to a much lesser degree. The hypothesis is that background spiritual factors enhance the effectiveness of conventional treatments to some extent, but are normally essential if people are to respond to spiritual healing.

On general psychological grounds, I would expect that cognitive and social processes are likely to be the chief background factors that are relevant to spiritual healing. Again, there is a helpful analogy with depression. Cognitive factors, such as an attributional style that involves taking failures personally, make people more vulnerable to depression; social factors, such as a lack of social support, are also relevant. Similarly, there are cognitive and relational aspects of spirituality that are likely to be conducive to healing. Let us briefly consider both.

Spirituality tends to give people a cognitive framework that enables them to make sense of a broad range of experiences, and to find meaning and significance in them, which seems likely to contribute to healing. An interesting example is pain. How much pain people experience is partly dependent on the extent of tissue damage but is also very substantially affected by attitudes and frameworks of meaning (Coakley and Shelemay 2007). Spiritual practices are likely to give rise to the kind of framework of meaning that in turn will reduce pain. Though there is much more to spiritual healing than pain reduction, it provides a helpful model of how cognitive processes can contribute to spiritual healing.

Spirituality also seems likely to be associated with a sense of social support that is conducive to spiritual healing, and Paul and Hannah Gilbert in this volume provide a very helpful scientific account of how that might work. Healing also arises in the context of a community that has a shared understanding of the significance of ailments and their alleviation, as Simon Dein indicates. Though the spiritual life may include forms of community that are helpful in themselves, I suspect that how spirituality enhances the sense of being supported by others is just as relevant. If spirituality tends to increase empathy, that will in turn lead to an enhanced sense of being supported by others. Those seeking spiritual healing will often have a sense of being supported by the unseen presence or energies of the spiritual world, whether or not that is conceptualized in conventional religious terms as a relationship with God.

Next there is the question of how the psychosocial processes that are conducive to spiritual healing might be mediated at a somatic level, so that they can give rise to physical healing. My scientific hunch is that psychoneuroimmunology (PNI) is the best bet for where to look for the somatic mediation of spiritual healing. Michael Boivin and Burton Webb have provided, in Chapter 8, a helpful indication of how psychoneuroimmunology can be linked to good health. It seems quite likely that the cognitive and social processes associated with spirituality help to give rise to the patterns of immunological activity that are conducive to health.

Though there is much more detailed research to be done, I suspect that this broad outline of a scientific account of the background factors relevant to spiritual healing will stand the test of time, and will gradually be fleshed out at a greater level of scientific detail. What is also needed, and is much more challenging to provide, is some kind of scientific account of how specific healing practices, such as the laying on of hands, can trigger healing.

THE IMPACT OF SPIRITUAL HEALING PRACTICES

In considering the impact of spiritual healing practices from a scientific point of view, I suggest that we will need a broader scientific paradigm than many people are yet willing to espouse. The last few chapters, in different ways, have offered ways of approaching this question. Though they take some kind of psychological approach to spiritual healing, I will argue against a narrowly psychological approach. Rather, we need a broader understanding of healing that includes the spiritual as well as the psychological.

Bruce Kinsey's chapter takes a psychodynamic perspective, and there are many ways in which psychodynamic psychology is potentially relevant to understanding spiritual healing. It might be thought that using psychodynamic psychology to understand spiritual healing implies that such healing is really nothing more than psychological healing. However, that doesn't necessarily follow. It is possible that the close intertwining of mind and body that psychosomatic medicine has discovered is part of a larger whole. If, as I have suggested, spirit can be distinguished from mind or psyche (though not separated from it), there could perhaps be an extended version of psychosomatics that we might call 'spirital-psycho-somatics' that would enable us to understand how closely intertwined spirit, psyche and body can all be. Phenomena such as hysterical conversion syndromes have shown a truly remarkable effect of mind on body. Perhaps an extended version of psychosomatics will enable us to understand a remarkable intertwining of spirit with both mind and body. Such an extended psychosomatics could enable us to develop some kind of scientific account of spiritual healing. The interest of psychodynamic psychology here lies not so much in what it currently offers, but in what an extended version of it, including the spiritual dimension, could contribute to the understanding of spiritual healing.

As was suggested in Chapter 1, the concept of 'flight into health' is particularly interesting from this point of view. If we make a distinction between soul and spirit (e.g. Hillman 1979), 'flight into health' seems likely to be working at the level of spirit rather than of soul (which may partly account for why it is distrusted by psychotherapists). My suggestion is that spiritual healing might be some kind of 'flight into health.' That may sound reductionist and diminishing, but it is not meant to be. Though there is clearly a danger of it being seen as somewhat superficial, there may be ways in which a 'flight into health' can be undertaken at a greater level of inner depth, and with more enduring consequences. Also, there is nothing in this concept that rules out the possibility of it being enhanced by some kind of transcendent spiritual grace.

The limited view of mental powers espoused by most contemporary science seems a particular problem in making scientific sense of spiritual healing. I am persuaded by the evidence that Rupert Sheldrake has presented for what he calls an 'extended mind' that is not strictly limited to the boundaries of the physical body. In a recent book (Sheldrake 2003) he provides convincing evidence that people know whether or not they are being stared at, even when the person staring is outside the range of sight. At least they can guess when they are being stared at with a level of accuracy that is consistently above chance. Sheldrake takes that as evidence for mental powers that seem to extend beyond the confines of the physical body. In my view, the scientific evidence for such phenomena is persuasive. I assume that such mental activity can make a contribution to spiritual healing. It is an approach consistent with the data on biopsychokinesis presented in the chapter by Marilyn Schlitz. David Leech has discussed the philosophical and theological issues on the interpretation of such parapsychological evidence earlier in this book.

I suggest that spiritual healing can be understood, in part, in terms of the enmeshing of the extended minds of healer and healee. It is important to emphasize here that I am not arguing for a purely mental basis of healing in the way that a mind–body dualist might. Just as I am sceptical of the idea of healing that is purely spiritual, so I am sceptical of the idea of healing being brought about solely at a mental level. In so far as mental powers are relevant to healing, there may be some kind of subtle interpenetration of mental or spiritual healing energy with the physical body. The point here is parallel to the one made above about psychosomatics. The interest of Sheldrake's concept of extended mind is not that it might offer a purely psychological account of spiritual healing. Rather, Sheldrake's way of understanding extended mental powers could point to a parallel way of understanding spiritual powers and the channelling of spiritual energy for healing energy.

In using parapsychology to point towards a possible scientific understanding of spiritual healing, I am rejecting the idea that parapsychology is concerned with processes that science could not possibly understand. Rather, I see parapsychology as concerned with processes that it would take an extended science to understand. If it is possible through concentrated mental activity to influence physiological processes, that may be part of what occurs in successful physical healing. Biopsychokinesis research doesn't normally consider how such effects could be further augmented by the healer deliberately channelling transcendent resources or energy, though in principle it could do so.

The approach I am suggesting here can be compared with that of Lawrence LeShan (1980) who proposes that there is a clairvoyant reality as well as an ordinary reality, and that spiritual healing needs to be understood in terms of the former. However, that way of framing things is too dualist for my taste. I would prefer to say that there are two or more aspects of reality that are intertwined, rather in the way that mind and brain are two intertwined aspects of the same reality. Different scientific approaches may be needed to understand the ordinary and clairvoyant aspects of reality, just as mind and brain require different scientific approaches. Understanding the intertwining of mental and physical in healing could be a step towards understanding how spiritual, mental and physical processes are all involved in spiritual healing.

LeShan (1980) makes a helpful distinction between two types of spiritual healing (see Bourne and Watts in Chapter 5). In 'Type 1' healing there is a deeply intense caring and an empathic sense of unity with the person being healed, but no attempt to do anything to the healee. The focus is on a purposeful unity of love between the healer and the healee. In 'Type 2' healing there is a specific endeavour to heal in which healers see themselves as agents or channels of healing energy. The healer seeks to bring about cure through the explicit channelling of healing energy; the healer has an additional role in facilitating the flow of quasi-physical energy from its source to the healee. Seen in this way, it makes sense that a basic resonance should be established first, before any such channelling is attempted. In accordance with that, LeShan makes the point that Type 2 healing should only be used where it builds on Type 1 healing. These two types seem to represent different kinds of enmeshment between the healer and healee, and it seems an important distinction to understand from a scientific point of view.

Many healing practices involve physical contact, in the form of the laying on of hands or in some other way between the healer and the healee. In some cases where hands are used, they are merely a 'sign' of healing, and are not regarded as essential to it. In other cases, hands are used as an actual 'instrument' of healing in a way that is thought to be indispensable to it. Hands are also sometimes used as an instrument of diagnosis as well as of healing. It may not always be evident to the casual observer whether hands are being used as a sign or as an instrument of healing. This is unrelated to whether the hands are placed in contact with the body of the healee, or merely close to it. The use of hands as an instrument of healing is an example of LeShan's Type 2 healing. Where they are used as just a sign of healing, the healing will usually be Type 1.

In considering procedures intended to bring about physical healing, it is useful to distinguish spiritual healing procedures (such as the laying on of hands) from prayer for healing. Spiritual healing includes prayer, but is more than prayer. Healing characteristically involves at least two people, the person who is seeking the cure, and the person who is promoting or conferring that on them. They work together. If it were not so, it would not be spiritual healing. If people pray on their own to recover, that is prayer but not spiritual healing proper. Equally, if a person prays for the healing of another, it is again prayer but not spiritual healing proper. The collaborative spiritual activity of the two key participants is a defining feature of spiritual healing procedures, even though healing may also come about through prayer alone.

If we follow the suggestion (Polkinghorne 1989) that prayer depends on a kind of resonance between God and the person who prays, analogous to a nuclear resonance, I would suggest that spiritual healing involves a kind of resonance that involves God, the healer and the healee. The healee is drawn into this resonance more explicitly than is the case with prayer, to make a threesome. Indeed, that is perhaps one of the key differences between spiritual healing and prayer. Such a resonance is something that could, in principle, be approached scientifically, though I assume that a scientific account would need to be complemented by a theological one about the purposes and grace of God.

SPIRITUAL HEALING AND MODERNITY

Next, I turn to consider how questions about spiritual healing are deeply embedded in contemporary debates about both science and health, and to try to put this debate in some historical context.

Spiritual healing is often presented in religious circles as though it were simply a continuation of what has been going on for 2,000 years or more. However, that is clearly not the case. The 'revival' of spiritual healing since the late nineteenth century has created something new and radically different from what occurred before. As Philip Clayton shows in Chapter 3, spiritual healing declined after the first few centuries of the Christian era, and what was left of the tradition of healing was spiritualized by Aquinas and others. When spiritual healing was revived, it was after a very long moratorium, and in a culture that was radically different in almost every way from that of the New Testament and the early Church.

Key changes occurred in the nineteenth century concerning both science and health that set the parameters for current approaches to spiritual healing. It was then that the dream was born that health problems could be alleviated through scientific advance. Prior to that, there had often been little prospect of effective treatment for health problems, and so there had been little hope that human beings could be spared disease and other ailments. The nineteenth century saw the birth of the dream of a really successful medical science.

However, the interesting thing is that the dream of such useful treatment was not tied exclusively to the advance of medical science. The alleviation of pain and illness was sought by a wide variety of new methods, and not exclusively from mainstream medical science. At the end of the nineteenth century, alongside scientific advance, there was the birth of a variety of approaches to healing through psychological, spiritual or other 'alternative' methods. It might be thought that the advances in scientific medicine that began towards the end of the nineteenth century would have driven out alternative approaches to healing. On the contrary, the birth of modern scientific medicine and the modern wave of interest in alternative medicine (including spiritual healing) are intertwined (Pattison 1989).

The alternatives to modern scientific medicine are very diverse, and cannot be considered as a single category. Indeed all that they have in common is that they are alternatives to modern medical science. Those who have an exclusive commitment to modern medical science will be resistant to all alternative approaches, including 'spiritual' healing. In contrast, those who think that modern medical science is valuable but limited will be disposed to take seriously the family of alternatives, though without necessarily embracing all of them uncritically.

It is regrettable that departures from medical science have come to be seen as 'alternative' in the way they have. The reasons why they have often been pursued outside the framework of modern medical science are complex, part intellectual and part sociological. However, it was surely unnecessary that such a sharp institutional separation should have occurred, and it has damaged both sides. Modern medical science, through not having to even consider alternative approaches to healing, has remained narrower than it would otherwise have been. On the other hand, alternative approaches, cut off from mainstream science, have become vulnerable to accusations of quackery, even though there may be much effective healing practice within them.

This raises many powerful and emotive issues that are frequently discussed in terms of 'modernism' and its alternatives. Medical science is clearly a product of 'modernity' and it is tempting to regard alternatives to it as 'post-modern'. However, that would misrepresent the chronology of their concurrent development. It would also be inappropriate to imply that modern medical science is outmoded. On the contrary, medical science has been of enormous help to humanity, and there are very few people who would not wish to take advantage of the huge benefits it has conferred. Talk about 'post-modernity', in connection with medicine and healing, or indeed anything else, implies a choice between modernist and post-modernist approaches.

My own view is that we should not be choosing between modernity and post-modernity, but rather looking to what David Ford (2007) has called the 'healing' of modernity. By such 'healing' I understand an emancipation and development of modernity that rescues it from some of its narrowness and excessive 'objectivity', a healing that opens up its potential without losing sight of its merits. The benefits of modern medical science are beyond question, but it is at least possible that a broadening of the paradigm of medical science would enable those benefits to be extended further. The split between 'scientific' and 'alternative' methods has mitigated against the healing of modernity in matters of medicine and healing.

CURRENT CONCEPTUALIZATIONS OF SPIRITUAL HEALING

Current concepts of spiritual healing in religious contexts have often contrasted it with the methods of modern medicine. Spiritual healing has usually been practised in conjunction with modern medicine, and there has often been a harmonious coexistence between them. Nevertheless, it remains the case that faith communities have seen spiritual healing as something radically different from the methods of modern medicine.

It is important to understand here that the revival of spiritual healing in modern times has been accompanied by radical changes in how it is understood. These changes are parallel to, and a special example of, the shift that has taken place in how miracles are understood. As we noted in Chapter 1, the concept of miracle changed with the development of modern science. Because science used not to exist in its present form, miracles used not to be contrasted with what was scientifically explicable. However, the development of modern science led to a narrowing and hardening of the concept of miracle in which it has increasingly been contrasted with the natural processes science could understand. That is also true of the concept of spiritual healing. In the early centuries of Christianity, spiritual healing was not contrasted with modern medicine, because modern medicine did not exist. When spiritual healing was revived from the nineteenth century onwards, it was contrasted with modern medicine in a new way.

So, we have an interesting paradox to consider. On the one hand, the revival of interest in alternative medicine and spiritual healing is closely intertwined with the development of modern scientific medicine as part of a new quasi-eschatological vision of universal health. On the other hand, spiritual healing has been contrasted sharply with the methods of modern medicine.

It is also important to understand how spiritual healing has been conceptualized differently in religious and non-religious settings. In non-religious contexts spiritual healing has been conceptualized in terms of energies or powers that are potentially capable of being understood within a broad and emancipated scientific paradigm. In contrast, the faith communities have emphasized that spiritual healing is outside anything that science could possibly understand. Practitioners of non-religious forms of spiritual healing look to alternative science for an account of what they are doing. Those who use religious forms of spiritual healing have given a theological account of it in terms of the grace and power of God.

My proposal is that we should develop both accounts, in parallel. As complementary perspectives, they will enable us to conceptualize spiritual healing of all kinds, both religious and non-religious, more adequately. I hope that an expanded scientific paradigm will give us an increasing scientific understanding of all forms of spiritual healing. In addition, I suggest that we should see all forms of spiritual healing in theological terms, whether or not that healing is explicitly religious, as arising within the grace and providence of God.

I do not expect this proposal to be greeted with enthusiasm by practitioners of either religious or non-religious forms of spiritual healing. Non-religious practitioners will probably be reluctant to view what they are doing in theological terms. However, developments in the concept of God in liberal Protestant theologies of the twentieth century – such as that of Paul Tillich – make it possible to work out a broad theology of spiritual healing that could be acceptable to such non-religious practitioners. I also recognize that those who use religious forms of spiritual healing will be resistant to any kind of scientific account of it, whether in terms of mainstream or alternative science. That would parallel the widespread theological protests at scientific approaches to intercessory prayer.

Contemporary theology seems to be running scared of science, and that shows itself in various ways. First, it is wary of being caught out making claims that are scientifically incredible. Second, it is wary of trying to establish its claims on any kind of scientific foundation in case the foundations give way. Third, it is wary of any flirtation with alternative science in case it results in theology being dismissed as 'wacky'. The result is that science is allowed, in practice, to exercise a tyranny over theological claims in a way that is usually not explicitly acknowledged. This is very strange when many theologians are disparaging about modernity (of which a narrow scientifically constrained worldview is a key part), and claim to have moved beyond it to a post-modern position. In practice, a rather narrow 'modern' view of science is still allowed to constrain theological claims.

Spiritual healing is a phenomenon that raises broad and significant issues. As we have seen, an adequate conceptualization of it will require several fault lines to be bridged. There will have to be:

1 a healing of the rift between modernity and so-called 'post-modernity';
2 a reconciliation between over-rigid mainstream science and an alternative science that is sometimes over-fanciful;
3 a deeper reconciliation between theology and science about divine action, one that goes beyond the physical sciences and engages more adequately with the human sciences, and with the relationship between divine and human agency;
4 a broader awareness of the totality of contemporary spiritual healing that transcends the split between religious and non-religious wings of contemporary culture.

All that is a tall order, and it is little wonder that an understanding of spiritual healing is very difficult. Nevertheless it is hoped that the present volume has made a significant contribution to this important task. It is precisely because spiritual healing is so challenging to conceptualize that efforts to do so may be particularly rewarding and bring widespread benefits.

Bibliography

PRIMARY TEXTS

Aquinas, Thomas 1975. *Summa contra Gentiles.* Pegis, A. C. (trans.), South Bend, IN: University of Notre Dame Press

Aquinas, Thomas 1990. *Summa Theologica.* Shapcote, L. (trans.), Chicago: Encyclopædia Britannica, Inc.

Athenagoras 2004. *A Plea for the Christians.* Pratten, B. P. (trans.), Whitefish, MT: Kessinger

Augustine 1999. *The Retractions.* Bogan, M. I. (trans.), Washington, DC: Catholic University of America Press

Augustine 2003. *City of God.* Bettenson, H. (trans.), revised edn. London: Penguin

Baba Qamma 1998. Neusner, J. (trans.), in *The Mishnah: A New Translation,* Neusner, J. (ed.), New Haven: Yale University Press, pp. 503–28

Berakhot 1998. Zahavy, T. and Avery-Peck, A. (trans.), in *The Mishnah: A New Translation,* Neusner, J. (ed.), New Haven: Yale University Press, pp. 3–14

Book of Concord: The Confessions of the Evangelical Lutheran Church, 2001. Kolb, R. and Wengert, T. J. (eds.), 2nd edn. Minneapolis, MN: Fortress Press

Calvin, John 1989. *Institutes of the Christian Religion.* Beveridge, Henry (trans.), Grand Rapids, MI: Eerdmans

Cassius, Dio 1914–27. 'Roman histories' in *Dio Cassius,* vols. I–IX. Cary, E. and Foster, H. B. (trans.), Cambridge, MA: Harvard University Press

Cato the Elder 1934. *On Agriculture.* Hooper, W. D. and Ash, H. B. (trans.), Cambridge, MA: Harvard University Press

Chrysostom, John 1966. *Chrysostom's Homilies against the Jews: An English Translation.* Maxwell, C. M. (trans.), University of Chicago Press

Descartes, René 1984. *Principles of Philosophy.* Miller, V. R. (trans.), Dordrecht: Kluwer Academic Publishers

Eusebius 1989. *The History of the Church: From Christ to Constantine.* Williamson, G. A (trans.), Louth, Andrew (ed.), New York: Penguin Books

Josephus 1927–8. 'The Jewish War' in *Josephus,* vols. II–IV. Thackeray, H. St. J. (trans.), Cambridge, MA: Harvard University Press

Josephus 1930–65. 'Jewish antiquities' in *Josephus*, vols. v–xiii. Thackeray, H. St. J., Marcus, R., Wikgren, A. and Feldman, L. H. (trans.), Cambridge, MA: Harvard University Press

Lucian 1921. 'Lover of lies' in Harmon, A. M. (trans.), *Lucian*, vol. iii, Loeb Classics, Cambridge, MA: Harvard University Press

Luther, M. 1955. *Luther: Letters of Spiritual Counsel.* Tappert, Theodore G. (ed. and trans.), London: SCM Press

Origen 1980. *Contra Celsum.* Chadwick, H. (trans.), Cambridge: Cambridge University Press

Sepher Yezirah: *A Book on Creation; or the Jewish Metaphysics of Remote Antiquity, with English Translation, Preface, Explanatory Notes and Glossary*, 1877. Kalisch, I. (trans.), New York: L. H. Frank & Co.

Suetonius 1914. 'Vespasian' in *Suetonius*, vol. ii. Rolfe, J. C. (trans.), Cambridge, MA: Harvard University Press

Tacitus, Cornelius 1997. *The Histories.* Levene, D. S. and Fyfe, W. H. (trans.), Oxford: Oxford University Press

Zalman, S. 1998. *The Tanya: Bi-Lingual Edition*, Mindel, N., Mangel, N., Posner, Z. I. and Schochet, J. I. (trans.), Brooklyn, NY: Kehot Publication Society

SECONDARY TEXTS

Achtemeier, P. J. 2008. *Jesus and the Miracle Tradition.* Eugene, OR: Cascade Books

Adler, H. M. and Hammett, V. B. 1973. 'The doctor–patient relationship revisited: An analysis of the placebo effect', *Annals of Internal Medicine* **78**: 595–8

Aldridge, D. 2000. *Spirituality, Healing and Medicine.* London: Jessica Kingsley

Alexander, F. and French, T. M. 1946. *Psychoanalytic Therapy.* New York: The Ronald Press Company

Ameling, A. 2000. 'Prayer: An ancient healing practice becomes new again', *Holistic Nursing Practice* **14**: 40–8

American Cancer Society 2005. *Cancer Facts and Figures.* Atlanta, GA: American Cancer Society

American Cancer Society 2006. *Cancer Facts and Figures.* Atlanta, GA: American Cancer Society

American Psychiatric Association 1992–4. *Diagnostic and Statistical Manual of Mental Disorders IV.* Washington, DC: American Psychiatric Association

Amundsen, D. and Ferngren, C. 1995. 'The perception of disease causality in the New Testament', *Aufstieg und Niedergang der römischen Welt*, vol. 2, 37.3: 2934–56

Anderson, A. H. and Hollenweger, W. J. (eds.) 1999. *Pentecostals after a Century: Global Perspectives on a Movement in Transition.* Sheffield: Sheffield Academic Press

Aragona, M., Muscatello, M. R., Losi, E., *et al.* 1996. 'Lymphocyte number and stress parameter modifications in untreated breast cancer patients with depressive mood and previous life stress', *Journal of Experimental Therapeutics and Oncology* 1: 354–60

Armstrong, K. 1993. *A History of God from Abraham to the Present: The 4,000 Year Quest for God.* London: Mandarin

Arrindell, W. A., Steptoe, A. and Wardle, J. 2003. 'Higher levels of depression in masculine than in feminine nations', *Behaviour Research and Therapy* 41: 809–17

Astin, J. A., Harkness, E. and Ernst, E. 2000. 'The efficacy of "distant healing": A systematic review of randomized trials', *Annals of Internal Medicine* 132: 903–10

Aune, D. E. 1980. 'Magic in early Christianity', *Aufstieg und Niedergang der römischen Welt* vol. 2,23.2: 1507–57

Avalos, H. 1999. *Health Care and the Rise of Christianity.* Peabody, MA: Hendrickson

Bailey, A. A. 1953. *Esoteric Healing.* New York: Lucis Publishing Company

Bailey, K. G. 2002. 'Recognizing, assessing and classifying others: Cognitive bases of evolutionary kinship therapy', *Journal of Cognitive Psychotherapy: An International Quarterly* 16: 367–83

Balint, M. 1964. *The Doctor, His Patient, and the Illness.* Madison, CT: International Universities Press

Barnes, L. and Sered, S. 2005. *Religion and Healing in America.* Oxford: Oxford University Press

Barnes, P. M., Powell-Griner, E., McFann, K. and Nahin, R. L. 2004. 'Complementary and alternative medicine use among adults', *CDC Advance Data Report* 343: 1–19

Barth, K. 1975. *Church Dogmatics,* vol. 4, part 2. Bromiley, G. W. (trans.), Torrance, T. F. (ed.), Edinburgh: T & T Clark

Bauckham, R. 2006. *Jesus and the Eyewitnesses: The Gospels as Eyewitness Testimony.* Cambridge: Eerdmans

Bauer-Wu, S. and Farran, C. J. 2005. 'Meaning in life and psycho-spiritual functioning', *Journal of Holistic Nursing* 23: 172–90

Baumeister, R. F. and Leary, M. R. 1995. 'The need to belong: Desire for interpersonal attachments as a fundamental human motivation', *Psychological Bulletin* 117: 497–529

Beauregard, M. and Paquette, V. 2006. 'Neural correlates of a mystical experience in Carmelite nuns', *Neuroscience Letters* 405: 186–90

Beecher, H. K. 1955. 'The powerful placebo', *Journal of the American Medical Association,* 159: 1602–6

Benedetti, F. 2008. *Placebo Effects: Understanding the Mechanisms in Health and Disease.* Oxford: Oxford University Press

Benedetti, F., Colloca, L., Torre, E., *et al.* 2004. 'Placebo-responsive Parkinson patients show decreased activity in single neurons of subthalamic nucleus', *Nature Neuroscience* 7: 587–8

Ben-Eliyahu, S. 2003. 'The promotion of tumor metastasis by surgery and stress: Immunological basis and implications for psychoneuroimmunology', *Brain Behavior and Immunity* 17 (Suppl. 1): 27–36

Bennett, G. and Bennett, K. M. 2000. 'The presence of the dead: An empirical study', *Mortality* **5**: 139–57

Benor, D. J. 1993. *Healing Research: Holistic Medicine and Spiritual Healing.* Munich: Helix Verlag

Benor, D. J. 2005. 'Healing', in *Parapsychology: Research on Exceptional Experience.* Henry, J. (ed.), Hove: Routledge, pp. 137–48

Benson, H. and Epstein, M. D. 1975. 'The Placebo effect: A neglected asset in the care of patients', *Journal of the American Medical Association* **232**: 1225–7

Benson, H., Dusek, J. A., Sherwood, J. B., *et al.* 2006. 'Study of the therapeutic effects of intercessory prayer (STEP) in cardiac bypass patients: A multicenter randomized trial of uncertainty and certainty of receiving intercessory prayer', *American Heart Journal* **151**: 934–42

Benz, E. 1983. *Parapsychologie und Religion: Erfahrungen mit übersinnlichen Kräften.* Freiburg im Breisgau: Herder

Berger, K. 1973. 'Die königlichen Messiastraditionen des Neuen Testaments', *New Testament Studies* **20**: 1–44

Berger, K. 1974. 'Zum Problem des Messianität Jesu', *Zeitschrift für Theologie und Kirche* **71**: 1–30

Bettencourt, E. 1968. 'Charisms', in *Sacramentum Mundi: An Encyclopedia of Theology*, vol. 1. Rahner, K. (ed.), New York: Herder and Herder, pp. 283–4

Black, D. M. 2006. (ed.) *Psychoanalysis and Religion in the 21st Century: Competitors or Collaborators?* London: Routledge

Blackburn, B. 1994. 'The miracles of Jesus', in *Studying the Historical Jesus: Evaluations of the State of Current Research.* Chilton, B. and Evans, C. A. (eds.), Leiden: E. J. Brill, pp. 353–94

Bloom, B. 2007. *Meaning-full Disease: How Personal Experience and Meanings Cause and Maintain Physical Illness.* London: Karnac

Boivin, M. J. 1991. 'The Hebraic model of the person: Towards a unified psychological science among Christian helping professionals', *Journal of Psychology and Theology* **19**: 157–65

Boivin, M. J. 2002. 'Finding God in Prozac or finding Prozac in God: Preserving a Christian view of the person amidst a biopsychological revolution', *Christian Scholar's Review* **32**(2): 159–76

Boivin, M. J. 2003a. 'Response to Kathleen Storm's reflection on "Finding God in Prozac or finding Prozac in God: Preserving a Christian view of the person amidst a biopsychological revolution"', *Christian Scholar's Review* **33**(1): 17–22

Boivin, M. J. 2003b. 'Can purpose be found in the assent of humankind? A review of Seymour W. Itzkoff's *The Inevitable Domination by Man: An Evolutionary Detective Story*', *Contemporary Psychology* **48**: 609–11

Boivin, M. J. and Webb, B. 2005. *Spirituality, Emotional Well-Being, Immunological Resilience, and Neuropsychological Function in Breast Cancer Patients: Final Report to the CCCU Collaborative Initiative Grant Program.* Wenham, MA: Center for Integration Studies, Gordon College

Bowlby, J. 1969. *Attachment and Loss*, vol. 1: *Attachment.* London: Hogarth Press

Bowlby, J. 1973. *Attachment and Loss, vol. 2: Separation, Anxiety and Anger.* London: Hogarth Press

Bowlby, J. 1988. *A Secure Base: Clinical Applications of Attachment Theory.* London: Routledge

Braud, W. and Schlitz, M. 1983, 'Psychokinetic influence on electrodermal activity', *Journal of Parapsychology* **47**: 95–119

Brennan, B. A. 1987. *Hands of Light: A Guide to Healing through the Human Energy Field.* New York: Bantam Books

Brennan, B. A. 1993. *Light Emerging: The Journey of Personal Healing.* New York: Bantam Books

Brody, H. 1995 'Placebo', in *Encyclopedia of Bioethics*, 2nd edn. Reich, W. T. (ed.), New York: Macmillan, pp. 1951–3

Brody, H. 1997. 'The doctor as therapeutic agent: A placebo effect research agenda', in *The Placebo Effect: An Interdisciplinary Exploration.* Harrington, A. (ed.), Cambridge MA: Harvard University Press, pp. 77–92

Brody, H. 2000. *The Placebo Response.* New York: Cliff Street Books

Broom, B. 2007. *Meaning-full Disease: How Personal Experience and Meanings Cause and Maintain Physical Illness.* London: Karnac

Brown, R. J. 2004. 'Psychological mechanisms of medically unexplained symptoms: An integrative conceptual model', *Psychological Bulletin* **130**: 793–812

Brown, W. S., Murphy, N. and Malony, H. N. (eds.) 1998. *Whatever Happened to the Soul? Scientific and Theological Portraits of Human Nature.* Minneapolis: Fortress Press

Bulger, R. J. 1990. 'The demise of the placebo effect in the practice of scientific medicine: A natural progression or an undesirable aberration?' *Transactions of the American Clinical and Climatological Association* **102**: 285–93

Bultmann, R. 1958. *Jesus and the Word.* Smith, L. P. and Lantero, E. H. (trans.), New York: Charles Scribner's Sons

Bultmann, R. 1987. *Rudolf Bultmann: Interpreting Faith for the Modern Era.* Johnson, R. A. (ed.), San Francisco: Collins

Bultmann, R. 1961. *Kerygma and Myth: A Theological Debate.* New York: Harper & Row

Butler, T., Pan, H., Epstein, J., *et al.* 2005. 'Fear-related activity in subgenual anterior cingulate differs between men and women', *Neuroreport* **16**: 1233–6

Butler, T., Pan, H., Tuescher, O., *et al.* 2007. 'Human fear-related motor neurocircuitry', *Neuroscience* **150**: 1–7

Byrd, R. C. 1988. 'Positive therapeutic effects of intercessory prayer in a coronary care unit population', *Southern Medical Journal* **81**: 826–9

Cacioppo, J. T., Berston, G. G., Sheridan, J. F. and McClintock, M. K. 2000. 'Multilevel integrative analysis of human behaviour: Social neuroscience and the complementing nature of social and biological approaches', *Psychological Bulletin* **126**: 829–43

Cacioppo, J. T., Hawkley, L. C., Rickett, E. M. and Masi, C. M. 2005. 'Sociality, spirituality, and meaning making: Chicago health, aging, and social relations study', *Review of General Psychology* **9**: 143–55

Cadbury, H. J. 1926. 'Lexical notes on Luke-Acts II: Recent arguments for medical language', *Journal of Biblical Literature* **45**: 190–209

Cadbury, H. J. 1937. *The Peril of Modernizing Jesus*. New York: Macmillan

Cannon W. B. 1942. 'Voodoo death', *American Anthropologist* **44**: 169–81

Capps, D. 2000. *Jesus: A Psychological Biography*. St Louis: Chalice Press

Capps, D. 2008. *Jesus the Village Psychiatrist*. Louisville, KY: Westminster John Knox

Carleton Paget, J. 2001. 'Some observations on Josephus and Christianity', *Journal of Theological Studies* **52**: 539–624

Carter, C. S. 1998. 'Neuroendocrine perspectives on social attachment and love', *Psychoneuroendocrinology* **23**: 779–818

Casement, P. 1985. *On Learning from the Patient*. London: Tavistock Publications

Cassidy, J. and Shaver, P. R. 1999. *Handbook of Attachment: Theory, Research and Clinical Applications*. New York: Guilford Press

Cassileth, B. R. 1984. 'Contemporary unorthodox treatment in cancer medicine: A study of patients, treatments and practitioners', *Annals of Internal Medicine* **101**: 105–12

Church of England 2000. *A Time to Heal: A Report for the House of Bishops on the Healing Ministry*. London: Church House Publishing

Clayton, P. 1989. *Explanation from Physics to Theology: An Essay in Rationality and Religion*. New Haven: Yale University Press

Clayton, P. 2006. *Mind and Emergence: From Quantum to Consciousness*. Oxford: Oxford University Press

Clayton, P. 2008. *Adventures in the Spirit: God, World, Divine Action*. Simpson, Z. R. (ed.), Minneapolis, MN: Fortress Press

Clayton, P. and Knapp, S. 2007. 'Divine action and the "argument from neglect"', in *Physics and Cosmology: Scientific Perspectives on the Problem of Natural Evil*. Murphy, N., Russell, R. J. and Stoeger, W. R. (eds.), Vatican City: Vatican Observatory Publications, pp. 179–94

Clayton, P. and Peacocke, A. (eds.) 2004. *In Whom We Live and Move and Have Our Being: Panentheistic Reflections on God's Presence in a Scientific World*. Grand Rapids, MI: Eerdmans

Coakley, S. and Shelemay, K. K. (eds.) 2007. *Pain and its Transformations: The Interface of Biology and Culture*. Cambridge, MA: Harvard University Press

Cohen, M. Z., Kahn, D. L. and Steeves, R. H. 1998. 'Beyond body image: The experience of breast cancer', *Oncology Nursing Forum* **25**: 835–41

Cohen, S. I. 1985. 'Psychosomatic death: Voodoo death in a modern perspective', *Integrative Psychiatry* **3**: 46–51

Collins, J. 1990. 'Is critical Biblical theology possible?' in *The Hebrew Bible and its Interpreters*. Propp, W. H., Halpern, B. and Freedman, D. N., (eds.), Winona Lake, IN: Eisenbrauns, pp. 1–17

Colloca, L. and Benedetti, F. 2001. 'Placebos and painkillers: Is mind as real as matter?', *Nature Reviews Neuroscience* **6**: 545–52

Colloca, L., Lopiano, L., Lanotte, M. and Benedetti, F. 2004. 'Overt versus covert treatment for pain, anxiety, and Parkinson's disease', *Lancet Neurology* **3**: 679–84

Coward, D. D. and Kahn, D. L. 2004. 'Resolution of spiritual disequilibrium by women newly diagnosed with breast cancer', *Oncology Nursing Forum* **31**(2): E24–E31

Cox, H. G. 1995. *Fire from Heaven: The Rise of Pentecostal Spirituality and the Reshaping of Religion in the Twenty-First Century.* Reading, MA: Addison-Wesley

Cozolino, L. 2007. *The Neuroscience of Human Relationships: Attachment and the Developing Brain.* New York: Norton

Crossan, J. D. 1991. *The Historical Jesus: The Life of a Mediterranean Jewish Peasant.* Edinburgh: T & T Clark

Crossan, J. D. 1994. *Jesus: A Revolutionary Biography.* San Francisco: Harper

Crossan, J. D. 1998. *The Birth of Christianity.* Edinburgh: T & T Clark

Csordas, T. J. 1996. 'Imaginal performance and memory in ritual healing', in *The Performance of Healing.* Laderman, C. and Roseman, M. (eds.), New York and London: Routledge, pp. 91–114

Csordas, T. J. 1997. *The Sacred Self: A Cultural Phenomenology of Charismatic Healing.* Berkeley, CA: University of California Press

Csordas, T. J. 2002. *Body/Meaning/Healing.* Basingstoke: Palgrave Macmillan

Damasio, A. R., Grabowski, T. J., Bechara, A., *et al.* 2000. 'Subcortical and cortical brain activity during the feeling of self-generated emotions', *Nature Neuroscience* **3**: 1049–56

Davidson, R. J. and Harrington, A. 2002. *Visions of Compassion: Western Scientists and Tibetan Buddhists Examine Human Nature.* New York: Oxford University Press

Davidson, R. J., Kabat-Zinn, J., Schumacher, J., *et al.* 2003. 'Alterations in brain and immune function produced by mindfulness meditation', *Psychosomatic Medicine* **65**: 564–70

Davies, S. 1995. *Jesus the Healer.* London: SCM

Davies, W. D. and Allison, D. 1991. *A Critical and Exegetical Commentary on the Gospel According to Saint Matthew,* vol. 2. Edinburgh: T & T Clark

De Forest, I. 1954. *The Leaven of Love: Development of the Psychoanalytic Theory and Technique of Sandor Ferenczi.* New York: Harper

De Letter, P. 1968. 'Anointing of the Sick', in *Sacramentum Mundi: An Encyclopedia of Theology,* vol. 1. Rahner, K. (ed.), New York: Herder and Herder, pp. 37–40

de Waal, F. B. M. 1996. *Good Natured: The Origins of Right and Wrong in Humans and Other Animals.* London: Harvard University Press

Dein, S. 1992. 'Millennium, Messianism and medicine among the Lubavitch of Stamford Hill', *International Journal of Social Psychiatry* **18**: 262–7

Dein, S. 2001. 'What really happens when prophecy fails?' *Sociology of Religion* **62**: 384–401

Dein, S. 2002. 'The power of words: Healing narratives amongst Lubavitch Hasidim', *Medical Anthropology Quarterly* **16**: 41–62

Dein, S. 2004. *Religion and Healing Among the Lubavitch Community in Stamford Hill, North London: A Case Study of Hasidism.* Lewiston, NY: Edwin Mellen Press

Dempster, M. W., Klaus, B. D. and Petersen, D. (eds.) 1999. *The Globalization of Pentecostalism: A Religion Made to Travel.* Oxford: Regnum Books

Depue, R. A. and Morrone-Strupinsky, J. V. 2005. 'A neurobehavioral model of affiliative bonding', *Behavioral and Brain Sciences* **28**: 313–95

Desjarlais, R. R. 1996. 'Presence', in *The Performance of Healing.* Laderman, C. and Roseman, M. (eds.), New York and London: Routledge, pp. 143–64

Devereux, G. (ed.) 1953. *Psychoanalysis and the Occult.* New York: International Universities Press

Dilley, F. B. (ed.) 1995. *Philosophical Interactions and Parapsychology: The Major Writings of H. H. Price on Parapsychology and Survival.* New York: St Martin's Press

Dossey, B. 2007. 'Integral nursing'. Talk given at the Integral Institute Showcase on Integral Medicine, Denver, CO

Dossey, L. 1993. *Healing Words: The Power of Prayer and the Practice of Medicine.* San Francisco: Harper

Dourley, J. 1997. 'Issues of naturalism and supranaturalism in Tillich's correlation of religious with psychological healing', *Studies in Religion* **26**: 211–22

Duling, D. C. 1975. 'Solomon, exorcism and the son of David', *Harvard Theological Review* **68**: 235–52

Dunn, J. D. G. 2003. *Christianity in the Making,* vol. 1: *Jesus Remembered.* Grand Rapids, MI: Eerdmans

Dunn, J. D. G. and McKnight, S. (eds.) 2005. *The Historical Jesus in Recent Research.* Winona Lake, IN: Eisenbrauns

Dupré, L. K. 2004. *The Enlightenment and the Intellectual Foundations of Modern Culture.* New Haven: Yale University Press

Easthope, G. 1986. *Healers and Alternative Medicine: A Sociological Examination.* Brookfield: Gower

Edelstein, E. J., Edelstein, L. and Ferngren, G. B. 1998. *Asclepius: Collection and Interpretation of the Testimonies.* Baltimore, MD: The Johns Hopkins University Press

Eitrem, S. 1966. *Some Notes on the Demonology in the New Testament.* 2nd edn. Uppsala: Almquist & Wiksells

Ellenberger, H. F. 1970. *The Discovery of the Unconscious: The History and Evolution of Dynamic Psychiatry.* New York: Basic Books

Engel, G. L. 1978. 'Psychologic stress, vasodepressor (vasovagal) syncope, and sudden death', *Annals of Internal Medicine* **89**: 403–412

Entralgo, P. L. 1970. *The Therapy of the Word in Classical Antiquity.* Rather, L. J. and Sharp, J. M. (trans.), New Haven: Yale University Press

Epperly, B. G. 2001. *God's Touch: Faith, Wholeness, and the Healing Miracles of Jesus.* Louisville, KY: Westminster John Knox Press

Ernst, E. 2001. 'Towards a scientific understanding of placebo effects', in *Understanding the Placebo Effect in Complementary Medicine: Theory, Practice and Research.* D. Peters (ed.), London: Churchill Livingston, pp. 17–29

Erzen, T. 2005. 'Sexual healing: Self-help and therapeutic Christianity in the ex-gay movement', in *Religion and Healing in America.* Barne, L. L. and Sered, S. S. (eds.), New York: Oxford University Press, pp. 265–80

European Union 2006. *Guidelines on Breast Cancer Screening* at: http://europa. eu/rapid/pressReleasesAction.do?reference=MEMO/06/161&format=HTML &aged=1&language=EN&guiLanguage=fr

Evans, F. J. 1985. 'Expectancy, therapeutic instructions, and the placebo response', in *Placebo: Theory, Research and Mechanisms.* White, L., Tursky, B. and Schwartz, G. E. (eds.), New York: Guilford Press, pp. 215–28

Eve, E. 2002. *The Jewish Context of Jesus' Miracles.* London: Continuum

Eve, E. 2005. 'Meier, miracle and multiple attestation', *Journal for the Study of the Historical Jesus* **3**: 23–45

Eve, E. 2008. 'Spit in your eye: The Blind Man of Bethsaida and the Blind Man of Alexandria', *New Testament Studies* **54**: 1–17

Eysenck, H. J. and Sargent, C. 1982. *Explaining the Unexplained: Mysteries of the Paranormal.* London: Weidenfield and Nicolson

Fanon, F. 1965. *The Wretched of the Earth.* London: Macgibbon and Kee

Ferrell, B. R., Grant, M. M., Funk, B. M., Otis-Green, S. A. and Garcia, N. J. 1998. 'Quality of life in breast cancer survivors: Implications for developing support services', *Oncology Nursing Forum* **25**: 887–95

Field, T. 2000. *Touch Therapy.* New York: Churchill Livingstone

Fiorenza, E. S. 1995a. *Jesus: Miriam's Child, Sophia's Prophet.* London: SCM

Fiorenza, E. S. 1995b. *In Memory of Her: A Feminist Theological Reconstruction of Christian Origins.* 2nd edn. London: SCM

Flusser, D. 1998. *Jesus.* Jerusalem: Magnes Press

Ford, D. 2007. *Christian Wisdom: Desiring God and Learning in Love.* Cambridge: Cambridge University Press

Frank, M. G., Hendricks, S. E., Johnson, D. R., Wieseler, J. L. and Burke, W. J. 1999. 'Antidepressants augment natural killer cell activity: In vivo and in vitro', *Neuropsychobiology* **39**: 18–24

Fredriksen, P. 2000. *Jesus of Nazareth, King of the Jews: A Jewish Life and the Emergence of Christianity.* London: Macmillan

Freud, S. 1955. *The Standard Edition of the Complete Psychological Works of Sigmund Freud,* vol. 2: *Studies on Hysteria.* J. Strachey (ed.), London: The Hogarth Press and the Institute of Psycho-Analysis

Frick, W. B. 1999. 'Flight into health: A new interpretation', *Journal of Humanistic Psychology* **39**(4): 58–81

Fricker, E. G. 1977. *God is My Witness: The Story of the World Famous Healer.* London: Arthur Barker

Frost, E. 1940. *Christian Healing: A Consideration of the Place of Spiritual Healing in the Church of Today in the Light of the Doctrine and Practice of the Ante-Nicene Church.* London: A. R. Mowbray

Funk, R. and the Jesus Seminar 1998. *The Acts of Jesus: The Search for the Authentic Deeds of Jesus.* San Francisco: Harper

Galipeau, S. A. 1990. *Transforming Body and Soul: Therapeutic Wisdom in the Gospel Healing Stories.* New York: Paulist Press

Gall, T. L. 2004a. 'The role of religious coping in adjustment to prostate cancer', *Cancer Nursing* **27**: 454–61

Gall, T. L. 2004b. 'Relationship with God and the quality of life of prostate cancer survivors', *Quality of Life Research* **13**: 1357–68

Gall, T. L. and Cornblat, M. W. 2002. 'Breast cancer survivors give voice: A qualitative analysis of spiritual factors in long-term adjustment', *Psycho-Oncology* **11**: 524–35

Gerhardt, S. 2004. *Why Love Matters: How Affection Shapes a Baby's Brain*. London: Brunner-Routledge

Gilbert, P. 1989. *Human Nature and Suffering*. Hove: Lawrence Erlbaum

Gilbert, P. 1993. 'Defence and safety: Their function in social behaviour and psychopathology', *British Journal of Clinical Psychology* **32**: 131–53

Gilbert, P. 1998. 'Suffering, evolution, and psychotherapy', in *Witness and Vision of the Therapist*. Feltham, C. (ed.), London: Sage, pp. 94–122

Gilbert, P. 2005. 'Compassion and cruelty: A biopsychosocial approach', in *Compassion: Conceptualisations, Research and Use in Psychotherapy*. Gilbert, P. (ed.), London: Brunner-Routledge, pp. 9–74

Gilbert, P. 2007. *Psychotherapy and Counselling for Depression*. London: Sage

Gilbert, P. 2009a. *Compassion Focused Therapy: Distinctive Features (CBT Distinctive Features)*. London: Routledge

Gilbert, P. 2009b. *The Compassionate Mind*. London: Constable Robinson

Goleman, D. 2003. *Destructive Emotions and How We Can Overcome Them: A Dialogue with the Dalai Lama*. London: Bloomsbury

Graber, M., Gordon, R. and Franklin, N. 2002. 'Diagnostic errors in medicine: What's the goal?', *Academic Medicine* **77**: 981–92

Greenson, R. 1969. *The Technique and Practice of Psychoanalysis*. London: Hogarth Press

Griffin, D. R. 1988. *The Re-enchantment of Science: Postmodern Proposals*. Albany, NY: State University of New York Press

Grinker, R. and Robbins, F. 1954. *Psychosomatic Case Book*. New York: Blakiston

Groddeck, G. 1950. *The Book of the It*. Collins, V. M. E. (trans.), London: Vision Press

Groddeck, G. 1977. *The Meaning of Illness*. London: Hogarth Press

Guirdham, A. 1964. *The Nature of Healing*. London: G. Allen & Unwin

Gutting, G. (ed.) 1980. *Paradigms and Revolutions: Appraisals and Applications of Thomas Kuhn's Philosophy of Science*. London: University of Notre Dame Press

Hahn, R. A. and Kleinman, A. 1983. 'Belief as pathogen, belief as medicine: "Voodoo death" and the "placebo phenomenon" in anthropological perspective', *Medical Anthropology Quarterly* **4**: 16–19

Harrell, D. E. 1975. *All Things are Possible: The Healing and Charismatic Revivals in Modern America*. Bloomington: Indiana University Press

Harrington, A. (ed.) 1997. *The Placebo Effect: An Interdisciplinary Exploration*. Cambridge, MA: Harvard University Press

Hart, G. D. 2000. *Asclepius, the God of Medicine*. London: Royal Society of Medicine Press

Helman, C. G. 2001. 'Placebos and nocebos: The cultural construction of belief', in *Understanding the Placebo Effect in Complementary Medicine:*

Theory, Practice and Research. Peters, D. (ed.), London: Churchill Livingston, pp. 3–16

Henry, W. P. and Strupp, H. H. 1994. 'The therapeutic alliance as interpersonal process', in *The Working Alliance: Theory, Research and Practice.* Horvath, A. and Greenberg, L. (eds.), New York: John Wiley, pp. 51–84

Hernandez-Reif, M., Ironson, G., Field, T., *et al.* 2004. 'Breast cancer patients have improved immune and neuroendocrine functions following massage therapy', *Journal of Psychosomatic Research* **57**: 45–52

Herzog, H., Lele, V. R., Kuwert, T., Langen, K. J., Rota Kops, E. and Feinendegen, L. E. 1990. 'Changed pattern of regional glucose metabolism during yoga meditative relaxation', *Neuropsychobiology* **23**: 182–7

Hess, D. J. 1993. *Science in the New Age: The Paranormal, Its Defenders and Debunkers, and American Culture.* Madison, WI: University of Wisconsin Press

Highfield, M. F. 1992. 'Spiritual health of oncology patients: Nurse and patient perspectives', *Cancer Nursing* **15**: 1–8

Highfield, M. F. 1997. 'Spiritual assessment across the cancer trajectory: Methods and reflections', *Seminars in Oncology Nursing* **13**: 237–41

Hillman, J. 1979. 'Peaks and vales: The soul/spirit distinction as basis for the differences between psychotherapy and spiritual discipline', in *Puer Papers*, Hillman, J. (ed.), Dallas: Spring Publications, 57–65

Hinde, R. A. 1999. *Why Gods Persist: A Scientific Approach to Religion.* London: Routledge

Hobart, W. K. 1882. *The Medical Language of St Luke.* London: Longmans, Green & Co

Holland, J. C. 2002. 'History of psycho-oncology: Overcoming attitudinal and conceptual barriers', *Psychosomatic Medicine* **64**: 206–21

Holland, J. C. 2006. 'An international perspective on the development of psychosocial oncology: Overcoming cultural and attitudinal barriers to improve psychosocial care', *Psycho-Oncology* **13**: 445–59

Holland, J. C., Kash, K. M., Passik, S., *et al.* 1998. 'A brief spiritual beliefs inventory for use in quality of life research in life-threatening illness', *Psycho-Oncology* **7**: 460–9

Hollenbach, P. 1981. 'Jesus, demoniacs, and public authorities: A socio-historical study', *Journal of the American Academy of Religion* **49**: 567–88

Houston, W. R. 1938. 'The doctor himself as a therapeutic agent', *Annals of Internal Medicine* **11**: 1416–25

Howard, J. K. 2001. *Disease and Healing in the New Testament: An Analysis and Interpretation.* Lanham, MD: University Press of America

Howe, D. 1999. 'The main change agent in psychotherapy is the relationship between therapist and client', in *Controversies in Psychotherapy and Counselling.* Feltham, C. (ed.), London: Sage, pp. 95–103

Hrobjartsson, A. and Gøtzsche, P. C. 2001. 'Is the placebo powerless? An analysis of clinical trials comparing placebo with no treatment', *New England Journal of Medicine* **344**: 1594–602

Hufford, D. J. 2005. 'An analysis of the field of spirituality, religion and health', (S/RH) at http://www.templetonadvancedresearchprogram.com/pdf/TARP-Hufford.pdf

Humphrey, N. 2002. 'Great expectations: The evolutionary psychology of faith healing and the placebo effect', in *The Mind Made Flesh: Essays from the Frontiers of Psychology and Evolution*. Humphrey, N. (ed.), Oxford: Oxford University Press, pp. 255–85

Idel, M. 1992. 'Reification of language in Jewish mysticism', in *Mysticism and Language*. Katz, S. (ed.), Oxford: Oxford University Press, pp. 42–79

Irwin, M. 1993. 'Stress-induced immune suppression: Role of the autonomic nervous system', *Annals of the New York Academy of Sciences* **697**: 203–18

Irwin, M. 1994. 'Stress-induced immune suppression: Role of brain corticotropin releasing hormone and autonomic nervous system mechanisms', *Advances in Neuroimmunology* **4**: 29–47

Irwin, M. 1999. 'Immune correlates of depression', *Advances in Experimental Medicine and Biology* **461**: 1–24

Irwin, M., Hauger, R., Patterson, T. L., Semple, S., Ziegler, M. and Grant, I. 1997. 'Alzheimer caregiver stress: Basal natural killer cell activity, pituitary-adrenal cortical function, and sympathetic tone', *Annals of Behavioral Medicine* **19**: 83–90

Jackson, E. N. 1989. *Understanding Health: An Introduction to the Holistic Approach*. London: SCM

Jarrett, G. and Boivin, M. J. 2000. *The Relationship between Fatigue, Depression, and Spiritual Wellbeing in Cancer Patients*. Tulsa, OK: Christian Association for Psychological Studies

Jarrett, G., Leep, R., Kabot, A., Brown, S. and Mingus, M. 1999. Depression, Fatigue, Insomnia, Anxiety, and Spiritual Beliefs in Cancer Patients: Examining the Interrelationships. Unpublished manuscript

Jenkins, R. A. and Pargament, K. I. 1995. 'Religion and spirituality as resources for coping with cancer', *Journal of Psychosocial Oncology* **13**: 51–74

Johnson, L. T. 1997. *The Real Jesus: The Misguided Quest for the Historical Jesus and the Truth of the Traditional Gospels*. San Francisco: Harper

Johnson, S. C. and Spilka, B. 1991. 'Coping with breast cancer: The roles of clergy and faith', *Journal of Religion and Health* **30**: 21–33

Jones, G. L. 2006. 'A basic spiritual assessment model', *Journal of Cancer Education* **21**: 26–7

Jung, C. G. 1998. *Answer to Job*. London: Routledge

Kaczorowski, J. M. 1990. 'Spiritual well being and anxiety in adults diagnosed with Cancer', *The Hospice Journal* **5**(3): 105–16

Kakar, S. 1985. 'Psychoanalysis and religious healing: Siblings or strangers' in *Journal of the American Academy of Religion* **53**: 841–53

Kamper, S. J., Machado, L. A. C., Herbert, R. D., Maher, C. G. and McAuley, J. H. 2008. 'Trial methodology and patient characteristics did not influence the size of placebo effects on pain', *Journal of Clinical Epidemiology* **61**: 256–60

Kaptchuk, T. 1998. 'Intentional ignorance: A history of blind assessment and placebo controls in medicine', *Bulletin of the History of Medicine* **72**: 389–433

Kasser, T. 2002. *The High Price of Materialism.* Cambridge, MA: MIT Press

Kaufman, Y., Anaki, D., Binns, M. and Freedman, M. 2007. 'Cognitive decline in Alzheimer disease: Impact of spirituality, religiosity, and QOL', *Neurology* **68**: 1509–14

Kelsey, M. T. 1973. *Healing and Christianity.* London: SCM

Kelsey, M. T. 1988. *Psychology, Medicine and Christian Healing.* San Francisco: Harper

Kendell, R. E. 1975. *The Role of Diagnosis in Psychiatry.* London: Blackwell Scientific Publications

Keshava, E. 2002. Reiki: Love Beyond Reason. Unpublished manuscript

Kidel, M. and Rowe-Leete, S. (eds.) 1988. 'The doctor verses King Canute: From Georg Groddeck to family therapy', in *The Meaning of Illness.* Kidel, M. and Rowe-Leete, S. (eds.), London: Routledge, pp. 53–72

Kiecolt-Glaser, J., McGuire, L., Robles, T. and Glaser, R. 2002. 'Psychoneuro-immunology and psychosomatic medicine: Back to the future', *Psychomatic Medicine* **64**: 15–28

Kienle, G. S. and Keine H. 1987. 'The powerful placebo effect: Fact or fiction?' *Journal of Clinical Epidemiology* **50**: 1311–18

Kienle, G. S. and Keine, H. 2001. 'A critical reanalysis of the concept, magnitude and existence of placebo effects', in *Understanding the Placebo Effect in Complementary Medicine: Theory, Practice and Research.* Peters, D. (ed.), London: Churchill Livingston, pp. 31–50

Kiesler, D. J. 1999. *Beyond the Disease Model of Mental Disorders.* New York: Praeger

Kirkpatrick, L. A. 2005. *Attachment, Evolution and the Psychology of Religion.* New York: Guilford

Kirsch, I. and Weixel, L. J. 1988. 'Double-blind versus deceptive administration of a placebo', *Behavioral Neuroscience* **102**: 319–23

Kleinman, A. and Sung, L. H. 1979. 'Why do indigenous practitioners successfully heal?' *Social Science & Medicine* **13**: 7–26

Koenig, H. G., McCollough, M. E. and Larson, D. B. 2001. *Handbook of Religion and Health.* Oxford: Oxford University Press

Kohut, H. 1977. *The Analysis of the Self.* New York: International Universities Press

Kootstra, J., Hoekstra-Weebers, J. E., Rietman, H., *et al.* 2008. 'Quality of life after sentinel lymph node biopsy or axillary lymph node dissection in stage I/II breast cancer patients: A prospective longitudinal study', *Annals of Surgical Oncology* **15**: 2533–41

Krieger, D. 1979. *The Therapeutic Touch: How to Use Your Hands to Help or Heal.* Englewood Cliffs, NJ: Prentice-Hall

Krippner, S. C. 2002. 'Conflicting perspectives on shamans and shamanism: Points and counterpoints', *American Psychologist* **57**: 962–77

Kropf, A. 1999. *Philosophie und Parapsychologie: Zur Rezeptionsgeschichte Parapsychologischer Phänomene am beispiel Kants, Schopenhauers und C. G Jung,*

Naturwissenschaft – Philosophie – Geschichte, II. Hucklenbroich, Peter (ed.), Hamburg: LIT

Krucoff, M., Crater, S. and Green, C. 2001. 'Integrative noetic therapies as adjuncts to percutaneous intervention during unstable coronary syndromes: Monitoring and actualization of noetic training (MANTRA) feasibility pilot', *American Heart Journal* **142**: 760–9

Krucoff, M., Crater, S., Gallup, D., *et al.* 2005. 'Music, imagery, touch, and prayer as adjuncts to interventional cardiac care: The monitoring and actualisation of noetic trainings (MANTRA) II randomised study', *Lancet* **366**: 211–17

Krupski, T. L., Fink, A., Kwan, L., *et al.* 2005. 'Health-related quality-of-life in low-income, uninsured men with prostate cancer', *Journal of Health Care for the Poor and Underserved* **16**: 375–90

Krupski, T. L., Sonn, G., Kwan, L., Maliski, S., Fink, A. and Litwin, M. S. 2005. 'Ethnic variation in health-related quality of life among low-income men with prostate cancer', *Ethnicity and Disease* **15**: 461–8

Kuhn, T. S. 1962. *The Structure of Scientific Revolutions.* Chicago: University of Chicago Press

Kydd, R. A. N. 2001. *Healing through the Centuries.* Peabody, MO: Hendrickson

Lademan, C. and Roseman, M. 1996. *The Performance of Healing.* London: Routledge

Laplanche, J. and Pontalis, J. B. 1973. *The Language of Psycho-Analysis.* London: Hogarth Press

Larson, D. B., Pattison, E. M., Blazer, D. G., Omran, A. R. and Kaplan, B. H. 1986. 'Systematic analysis of research on religious variables in four major psychiatric journals, 1978–1982', *The American Journal of Psychiatry* **143**: 329–34

Larson, D. B., Swyers, J. P. and McCullough, M. E. (eds.) 1998. *Scientific Research on Spirituality and Health: A Consensus Report.* Rockville, MD: National Institute for Healthcare Research

Lawrence, P. H. 1997. *Christian Healing.* Bristol: Terra Nova

Lazar, S. W., Bush, G., Gollub, R. L., Fricchione, G. L., Khalsa, G. and Benson, H. 2000. 'Functional brain mapping of the relaxation response and meditation', *Neuroreport* **11**: 1581–5

Leach, C. W., Spears, R., Branscombe, N. R. and Dossje, B. 2003. 'Malicious pleasure: Schadenfreude at the suffering of another group', *Journal of Personality and Social Psychology* **84**: 932–43

Leader, D. and Corfield, D. 2007. *Why do People Get Ill?* London: Hamish Hamilton

LeShan, L. 1980. *Clairvoyant Reality: Towards a Theory of the Paranormal.* Wellingborough, UK: Turnstone Books

Lester, D. 1972. 'Voodoo death: Some new thoughts on an old phenomenon', *American Anthropologist* **74**: 386–90

Levine, F. 2001. *Practical Kabbalah.* http://kabbalah.fayelevine.com

Littlewood, R. and Dein, S. 1995. 'The effectiveness of words: Religion and healing among the Lubavitch of Stamford Hill', *Culture, Medicine and Psychiatry* **19**: 339–83

Longrigg, J. 2000. 'Epilepsy in ancient Greek medicine: The vital step', *Seizure: European Journal of Epilepsy* **9**: 12–21

MacNutt, F. 1989. *Healing.* London: Hodder and Stoughton

Macquarrie, J. 1977. *Principles of Christian Thought, 2nd edn.* New York: Scribner

Maddocks, M. 1990. *The Christian Healing Ministry.* London: SPCK

Maddocks, M. 1992. *Twenty Questions about Healing.* London: SPCK

Maier, S. F. and Watkins, L. R. 1998. 'Cytokines for psychologists: Implications of bidirectional immune-to-brain communication for understanding behavior, mood, and cognition', *Psychological Review* **105**: 83–107

Mainprice, J. 1974. *Marital Interaction and Some Illnesses in Children.* London: Institute of Marital Studies, Tavistock Centre

Marsden, G. M. 1997. *The Outrageous Idea of Christian Scholarship.* Oxford/New York: Oxford University Press

Martimort, A. G. 1961. *L'Église en prière: introduction à la liturgie.* Paris: Desclée

Martimort, A. G. 1986. *The Church at Prayer: An Introduction to the Liturgy.* O'Connell, M. (trans.), Collegeville, MN: Liturgical Press

Martin, P. 1997. *The Sickening Mind: Brain, Behavior, Immunity and Disease.* London: Flamingo

Mathews, T. F. 1999. *The Clash of Gods: A Reinterpretation of Early Christian Art.* Princeton: Princeton University Press

Maxwell, J. 1996. 'Nursing's new age?' *Christianity Today* **40**: 96–9

May, E. and Vilenskaya, L. 1994. 'Some aspects of parapsychological research in the former Soviet Union', *Subtle Energies* **3**: 1–24

Mayberg, H. S., Liotti, M., Brannan, S. K., *et al.* 1999. 'Reciprocal limbic-cortical function and negative mood: Converging PET findings in depression and normal sadness', *American Journal of Psychiatry* **156**: 675–82

Mayberg, H. S., Robinson, R. G., Wong, D. F., *et al.* 1988. 'PET imaging of cortical S2 serotonin receptors after stroke: Lateralized changes and relationship to depression', *American Journal of Psychiatry* **145**: 937–43

McCain, N. L. 2005. 'Psychoneuroimmunology, spirituality, and cancer', *Gynecologic Oncology* **99**(3): S121

McCain, N. L., Gray, D. P., Walter, J. M. and Robins J. 2005. 'Implementing a comprehensive approach to the study of health dynamics using the psychoneuroimmunology paradigm', *Advances in Nursing Science* **28**: 320–32

McClenon, J. 1997. 'Spiritual healing and folklore research: Evaluating the hypnosis/placebo theory', *Alternative Therapies in Health and Medicine* **2**: 61–6

McClenon, J. 2001. *Wondrous Healing: Shamanism, Human Evolution and the Origin of Religion.* DeKalb, IL: Northern Illinois University Press

McDougall, J. 1989. *Theatres of the Body.* London: Free Association Books

McMahon, C. E. 1975. 'The "Placebo Effect" in renaissance medicine', *Journal of the American Society of Psychosomatic Dentistry and Medicine* **22**: 3–9

Meehl, P. E. 1958. *What, Then, Is Man?* St Louis, MI: Concordia Publishing House

Meek, G. W. 1977. 'Teaching cancer patients to accelerate their healing', 'Teaching people to become healers', and 'Towards a general theory of healing', in Meek, G. W. (ed.), *Healers and the Healing Process: A Report on 10 Years of Research by 14 World Famous Investigators.* London: Theosophical Publishing House, pp. 158–61, 162–70, 193–235

Meggitt, J. J. 1998. 'Review of Bruce Malina, *The Social World of Jesus and the Gospels*', *Journal of Theological Studies* **49**: 215–19

Meggitt, J. J. 2006. 'Magic, healing and early Christianity: Consumption and competition', in *The Meanings of Magic: From the Bible to Buffalo Bill.* Wygant, A. (ed.), New York: Berghahn Books, pp. 89–114

Meier, J. P. 1991–2009. *A Marginal Jew: Rethinking the Historical Jesus,* 4 vols. (1991, 1994, 2001, 2009). Anchor Bible Reference Library. New York: Doubleday

Meissner, W. W. 1987. *Life and Faith.* Washington, DC: Georgetown University Press

Meyers, E. M. 1997. 'Jesus and his Galilean context', in *Archaeology and the Galilee.* Edwards, D. R. and McCollough, T. (eds.), Atlanta, GA: Scholars Press, pp. 57–66

Mikulincer, M. and Shaver, P. R. 2007. *Attachment in Adulthood: Structure, Dynamics, and Change.* New York: Guilford

Miller, F. G. and Kaptchuk, T. J. 2008. 'The power of context: Reconceptualising the placebo effect', *Journal of the Royal Society of Medicine* **101**: 222–5

Miller, F. G. and Rosenstein, D. L. 2006. 'The nature and power of the placebo effect', *Journal of Clinical Epidemiology* **59**: 331–5

Miller, W. R. and Thorsen, C. E. 2003. 'Spirituality, religion, and health: An emerging research field', *American Psychologist* **58**: 24–35

Moene, F. C. and Roelofs, K. 2008. 'Hypnosis in the treatment of conversion and somatization disorders', in *The Oxford Handbook of Hypnosis: Theory, Research and Practice.* Nash, M. R. and Barnier, M. J. (eds.), Oxford: Oxford University Press, pp. 625–45

Moerman, D. 1983. 'Physiology and symbols: The anthropological implications of the placebo effect', in *The Anthropology of Medicine: From Culture to Method.* Ramanucci-Ross, L., Moerman, D. and Tancredi, L. R. (eds.), Westport: Bergin and Garvey, pp. 156–67

Moerman, D. 2002. *Meaning, Medicine and the 'Placebo Effect'.* Cambridge: Cambridge University Press

Moltmann, J. 1985. *God in Creation: An Ecological Doctrine of Creation.* London: SCM

Money, M. 2001. 'Shamanism as a healing paradigm for complementary therapy', *Complementary Therapies in Nursing and Midwifery* **7**: 126–31

Moseley, J. B., Wray, N. P., Kuykendall, D., Willis, K. and Landon, G. 1996. 'Arthroscopic treatment of osteoarthritis of the knee: A prospective, randomized, placebo-controlled trial', *The American Journal of Sports Medicine* **24**: 28–34

Moyé, L. A., Richardson, M. A., Post-White, J. and Justice, B. 1995. 'Research methodology in psychoneuroimmunology: Rationale and design of the IMAGES-P clinical trial', *Alternative Therapies in Health and Medicine* **1**(2): 34–9

Murphy, N. 1998. 'Nonreductive physicalism: Philosophical issues', in Brown, W. S., Murphy, N. and Malony, H. N. (eds.), pp. 127–48

Myers, C. 1990. *Binding the Strongman: A Political Reading of Mark's Story of Jesus*. New York: Orbis

Nabokov, I. 2000. *Religion against the Self: An Ethnography of Tamil Rituals*. Oxford: Oxford University Press

Nash, C. B. 1982. 'ESP of present and future targets', *Journal of the Society for Psychical Research* **51**: 374–7

Neusner, J. 1989. 'Introduction', in *Religion Science and Magic: In Concert and Conflict*. Neusner, J., Frerichs, B. and Flesher, P. V. McC. (eds.), New York: Oxford University Press, pp. 3–7

Newberg A. B. 2004. 'Field analysis of the neuroscientific study of religious and spiritual phenomena'. http://metanexus.net/magazine/ArticleDetail/tabid/68/id/9468/Default.aspx

Newberg, A. B. and Iversen, J. 2003. 'The neural basis of the complex mental task of meditation: Neurotransmitter and neurochemical considerations', *Medical Hypotheses* **61**: 282–91

Newberg, A. B., Alavi, A., Baime, M., Pourdehnad, M., Santanna, J. and d'Aquili, E. 2001. 'The measurement of regional cerebral blood flow during the complex cognitive task of meditation: A preliminary SPECT study', *Psychiatry Research* **106**: 113–22

Newberg, A. B., Pourdehnad, M., Alavi, A. and d'Aquili, E. G. 2003. 'Cerebral blood flow during meditative prayer: Preliminary findings and methodological issues', *Perceptual and Motor Skills* **97**: 625–30

Niebuhr, H. R. 1960. *Radical Monotheism and Western Culture*. New York: Harper & Bros

Nigal, G. 1994. *Magic, Mysticism and Hasidism: The Supernatural in Jewish Thought*. Northvale, NJ: Jason Aronson

Nisbett, R. E., Peng, K., Choi, I. and Norenzayan, A. 2001. 'Culture and systems of thought: Holistic versus analytic cognition', *Psychological Review* **108**: 291–310

Novack, D. H. 1987. 'Therapeutic aspects of the clinical encounter', *Journal of General Internal Medicine* **2**: 346–55

Nutton, V. 2002. 'The unknown Galen: Galen beyond Kühn', *Bulletin of the Institute of Classical Studies* Suppl. **77**

Nutton, V. 2004. *Ancient Medicine*. London: Routledge

Oremland, J. D. 1972. 'Transference cure and flight into health', *International Journal of Psychoanalytic Psychotherapy* **1**: 61–75

Owens, C. and Dein, S. 2006. 'Conversion disorder: The modern hysteria', *Advances in Psychiatric Treatment* **12**: 152–7

Panksepp, J. 1998. *Affective Neuroscience: The Foundations of Human and Animal Emotions*. Oxford: Oxford University Press

Pargament, K. I., Ensing, D. S., Falgout, K., *et al.* 1990. 'God help me (I): Religious coping efforts as predictors of the outcome to significant negative life events', *American Journal of Community Psychology* **18**: 793–824

Pargament, K. I., Ishler, K., Dubow, E. F., *et al.* 1997. 'Methods of religious coping with the Gulf War: Cross-sectional and longitudinal analyses', *Journal of Scientific Study of Religion* **33**: 347–61

Pattison, S. 1989. *Alive and Kicking: Towards a Practical Theology of Illness and Healing.* London: SCM

Pearson, M. A. 1996. *Christian Healing: A Practical and Comprehensive Guide.* London: Hodder and Stoughton

Perrin, N. 1976. *Rediscovering the Teaching of Jesus.* New York: Harper and Row

Phan, K. L., Wager, T. D., Taylor, S. F. and Liberzon, I. 2004. 'Functional neuroimaging studies of human emotions', *CNS Spectrums* **9**: 258–66

Phillips, A. 1995. *Terrors and Experts.* London: Faber and Faber

Pilch, J. J. 2000. *Healing in the New Testament: Insights from Medical and Mediterranean Anthropology.* Philadelphia, PA: Fortress

Piper, R. A. 2000. 'Satan, demons and absence of exorcisms in the Gospel of John', in *Christology, Controversy and Community: New Testament Essays in Honour of David, R. Catchpole.* Horrell, D. and Tuckett, C. M. (eds.), Leiden: E. J. Brill, pp. 253–78

Plantinga, A. 1996. 'Science: Augustinian or Duhemian?' *Faith and Philosophy* **13**: 368–94

Plantinga, A. 2000. *Warranted Christian Belief.* Oxford: Oxford University Press

Polkinghorne, J. C. 1989. *Science and Providence: God's Interaction with the World.* London: SPCK

Polkinghorne, J. C. 1996. *Scientists as Theologians: A Comparison of the Writings of Ian Barbour, Arthur Peacocke and John Polkinghorne.* London: SPCK

Porterfield, A. 2005. *Healing in the History of Christianity.* Oxford: Oxford University Press

Preuss, J. 1978. *Biblical and Talmudic Medicine.* New York: Sanhedrin Press

Radin, D. I. 2006. *Entangled Minds: Extrasensory Experiences in a Quantum Reality.* New York: Simon & Schuster

Radin, D. I., Stone, J., Levine, E., *et al.* (in press). 'Effects of motivated distant intention on electrodermal activity', *Explore: The Journal of Science and Healing*

Ramírez-Johnson, J., Fayard, C., Garberoglio, C. and Ramírez, C. M. J. 2002. 'Is faith an emotion? Faith as a meaning-making affective process: An example from breast cancer patients', *American Behavioral Scientist* **45**: 1839–53

Reed, P. G. 1987. 'Spirituality and well-being in terminally ill hospitalized adults', *Research in Nursing and Health* **10**: 335–44

Reid J. and Williams, N. 1984. '"Voodoo death" in Arnhem Land: Whose reality?' *American Anthropologist* **86**: 121–33

Remus, H. 1983. *Pagan–Christian Conflict over Miracles in the Second Century.* Cambridge, MA: Philadelphia Patristic Foundation

Remus, H. 1992. 'Miracle: New Testament', in *Anchor Bible Dictionary*, vol. 4. New York: Doubleday, pp. 856–69

Remus, H. 1997. *Jesus as Healer.* Cambridge: Cambridge University Press

Roberts, L., Ahmed, I. and Hall, S. 2000. 'Intercessory prayer for the alleviation of ill health', *Cochrane Database Systematic Reviews* **2** (online)

Roseman, M. 2003. 'Remembering to forget: The aesthetics of longing', in *Shamanism: A Reader*. Harvey, G. (ed.), New York and London: Routledge, pp. 186–202

Samuel, A. 1985. *Jung and the Post Jungians*. London: Routledge and Kegan Paul

Sanders, E. P. 1985. *Jesus and Judaism*. London: SCM

Sanders, E. P. 1992. 'Jesus in historical context', *Theology Today* **50**: 429–48

Sanders, E. P. 1993. *The Historical Figure of Jesus*. London: Allen Lane

Sanford, A. 1966. *Healing Gifts of the Spirit*. Evesham: James

Sarafino, E. 2003. *Health Psychology: Biopsychosocial Interactions*, 4th edn. Chichester: Wiley

Sardar, Z. 1989. *Explorations in Islamic Science*. London: Mansell

Saudia, T. L., Kinney, M. R., Brown, K. C. and Young-Ward, L. 1991. 'Health locus of control and helpfulness of prayer', *Heart Lung* **20**: 60–5

Saunders, N. 2002. *Divine Action and Modern Science*. Cambridge: Cambridge University Press

Savage, S. and Boyd-Macmillan, E. 2007. *The Human Face of Church: A Social Psychology and Pastoral Theology Resource for Pioneer and Traditional Ministry*. Norwich: Canterbury Press

Schleiermacher, F. 1975. *The Life of Jesus*. Gilmour, S. M. (trans.), Verheyden, J. C. (ed.), Philadelphia: Fortress Press

Schlitz, M. 2007. 'Healing and wholeness: Mapping an integral approach to healthcare', *Unified Energetics* **3**: 58

Schlitz, M. 2008. 'The integral model: Answering the call for whole systems healthcare', *Permanente Journal* **12**(2): 61–8

Schlitz, M. and Braud, W. 1985. 'Reiki plus natural healing: An ethnographic and experimental study', *Psi Research* **4**: 100–23

Schlitz, M. and Braud, W. 1997. 'Distant intentionality and healing: Assessing the evidence', *Alternative Therapies in Health and Medicine* **3**: 62–73

Schlitz, M. J. and LaBerge, S. 1997. 'Covert observation increases skin conductance in subjects unaware of when they are being observed: A replication', *Journal of Parapsychology* **61**: 185–96

Schlitz, M. and Lewis, N. 1996. 'The healing powers of prayer', *Noetic Sciences Review, summer:* 29–33

Schlitz, M. and Radin, D. I. 2007. 'Prayer and intention in distant healing: Assessing the evidence', in *Whole Person Healthcare*, vol. 2: *Psychology, Spirituality, and Health*. Serlin, A., Rockefeller, K. and Brown, S. (eds.), Westport, CT: Praeger, pp. 177–90

Schlitz, M., Amorok, T. and Micozzi, M. 2005. *Consciousness and Healing: Integral Approaches to Mind Body Medicine*. St Louis, MO: Elsevier Churchill Livingston

Schlitz, M., Radin, D., Malle, B. F., Schmidt, S., Utts, J. and Yount, G. L. 2003. 'Distant healing intention: Definitions and evolving guidelines for laboratory studies', *Alternative Therapies in Health and Medicine* **9**(3) Suppl: A31–43

Schmidt, S., Schneider, R., Utts, J. and Walach, H. 2004. 'Distant intentionality and the feeling of being stared at', *British Journal of Psychology* **95**: 235–47

Schlitz, M., Vieten, C. and Amorok, T. 2008. *Living Deeply: The Art and Science of Transformation.* Berkeley, CA: New Harbinger

Scholem, G. 1965. *On the Kabbalah and its Symbolism*, New York: Shocken

Scholem, G. 1974. *Kabbalah*, New York: Quadrangle

Schore, A. N. 1994. *Affect Regulation and the Origin of the Self: The Neurobiology of Emotional Development.* Hillsdale, NJ: Lawrence Erlbaum

Schore, A. N. 2001. 'The effects of early relational trauma on right brain development, affect regulation, and infant mental health', *Infant Mental Health Journal* **22**: 7–66

Schweitzer, A. 2001. *The Quest of the Historical Jesus.* Montgomery, W., Coates, J. R., Cupitt, S. and Bowden, J. (trans.), Bowden, J. (ed.), Minneapolis, MN: Fortress Press

Seeman, T. E., Dubin, L. F. and Seeman, M. 2003. 'Religiosity/spirituality and health: A critical review of the evidence for biological pathways', *American Psychologist* **58**: 53–63

Segal, Z. V., Williams J. M. G. and Teasdale, J. 2002. *Mindfulness-Based Cognitive Therapy for Depression: A New Approach to Preventing Relapse.* New York: Guilford Press

Sephton, S. E., Koopman, C., Schaal, M., Thoresen, C. and Spiegel, D. 2001. 'Spiritual expression and immune status in women with metastatic breast cancer: An exploratory study', *The Breast Journal* **7**: 345–53

Shapiro, A. and Shapiro, E. 1997. *The Powerful Placebo: From Ancient Priest to Modern Physician.* Baltimore: Johns Hopkins University Press

Shaw, B. 1911. *The Doctor's Dilemma: Getting Married, and the Shewing-Up of Blanco Posnet.* New York: Brentano's

Sheils, W. J. (ed.), 1982. *The Church and Healing: Papers Read at the Twentieth Summer Meeting and the Twenty-First Winter Meeting of the Ecclesiastical History Society.* Oxford: Published for the *Ecclesiastical History Society* by Blackwell

Sheldrake, R. 2003. *The Sense of Being Stared at and Other Aspects of the Extended Mind.* London: Hutchinson

Shelley, B. L. 2000. 'Miracles ended long ago – or did they?' *Christian History* **67**: 43–4

Sicher, F., Targ, E., Moore, D. and Smith, H. S. 1998. 'A randomized double-blind study of the effect of distant healing in a population with advanced AIDS: Report of a small scale study', *Western Journal of Medicine* **169**: 356–63

Sloan, R. P. 2005. 'Field analysis of the literature on religion, spirituality and health' at http://templetonadvancedresearchprogram.com/pdf/TARP-sloan.pdf

Smith, E. D., Stefanek, M. E., Joseph, M. V. and Verdieck, M. J. 1993. 'Spiritual awareness, personal perspective on death, and psychosocial distress among cancer patients: An initial investigation', *Journal of Psychosocial Oncology* **11**(3): 89–103

Smith, E. W. L., Clance, P. R. and Imes, S. 1998. *Touch in Psychotherapy: Theory, Research and Practice.* New York: Guilford Press

Smith, M. 1978. *Jesus the Magician.* London: Gollanz

Snel, F. W. J. J., van der Sijde, P. C. and Wiegant, F. A. C. 1995. 'Cognitive styles of believers and disbelievers in paranormal phenomena', *Journal of the Society for Psychical Research* **60**: 251–7

Solfvin, J. 1984. 'Mental healing', *Advances in Parapsychological Research* **4**: 31–63

Solomon, N. 1999. 'From folk medicine to bioethics in Judaism' in *Religion, Health and Suffering*. Hinnells, J. and Porter, R. (eds.), London: Kegan Paul International, pp. 166–86

Spiegel, D. 2004. 'Placebos in practice', *British Medical Journal* **329**: 927–8

Stanton, G. 2001. 'Message and miracles', in *The Cambridge Companion to Jesus*. Bockmuehl, M. (ed.), Cambridge: Cambridge University Press, pp. 56–71

Stanton, G. 2002. *The Gospels and Jesus*. Oxford: Oxford University Press

Stenmark, M. 2004. *How to Relate Science and Religion: A Multidimensional Model*. Grand Rapids, MI: Eerdmans

Sterling, G. 1993. 'Jesus as exorcist: An analysis of Matthew 17:14–20; Mark 9:14–29; Luke 9:37–43a', *Catholic Biblical Quarterly* **55**(4): 67–93

Sternberg, E. M. 2002. 'Walter B. Cannon and "Voodoo Death": A perspective from 60 years on', *American Journal of Public Health* **92**: 1564–6

Strange, J. F. 1997. 'First century Galilee from archaeology and from the texts', in *Archaeology and the Galilee: Texts and Contexts in the Graeco-Roman and Byzantine Periods*. Edwards, D. R. and McCollough, C. T. (eds.), Atlanta, GA: Scholars Press, pp. 39–49

Strauss, D. F. 2006. *The Life of Jesus Critically Examined, 3 vols*. Eliot, G. (trans.), London: Continuum

Suarez, M., Raffaelli, M. and O'Leary, A. 1996. 'Use of folk healing practices by HIV-infected Hispanics living in the United States', *AIDS Care: Psychological and Socio-medical Aspects of AIDS/HIV* **8**: 683–90

Symonds, L. L., Gordon, N. S., Bixby, J. C. and Mande, M. M. 2006. 'Right-lateralized pain processing in the human cortex: An fMRI study', *Journal of Neurophysiology* **95**: 3823–30

Tambiah, S. 1968. 'The magical power of words', *Man* **3**: 175–208

Tambiah, S. 1990. *Magic, Science, Religion and the Scope of Rationality*. Cambridge: Cambridge University Press

Targ, E. F. and Levine, E. G. 2002. 'The efficacy of a mind-body-spirit group for women with breast cancer: A randomized controlled trial', *General Hospital Psychiatry* **24**: 238–48

Targ, R. and Katra, J. 1999. *Miracles of Mind: Exploring Non Local Consciousness and Spiritual Healing*. Novato, CA: New World Library

Theissen, G. 1983. *Miracles Stories of the Early Christian Tradition*. Edinburgh: T & T Clark

Theissen, G. and Merz, A. 1998. *The Historical Jesus: A Comprehensive Guide*. London: SCM

Thomas, O. C. 2006. *What is it that Theologians Do, How They Do it, and Why: Anglican Essays*. Lewiston, NY: Edwin Mellen Press

Thorne, B. 2002. *The Mystical Power of Person-Centred Therapy: Hope beyond Despair*. London: Whurr

Tilburt, J.C., Emanuel, E.J., Kaptchuk, T.J., Curlin, F.A. and Miller, F.G. 2008. 'Prescribing "placebo treatments": Results of national survey of US internists and rheumatologists.' *British Medical Journal* **337**: A1938

Toner, P. (1909). 'Extreme unction', in *The Catholic Encyclopedia*. New York: Robert Appleton Company

Totton, N. 2003. *Psychoanalysis and the Paranormal: Lands of Darkness*. London: Karnac

Trachtenberg, J. 1977. *Jewish Magic and Superstition: A Study in Folk Religion*. New York: Atheneum

Trevarthen, C. and Aitken, K. 2001. 'Infant intersubjectivity: Research, theory, and clinical applications', *Journal of Child Psychology and Psychiatry* **42**: 3–48

Twelftree, G.H. 1999. *Jesus the Miracle Worker: A Historical and Theological Study*. Leicester: InterVarsity Press

Twelftree, G.H. 2007. *In the Name of Jesus: Exorcism Among Early Christians*. Grand Rapids, MI: Baker Academic

Uväns-Morberg, K. 1998. 'Oxytocin may mediate the benefits of positive social interaction and emotions', *Psychoneuroendocrinology* **23**: 819–35

Vermes, G. 1973. *Jesus the Jew*. London: Collins

Vickers, A.J. 1996. 'Can acupuncture have specific effects on health? A systematic review of acupuncture antiemesis trials', *Journal of the Royal Society of Medicine* **89**(6): 303–11

Walach, H. 2005. 'Generalized entanglement: A new theoretical model for understanding the effects of complementary and alternative medicine', *Journal of Alternative and Complementary Medicine* **11**: 549–59

Wallis, C. 1996. 'Faith and healing', *Time* (online), June 24.

Walliss, J. 2001. 'Continuing bonds: Relationships between the living and the dead in contemporary spiritualism', *Mortality* **6**: 127–45

Walsh, R. 2005. 'The practices of essential spirituality', in *Consciousness and Healing*. Schlitz, M., Amorok, T. and Micozzi, M. (eds.), St Louis, MO: Elsevier Churchill Livingston, pp. 294–303

Wang, S. 2005. 'A conceptual framework for integrating research related to the physiology of compassion and the wisdom of Buddhist teachings', in *Compassion: Conceptualisations, Research and Use in Psychotherapy*. Gilbert, P. (ed.), London: Brunner-Routledge, pp. 75–120

Watts, F.N. (ed.) 1998. *Science Meets Faith*. London: SPCK

Watts, F.N. (ed.) 2001. *Perspectives on Prayer*. London: SPCK

Watts, F.N. 2002. *Theology and Psychology*. Basingstoke: Ashgate

Watts, F.N. and Bennett, D.H. 1983. *Theory and Practice of Psychiatric Rehabilitation*. Chichester: John Wiley

Weatherhead, L.D. 1951. *Psychology, Religion, and Healing: A Critical Study of all the Non-physical Methods of Healing, with an Examination of the Principles Underlying them and the Techniques Employed to Express them, Together with Some Conclusions Regarding Further Investigation and Action in this Field*. London: Hodder and Stoughton

Webb, R. L. 2006. 'Jesus heals a leper: Mark 1:40–45 and Egerton Gospel 35–47', *Journal for the Study of the Historical Jesus* **4**: 177–202

Weze, C., Leathard, H. L., Grange, J., Tiplady, P. and Stevens, G. 2004. 'Evaluation of healing by gentle touch in 35 clients with cancer', *European Journal of Oncology Nursing* **8**: 40–9

Wheelis, A. 1949. 'Flight from insight', *American Journal of Psychiatry* **105**: 915–19

White, L., Tursky B. and Schwartz, G. E. 1985. *Placebo: Theory, Research and Mechanism.* London: Guilford Press

Wimber, J. and Springer, K. 1987. *Power Healing.* London: Hodder and Stoughton

Winnicott, D. W. 1953. 'Transitional objects and transitional phenomena: A study of the first not-me possession', *International Journal of Psychoanalysis* **34**: 89–97

Wirth, D. P. 1995. 'The significance of belief and expectancy within the spiritual healing encounter', *Social Science & Medicine* **41**: 249–60

Wolf, S. 1959. 'The pharmacology of placebos', *Pharmacology Review* **11**: 689–704

World Health Organization 1992–4. *International Statistical Classification of Diseases and Related Health Problems (ICD-10).* Geneva: World Health Organization

Worrall, A. A. and Worrall, O. N. 1969. *The Gift of Healing: A Personal Story of Spiritual Therapy.* London: Rider

Worthington, E. L., Jr., O'Connor, L. E., Berry, J. W., Sharp, C., Murray, R. and Yi, E. 2005. 'Compassion and forgiveness: Implications for psychotherapy', in *Compassion: Conceptualisations, Research and Use in Psychotherapy.* Gilbert, P. (ed.), London: Brunner-Routledge, pp. 168–92

Yalom, I. 1995. *The Theory and Practise of Group Psychotherapy.* New York: Basic Books

Yates, J. W., Chalmer, B. J., James, P., Follansbee, M. and McKegney, F. P. 1981. 'Religion in patients with advanced cancer', *Medical and Pediatric Oncology* **9**: 121–8

Young, A. 1981. *Spiritual Healing: Miracle or Mirage?* Marina del Rey, CA: DeVorss

Young-Eisendrath, P. and Miller, M. E. 2000. *The Psychology of Mature Spirituality: Integrity, Wisdom, Transcendence.* London: Brunner-Routledge

Zinnbauer, B. J. and Pargament, K. I. 2005. 'Religiousness and spirituality', in *Handbook for the Psychology of Religion.* Paloutzian, R. and Park, C. (eds.), New York: Guilford Press, pp. 21–42

Index